WILD PRIDE MONTANA

WILD PRIDE MONTANA

A TRAPPERS JOURNEY

TOBY WALRATH

To order additional copies of this book, contact:
Xlibris Corporation
1-888-795-4274
www.Xlibris.com
Orders@Xlibris.com
115001

Contents

Dedication

This book is dedicated to the many hardworking trappers of Montana who continue to fight to preserve their culture and their way of life—the most honest, sincere, and genuine nature lovers I have ever known.

And in memory of Keith Floyd Walrath Sr., a man who taught me and others how to slow down, truly observe, and appreciate all that is in nature. My trapping partner and mentor, I called him Dad.

Foreword

As a young boy growing up in rural America, my father and I spent most of our time together in nature. Under his tutelage, I gained an appreciation for wildlife that I carried into adulthood. The outdoor people in my life have ranged from knowledgeable wool-clad woodsmen to high-tech mountaineers. Likewise, I have had an equally varied range of wilderness experiences. From cold nights spent sleeping in four-season tents high on alpine slopes with synthetic snowshoes and trekking poles and pushing forward with headlamps and crampons with hopes of a summit before noon to leather-laced wood-framed snowshoes and hand-carved walking sticks deep in the remote wilds on a trapline.

So much is misunderstood about wild people who are drawn to wild places. Hunters, trappers, mountain climbers, anglers, backpackers, skiers, and other outdoor adventurers are drawn to the outdoors with one commonality: to become immersed in nature, to feel it, to live it—not just to observe and lay claim to another visit. That is not enough. They are there because they need to experience it, to let nature seep into their pores, and let the unnatural dissipate out. The sting of winter on their faces and the heat of the sun reflecting off the snow await them. It's exciting to share an adventure with another wild soul or go it alone. The thrills of being high on a mountain top or cutting a fresh cougar track in the snow and listening to the low bawl of hounds is equally thrilling for those involved. So it is with trappers. Fresh tracks in snow, traps set, anticipation. Either the trapper got it right or he didn't. Either the trap will catch or it won't. Traps can freeze solid in the ground. Driving rain can wash the scent away. The animal may visit the set but never step in the trap or may never return at all.

I have been fortunate to have taken part in so many outdoor pursuits and to have met so many outdoorsy people, each with such varied perspectives. These people have shaped my life and my environmental ethics. Earliest memories of my youth are filled with sights and sounds of nature. My first trapping experiences were humbling as were my first experiences hiking with large groups of urban gearheads who marveled at my knowledge of wildlife and laughed at my army surplus clothing and flashlights while they sported the latest in Gore-Tex and microfleece attire and lithium battery headlamps.

I have enjoyed my time spent hiking mile after mile on trails for weeks at a time, canoeing through vast expanses of wilderness and summiting mountain peaks simply for the sake of being there. I've shared meteor showers with friends as we lay on our backs atop a small mountain and listened to a whip-poor-will sing its repetitive song with a line cast in the water, waiting for a bullhead to bite. I've spent restless nights turning in anticipation of the opening day of deer season and have driven in the dark for hours to get a good spot on the river when the salmon were running. I've spent all day building a duck blind in just the right spot for the annual migration. I've skied along forest service roads under the moonlight and dropped a fishing line into an eight-inch hole in the ice of a remote backcountry lake.

All of these experiences added to my appreciation of nature, immersed me in the very thing that makes us human. This is a story about a person who grew up loving nature and wanted nothing more than to spend all his time becoming more proficient figuring it out. It's about a trapper who learned the fundamentals of life through trapping, hunting, and fishing. And who later met extraordinary men and women in a state 2,500 miles away who inspired him to write about their efforts to keep their traditions alive in order to pass on their legacy to future generations.

These people are not famous; they are not the types who sit with perfect posture while listening to classical music and sipping tea. They don't drive fancy sports cars or spend thousands on rare art. They are more likely to be saddling up horses at a trailhead or launching a raft onto a river than they are to be sitting at home on a Saturday morning watching television. Their idea of wildlife is not a partial understanding; it is complete. They know when and where animals will be at different times of the year and fill one freezer with meat and another with fur. Their culture is not governed by rules of proper etiquette; rather, it is the result of generations flowing with the tides of nature.

They live by the laws of the land while keeping their eyes on the laws of man. They are students of nature and loyal servants of wild places and wildlife. There are those who pretend to be trappers, who place traps on forest floors in hopes of making a financial gain with complete disregard for the long-standing traditions of trapper's cherished heritage. This book is not about them. They will never be in the trapping fraternity. This book is about real trappers who put learning about wildlife first—who enjoy being immersed in the natural ecosystem and appreciate the experience of trapping simply because it adds to their appreciation of wild animals. This is the story of modern-day wildlife enthusiasts whose lives revolve around a true love for nature.

Trapper's interest in nature and natural systems is far more involved than the simplistic entrepreneurial spirit required to only take from the resource for a product. Trappers actively participate in scientific studies, aid wildlife managers in assessing wildlife health and alleviate population booms that threaten wildlife production areas and public safety. The skills that trappers have are the culmination of dozens of generations where primitive skills have been preserved and are now being used for modern day conservation. The dedication to preserving these skills is apparent in the continuous outreach and educational events paid for by trappers' own time and money. Trappers aren't hiding away hoping their livelihood will be preserved, they are educating others, promoting their skills and cherishing their rich heritage.

Since time began, man has hunted, trapped and fished for sustenance. It is his natural place to live among the creatures of the forests. It has only been in the last one hundred years of earth's history that the idea of man should separate from nature and only live among man began to grow and only within a few isolated cultures. Even as we move away from nature at this rapid rate, too fast to comprehend the impact of such a rash decision, we move animals into our lives and our homes. Perhaps on some primordial level humans can't let go of our connection with animals, we know that it is unnatural to move away so we invite them in and rationalize that we need pets, not to maintain connectivity to the animals man has relied on for sustenance for thousands of years but for companionship.

As time moves on and society continues to separate from nature becoming encapsulated in concrete and high rise buildings where the only known source of food is found at the grocery store and clothing from the shopping mall, preserving the outdoor skills of trappers, hunters and anglers becomes ever more important. Without the preservation of primitive living skills through people immersed in the natural cycles of nature the connectivity of man to his environment would be severed.

The worst possible outcome of human progression from uncivilized cave dwellers to modern city inhabitants would be one where man is only an observer of nature as if the trees and mountains were but a theater, the animals of the forest no longer sustenance reduced instead to the status of zoo animals. Their habits studied from afar and referenced in the pages of a book to be sure man will remember how animals once were. It will be through the preservation of the skills of hunter and gatherer developed over centuries that will keep man cognizant of the true importance of our natural world.

Perhaps this is the story of man's last ditch effort to remain connected to nature in a way that continues to keep man rooted in the earth. Or maybe it is one of natural history, a snapshot in time in the ever changing evolution of human culture. It might just be the simple story of a kid who grew up in rural America trapping, hunting and fishing and who wants nothing more than to protect and share his love of the outdoors. Regardless of what this story is or will become, it is a true account of a Montana trapper's journey written from the heart.

Chapter 1

Human Economy

The bird a nest, the spider a web, man friendship

—William Blake

A middle-aged woman stepped down onto the metal steps of a train on a foggy spring morning. She had just returned from a trip where she bought needed supplies for the coming year. At home, her family waited. It had been a nice reprieve from her day-to-day chores, but she was anxious to get back home. The bag hanging from her shoulder contained material she would use to make clothes for her children, new needles and thread, fine wool yarn, and three new steel-jawed foothold traps.

Before leaving on this trip, her husband had asked if she would bring with her two dozen muskrat pelts; a request she reluctantly agreed to. While in town, she found a fur buyer who paid her for the furs. She was surprised at the substantial figure, twice her husband's weekly pay from the talc mine. Looking at the money in her hand, she asked how much traps cost.

The year was 1927. The woman was my grandmother, Grace May Walrath, a woman I loved as a young boy. The fur trapper was my grandfather, Franklin Robert, a man I never met but who influenced my life through his legacy of trapping, hunting, and fishing.

Over fifty years later, I stood in our neighbor's frog pond with knee-high rubber boots and a toy gun over my shoulder. Suddenly a familiar voice came seemingly out of nowhere, "What are you doing young man?" my mother asked.

"Hunting rabbits," I stated firmly.

"Well, you should look for those rabbits a little closer to home young man!"

My mother continued trying to keep me from wandering deep into the woods and forests until I was a grown man. She finally gave up, but I never did.

A few years after she found me over a half mile from home "hunting for rabbits", I found several long-spring traps hanging in the horse barn. I had no idea what they were or what they were used for, but I thought they were pretty neat. When my dad came home from work, I asked him what they were. He told me they were number 1 Victor long-spring traps that he used to trap muskrats. I didn't know what a muskrat was. My father had stopped trapping a few years before, partly because my older brothers were no longer around to go with him.

He showed me how the traps were set as he carefully pushed the spring down and opened the jaws. The "dog," as he called it, was flipped over one jaw and pressed under the pan. As long as the dog was over the jaw this way, the spring was held fast. Then he showed me how the trap snapped shut. "This is like a muskrat's foot," he said as he held a stick over the trap pan. "When the 'rat steps on it, it catches his foot and holds him there until you get back."

I asked him to set and reset that trap over and over. Each time he sprung the trap, I was just as excited as the first time. There weren't any muskrats around that I knew of, but after thinking about it for several minutes, I had a revelation. You see, I lived in the middle of a dense, forested old farmland reclaimed by nature. It was bad for the farmers who once etched out a living there but really good for the rodents, raccoons, white-tailed deer and—"Dad!" I exclaimed. "Can these traps catch rabbits?"

He laughed and said, "Oh! I suppose they probably could." He didn't take me too seriously at that young age but didn't wish to prevent my wild wheels from turning. He patted me on the head and went into the house for dinner.

It took some practice, but eventually, I was able to set the traps and figured I could use a carrot from the kitchen for bait. With no instruction, I set several traps on my family's property. The summer went on, turned to fall, and before I knew it, the ground was blanketed in snow. I eventually gave up interest and thought it was impossible to catch a rabbit.

A few years went by and my family moved back to the Adirondack Mountain foothills in New York State. Not the metropolis pictured in the minds of millions with big city lights, tall skyscrapers, and hordes of people. The New York I knew was mountainous rugged country with dense forests and rivers, surrounded by miles of almost impenetrable swamps. Small creeks rushed into flowing rivers. Beaver ponds were not hard to find and neither were trappers.

Main Street had a bar, a grocery and convenience store, a small diner, a town hall, a hardware store, a four-lane bowling alley, and the occasional TV repair shop/video rental/bottle redemption combo store. Of course, there were three churches in town and two small gas stations. That was about it. The local bar held a big buck contest each year, and the winner was determined by the weight of the heaviest buck. All through November, hunters would pull up to the front of the bar and hoist their buck up on the scales. I couldn't wait to see the deer arrive and I would ride my bicycle downtown each day to see what came in.

Throughout the summers of my youth, whenever Dad wasn't working, we camped and fished in the thick mountain country near our home. It was an average weekend when he and I would hike into a lake or drive somewhere to pick berries, catch fish, or look for deer sign. We trolled for walleyes in local lakes from his motorboat or rowed across a quiet lake, catching trout. We would fish through the ice in winter, sit on the banks of the river in spring with a warm campfire, rods leaned against forked sticks, waiting for a bite. I hardly have a memory of time spent with my Dad when we weren't enjoying nature together. But when deer season came, he went alone. I wasn't old enough to hunt deer yet, and it was the only time of year he didn't take me along.

It was at these times that I wished I could hunt and spend more time with the man whose woodsman skills I admired so much. His storytelling could go on for hours, and it seemed like there wasn't anything he didn't know about. Every tree, every fern, every wild animal, he knew what it was. Every track or scat on the forest floor told a story, and he would kneel down and read it to me. The stories that unfolded told us which animal was there, where it came from, and where it was going. He taught me to slowdown and look, to really see what was going on around us. It wasn't the superficial one-dimensional understanding received from the pages of a book. It was up close and personal. I can't imagine my life without placing my hand over a raccoon track along a riverbank and following it to learn about wild animals.

We would sit for hours waiting for deer to enter the fields near our home in the evenings all summer long and take turns with binoculars to see the spots on the fawns and the antlers on the bucks. Wild turkeys and grouse, red fox and muskrats, it didn't matter, he loved to watch them and marveled at their ability to survive in the harsh winters of the Adirondack Mountains. He knew how to shoot straight and rarely missed. He could cut down trees and make a soft bed and a campfire. He too possessed the abilities to survive in the harsh elements, and he shared them freely.

It didn't take long for me to think of my options when the leaves started turning and my father disappeared into the forests in pursuit of deer. Those old traps had to be around somewhere! I managed to drum up several traps, and my school library had the *Trapper and Predator Caller* magazine available for students to read. I read like there was no tomorrow. I planned and prepared all summer and early fall and I couldn't wait until trapping season opened. I was determined to catch something! I read about trapping raccoons and collected corn and fish. *The perfect bait*, I thought. Then the season finally opened.

The Oswegatchie River was flowing high due to a dam upstream on the river which unnaturally controlled the water flow. I was forced to make alternative sets. Leaning a small log against a tree, I notched out the perfect place for a trap. Above it, about eighteen inches, I nailed a piece of corn to the log. I made my way through the thick edge of a hayfield and laid corn out all over the ground and staked two traps amid the bait. This was sure to lure a raccoon in! How could any 'coon resist?

The next morning, I was anxious to check my traps, but I had to go to school and checking would take too long. As soon as the school bus pulled up to my door, I wasted no time throwing my backpack in the front door, greeted my mother with a quick hello, and sped off on my bicycle to catch my first 'coon!

At least that's what I thought was going to happen. Without a mentor to teach me, I didn't know yet how to trap. I removed my trap from there and decided I would make a type of set I had seen somewhere that I knew had to work. I hung bait from a tree on the edge of the hayfield and laid the trap under it instead. I recalled from an antiquated trapping book that this set was good for fox. *There has to be a fox around here somewhere*, I thought.

When my new masterful set was complete, I ran to the corn set. This one had to have worked because as everyone knows, raccoons love corn, and I had seen raccoons in this field before. As I made my way up the drainage and into the field, I didn't see anything. As I got closer, I noticed that all my traps were sprung. *How could this be?* I thought to myself. Closer inspection revealed deer tracks and lots of them. The corn, I quickly learned, attracts deer very well and those traps wouldn't hold them. I envisioned a small group of deer smelling the corn and walking in then suddenly dancing around as traps sprung harmlessly at their feet. I reset the traps and, disappointed in my day's apparent failure, made my way back home.

After about a week of catching nothing, I decided that I needed to try something new. As I made my way out of the woods and back to the road where my bicycle lay, I came across a rather large hole in the ground. It had my curiosity perked. The hole was about ten inches in diameter, and the fresh dirt revealed a track. A raccoon track! I quickly set a number 1 long spring in front of the hole and wired it a nearby tree. This was going to work! And the best part was that the next day was Saturday! I could be there first thing in the morning!

I was restless all night. I just knew that raccoon would be back, and that trap was going to catch it! At first light, I woke up and was out the door before my parents even knew I was up. I sped down the rural road to where the creek crossed under it, threw my bike down, and ran to the first trap. I didn't see anything at the hole but noticed that the ground was covered in dirt and looked a little torn up. *What had happened*, I thought? I made my way closer and closer still. Then suddenly I noticed—the trap was gone! The wire was fastened hard to the tree on one end and disappeared into the hole on the other end. I carefully grabbed the wire and tugged. Something tugged back! I had trapped a raccoon! I pulled the wire but to no avail. That 'coon wanted no part of getting pulled out of the hole.

I had no idea what to do. Even if I got him out of there, what then? I was still too young to carry a gun other than my BB gun by myself—my mother's rules. I was going to have to figure this out. I quickly checked my other traps and found them undisturbed, so I ran back to my bicycle and sped home as fast as I could. My mother was surprised to see me come in the front door and would have scolded me were it not for my excited tale of my first raccoon. I begged her to let me take the .22 rifle to shoot my prized furbearer but the rules were clear—no.

I would have to get my older sister to accompany me. Trish was all of thirteen years old, still three years older than me, and my mother knew I would listen to her if she would just please come help me get this raccoon!

It seemed like hours waiting for Trish to get ready and ride to my trapline with me, although it was more like ten minutes. With my dad's .22 rifle across my handlebars, Trish and I rode across town and to the field where I had my first animal awaiting. The situation was a little tough because the 'coon was dug in deep, and I couldn't pull it out. I had apparently given it too much wire, and it was really in there. The correct trapping method is to stake the trap securely on a short chain, but I hadn't learned that yet.

Trish and I devised a plan that involved a stout stick and her leveraging it against the bank above the hole, one end under her weight, the other end with wire wrapped around it solidly enough to pry the trap and 'coon out of the hole far enough for me to get a .22 round into the 'coons vitals.

It was going along quite well. The 'coon was slowly coming to the surface, and I was ready. I saw the trap chain first and then the foot came up out of the hole along with the trap. Trish was really straining now and had all her weight on the stick. It was up to me to put a well-placed shot on the raccoon as soon as I had a chance.

As the foot emerged, I remember thinking, *man, that's a lot darker than I thought it would be.* Suddenly the 'coon popped out of the hole. This "coon" was black and white, and I knew immediately what that meant. I jumped back just in time for the skunk to lift its tail and spray my sister head on. She screamed like only a thirteen-year-old girl can but didn't remove her weight from the short stick holding the skunk in position. I made a quick shot that put the skunk down quickly but not before releasing another 4:4:3 ratio dose of crotyl mercaptan, isopentyl mercaptan, and methyl crotyl disulfide, aka skunk pee.

Trish and I learned that skunks are excellent diggers but needless to say, that was the only time she ever helped me on my trapline. I brought the skunk home and skinned it out. Quite proud of my accomplishment, I fleshed, stretched and hung it on the front porch. I don't think my mother held the skunk in the high regard that I did!

I kept trapping without much success but bought more traps with money that I earned from selling night crawlers to local fisherman. A painted plywood sign in front of my house read: Night crawlers 50¢ per dozen. I caught the night crawlers by walking around town in yards and grass-covered parking lots with a flashlight in one hand and a can in the other. On warm and rainy summer nights, I could pick up to one thousand crawlers in a single evening. I filled large washtubs with moss which I dug from a nearby cedar swamp. Coffee grounds and potato peels fed them all summer.

A few other boys in town took interest in trapping, and I had friends accompany me while I set traps. Occasionally, one would be excited and want to check every day for a while. But as the seasons went on and the traps remained empty, many of my friends lost interest. There were plenty of other things to do like school sports, hunting, and homework. As for me, spending all my time walking along the river and studying tracks and scat was the greatest thing ever. I never lost interest; I loved the outdoors and spent all my time playing in the woods.

When a local boy whom I went to school with drowned in the river, it was tragic. His name was Tommy, and he was about the same age as me, and he was also a trapper. His older brother, Donnie, missed his brother and the traplines they shared. Which is why, I realized years later, he took me trapping with him. He was about four years older than me, and I looked up to him. He knew how to trap muskrats and mink, and we spent several weeks together trapping. I have photos of me as a youngster with my first muskrats, thanks to Donnie.

When Donnie moved on, I tried to catch beavers but couldn't. I tried for weeks during the fall but to no avail. Dad gave me advice but was too busy at work and deer hunting to trap with me. Then he developed heart trouble and was forced to retire. It was this life-changing event that started changing my success as a trapper, and as I would learn, was the start of memorable relationships woven together with the reeds of traplines.

In the spring of 1991, Dad bought me an ash wood-woven pack basket, traps suitable for catching beaver which included three number 3 double long-spring traps, two number 330 body gripping traps, and the best part of all, he took me trapping. The next few years were made of my fondest memories and influenced the course of my life perhaps more than any other.

Dad was an excellent teacher and knew to start with the basics. He told stories of his traplines and trapping partners from days gone by that captivated me and really got me excited. Then he signed us both up for a trapper education class which consisted of three days instruction and two evenings of listening to the instructor talk about laws, ethics, responsible trapping, and types of equipment and their uses.

There was one field day when we got to observe experienced trappers make sets and ask questions about why they were set a certain way and how to be selective about which animal we trapped and how to avoid non-target animals. It opened my eyes to a whole new level of understanding. These trappers taught us to place traps to the left or right of a beaver slide because beaver feet are not in the center of their body. For otters, they set the traps deep about ten inches from the bank and under eighteen inches of water to ensure a hind foot catch

The drowning slides they made were with 9-11 gauge wire or cable, and they attached one end to a heavy cement block. On the end of their trap chains, a piece of angle iron was attached with a hole drilled in the *L*. By sliding the 9-gauge wire through the hole in the angle iron, it would slide down the wire to the bottom but would kink and not allow the trap to slide back up the wire. All advice Dad had given me countless times, but like so many young boys, I wasn't very adept at listening. It took being shown how to trap correctly by experienced trappers to really know how. An experienced teacher is the most important aspect of a new trapper's education.

When a beaver steps in a trap, its first instinct is to dive, it's a natural defense mechanism, but when the trap chain and trap—beaver attached, reaches the bottom of the slide wire, it can't go anywhere. This kills the beaver quickly. The alternative is a large body-gripping trap which slams shut on the beaver's neck. It is simple, but effective. However, the body grip trap is not always feasible, and beavers have been known to develop wariness around traps just like their distant cousins who wreak havoc in homes across America: the mouse. The foot trap still has a necessary place in the trapper's tool box, just as it did over one hundred years ago.

The instructors made dirt hole sets for canine species like the red fox and coyote and informed students that these would work for bobcats, fishers, and skunks. I already had a disposition toward skunks but listened anyway. The instructors used a small trowel to dig out a section of topsoil and set it aside. The resulting hole in the ground, called a trap bed, was slightly larger than the trap which was about four-and-a-half inches wide when set. A hole two inches in diameter and about ten inches deep was dug at an angle right at the edge of the trap bed and a teaspoon-sized gob of gland lure consisting of ground up fox or coyote glands, preservative, and antifreeze agents like glycerin or salt among other really ripe ingredients were placed at the bottom of the hole. The trap was bedded solidly four inches back, and to the right of the hole, a wad of grass was placed under the pan of the trap.

Next, he took the dirt from the topsoil he removed to make the trap bed and placed it in a sifter. The sifter was merely a wood frame with wire mesh stapled to the bottom. He placed the sifter filled with dirt over the trap and shook it, causing fine dirt to cover the trap until it was hidden. The wad of grass was to prevent dirt from getting under the pan. The airspace created by the grass would allow the pan to function. Genius!

All the books and magazine articles I had read didn't add up to watching someone do it. If only I had taken the education class before my first attempts at trapping on my own. I began to realize the true importance of trapper education and a good mentor.

Dad knew most of what these instructors were teaching, but he wanted to be part of my interests and hadn't ever been to a trapper education class because it wasn't mandatory for him thirty years ago. It was great to have Dad there with me. We took an exam at the end of the class and he got a higher grade than I did, four percentage points higher, in fact. It's funny, the things you remember even years later. The thing that I remember most is that he was there and we enjoyed our time together as we would for many seasons to come.

A few weeks later, we were out on a beaver pond, setting traps, finally! Dad got permission to trap a fairly large piece of private land where the beaver were numerous. At the same time, my nephew Tony who being two years older than me and more like a brother in our youth, was learning to trap with my much older sister's husband, Mike. I secretly wanted to catch a beaver before he did but didn't let on too much.

After a week of trap checks, we had what amounted to a handful of sprung traps. We found where the beaver were breaking through the ice along the flooded waterline. The water had dropped over the winter, leaving an air space between the thick ice and the surface of the water. The hole in the ice was big enough that I could fit my head and shoulders inside and peer in. I could see remnants from saplings, all the bark chewed off and floating. There were beaver tracks in the mud where the water had dropped and it smelled like beaver castor. I was amazed at the world that lived below the ice in winter. It was obvious that below the ice, there was more activity than above it.

Outside of this underworld, farther upstream were beaver dams made of mud, sticks, and debris. Water trickled slowly over the dams except for a few places where it seemed to flow like a small stream. Below the dams on these places were channels etched out of the heavy mud. Closer inspection revealed that these areas were worn by beaver activity. The channels, no doubt, were formed by beavers pulling small logs over the dams and back to their food caches or feeding sites. The beaver were clearly swimming to the edge of the creeks and ponds to get to fresh saplings and chewing them down. The tracks in the remaining spring snow told the story.

Dad explained how the beaver would cut down trees and store them in front of their lodges, which he called houses, and during the deep freeze of winter, they would only have to swim out several feet to retrieve a piece. They would then eat all the bark off inside their house and push it out the hole. All the bright white sticks with bark removed sunk in the water or floating nearby, indicated the whereabouts of beaver or where they planned to eat next. The things I learned about wild animals while trapping stuck and my passion for learning about them grew.

I worked my way up the flow to a large tree root that stuck up over five feet next to the water's edge. I had placed a number 3 double long-spring trap in there a week ago, and so far, every check I found that it was sprung and empty. I peered into the hole and the trap was gone. *Oh, great*, I thought. *Here we go again*. But this time, when I pulled on the wire, it felt heavy. I tugged and then pulled in the wire steadily. I was pulling pretty hard when suddenly fur emerged from the water. "I got one!" I yelled.

"Well, all right, I told ya one was going to come back here and get caught in that trap. You can't get discouraged," he said.

Wow! I finally had my first beaver, and it seemed big. Much bigger than any muskrat I had ever caught. I couldn't wait to get home and show my mother and Tony! This was one of the most memorable moments of my life, even now. Dad was proud and I'll bet relieved a little that we had finally caught one. The conditions had been tough, and we didn't have a lot of traps. But I could not have been happier in that moment.

The fur was thick and winter prime. It had huge webbed feet with a groomer toe nail and long claws. I marveled at the creature in a bittersweet moment, similar to hunting my first deer. Every hunter and trapper experiences that feeling of success tinged with remorse for killing an animal. It is part of nature, of hunting, fishing and trapping as man is meant to do. At the time, it was a real challenge, and I had to work for it. I had spent several seasons trying to catch one, but it took someone who knew how to trap and was willing to show me to be successful. That is one reason so many people trap for one or two seasons and quit. Trapping is hard. It takes time and dedication to become proficient at it. New trappers need a mentor, period. My understanding of the need for trapper education was sparked by this experience. Even at a young age, I got it, although I had no idea how much it would mean to me later.

When we got home, my dad showed me how to skin and remove the flesh from the beaver pelt. All we had was a small hand-fleshing tool that I had for muskrats, and with no plywood to stretch it out on, I used the inside of our wood garage door. I used roofing nails and tacked the nose of the pelt to the door at about eye level. Next, I put a nail on the outer edges of each side, followed by one at the tail. Slowly, I scraped fat off the beaver and kept adding nails to make it round. I scraped that beaver for over an hour and still couldn't quite get the meat and fat off. I insisted that I do it myself, and Dad let me. It didn't come out all that good, but I thought it was good enough.

Dad hadn't trapped much since I had been born and no longer had his tools of the trade. I had resparked his enthusiasm, and we kept trapping until we had twenty beavers and twenty muskrats. One set for beaver stood out as the primary producer. Below a large beaver dam about 120 feet in length and a full six feet over the creek which it dammed, a tree had fallen across the water, leaving about three feet between the top of the tree and the opposite bank. Dad and I used sticks to wedge in between the limbs of the tree and stuck them hard into the creek bottom. We then fastened a number 330 body gripping trap at the end of the tree where the only opening remained. I remember that in this one trap, we caught eleven beavers in twelve days. In fact, on the day we didn't catch one in it, I was surprised.

One morning, we pulled up to the creek and could see a beaver sitting on the ice just off the bank. As I walked down the bank, it jumped into the water and swam upstream, causing the ice above its wake to creak and groan. When it got below the dam, the water was open, and I watched it run up the dam on a section worn from so many beavers traveling over it. "We have trap up there!" I yelled.

"Yup, sure do," Dad replied. When the beaver got to the top of the dam, I saw it slap its tail and water flew. I ran to the top of the dam, and when I got there, the chain of the trap was stuck on one of the stake sticks I had used to hold the top of the slide wire in place. I reached down and pulled the chain off, and the beaver dove. It was dead in a minute, just like the first deer I shot with an arrow.

My family was sustained in large part by the food we got from the forest. We ate deer, small game and fish and picked wild leeks and fiddleheads in spring. We tapped sugar maple trees and boiled hundreds of gallons of sap each year in February and March to make delicious maple syrup. Blueberries, raspberries, and black caps were picked by the bucket loads and made into pies, added to pancakes, or eaten fresh. Now I was catching animals and selling the fur. It was hard work, but I loved it. We averaged about $20.00 per beaver pelt and about $3.50 for each muskrat for a total of $470.00. That may not seem like much, but at the time, it was a significant financial help, and I was able to buy things that I needed with my own money. And I loved learning about wildlife through firsthand experience.

As new seasons came and went, Dad and I trapped more and more fur together. Eventually, I was successfully trapping on my own and he came along less and less due to health issues. Tony continued to trap, and for a time, worked for a landscaping company during summer. He and Mike spent a month in spring trapping. They would stay in a trapper's camp deep in the woods until seasons end, and again in fall once the demands of landscaping were complete. They produced a lot of fur doing this, and it helped substantially with their finances. In that area of New York State, there aren't many options for work in winter, and unemployment checks only go so far.

Their stories of weeks spent in the woods in a makeshift camp and all the adventure that comes with it were thrilling. I would eventually get my chance too, but it would be years later.

Chapter 2

On the Line

Free enterprise is essentially a formula not just for wealth creation, but for life satisfaction.

—Arthur C. Brooks

During my senior year of high school, Tony and I trapped on a dairy farm with a very high number of muskrats, mink, and raccoons. It was not uncommon to walk that line and have ten to fifteen muskrats in one day. The fur prices were stable, and we were getting around $4 each for muskrats, $18 for mink and several raccoon pelts broke the $25 mark. If we placed the muskrat carcasses in plastic bags provided by the fur buyer, we were given 75¢ for two. The muskrats were sold to restaurants in western New Jersey and New York City. The fur buyer told me that they were marketed as marsh rabbits. They primarily eat vegetation and are actually very clean animals. There is no reason why they wouldn't taste good.

Our trapline was about 3 miles long and it was best to be dropped off at one end of the creek system and get picked up on the other. We took turns checking the line every day and would meet at my house to skin and stretch the pelts in my basement. We trapped the most muskrats I have ever trapped in a single season that year. It was a lot of fun to be outside every day trudging through the swamps, and I looked forward to the evening skinning sessions. We didn't have much money and my hip waders were ripped, duct-taped, ripped, and so on until it was pointless to even try. Eventually, we both ended up just getting wet every day, and it was a challenge to stay dry for as long as possible.

The bogs we trapped in were comprised of grass hummocks that moved and shifted when we jumped on them. They were surrounded by three to four feet of water which made for an exciting game of hop the hummocks until we got wet. It was inevitable, which wasn't too bad on a 50-degree spring day, but when temps dropped below freezing, that was a different story. Despite all the wet cold conditions, I was never sick in high school and never missed a day due to illness. However, I did miss a few due to hunting season and the salmon run out of Lake Ontario!

One day while Tony was checking the line on his own, we had an otter in a trap set for beavers. Otters were abundant but trap wary, and we had never caught one before. It was a rare event and one of the few photos I ever took of an animal we trapped. The river otter is a unique animal with beautiful sleek fur and a powerful build. They were made to hunt in the water and are awesome to watch. We were very proud of that otter, and at the time, they were selling for $60-$100. That made it even better for a couple of poor kids.

The fur buyer we sold our furs to lived about thirty-five miles away. His name was Lonnie, and he always gave us a fair price. It was an exciting event to go to the fur buyers. We would gather our furs and put them in the back of the car and make the one-hour drive. When we walked in to the building where Lonnie bought and sold fur, it was incredible. There were hundreds of pelts hanging to dry, everything imaginable. Beavers were on metal hoops stacked fur-to-fur, skin-to-skin, and otters tacked perfectly on basswood stretchers leaned against the wall. They seemed so big! Fox, coyotes, raccoons, and countless muskrat and mink pelts hung from heavy cable stretched across the room above our heads. There were thousands of dollars' worth of furs hanging in there. Much of the fur was caught, fleshed, and stretched by Lonnie. Others were purchased from trappers who sold their animals "in the round" which means they weren't skinned, fleshed, or stretched. Lonnie would look at the animal in the round and make an assessment what it would be worth skinned, fleshed and stretched on a forming board or as he called it "put up," less a fee for doing the putting up himself.

We always put our fur up ourselves and took pride in it. There are very specific ways to put up each type of fur to bring the most value. Lonnie gave us tips and tricks as to how to go about improving the quality of our furs. For example, raccoon are case or tube skinned which means the pelt ends up shaped like a sock versus open like a beaver. The classic beaver pelt depicted in mountain man scenes shows the round pelts shaped by weaving leather strips through the edges and wrapping them around lashed willow branches hanging outside the camp or on the cabin wall, and this is still the method used today sans the willow hoops and leather lacing.

Nowadays, trappers use metal hoops with hooks, or plywood and nails, to get the same effect. The hair on a raccoon is thickest on its lower back, and fur buyers like to see the hair quickly and easily when grading. This is made easier by the fur handler, in this case, us, by cutting a window out of the belly area of the pelt to allow the back hair to be seen after the hide is stretched fur side in. There is a specific way to cut the window out. Too small and the window is no good. Too big, and the grade of the pelt can be decreased. Likewise, a muskrat pelt should have a little flesh left on the skin. Take too much off, get it too clean, and you can damage the hide. Leave too much on it can grease burn. The more we went to Lonnie, the better the quality of our fur became.

As daylight diminishes in autumn, the under fur of furbearing animals becomes thicker or prime and long guard hairs lengthen. Depending on the time of year the animal was trapped, the quality of the pelt can be really good or various levels of not-so-good. Trapping season dates are set to have them overlap the time when fur is most prime. Many regulated trapping seasons don't start until November or December. This makes trapping more difficult because the snow is deep and the temperatures are cold, but the fur is at its best, which is important for sales and the trapper's ethic to get the most out of every animal he catches.

Local fur buyers make a return on their investment in several ways. One way is to predict what the international market is going to be and pay accordingly. There are numerous state and national auctions, and like any industry, some sales attract bigger buyers with more money to spend. It can be a gamble, but fur buyers send or take the fur they've purchased to the large auction houses and put it on the world market. Hopefully they have done their homework and make a profit. Guess it wrong, and they could lose.

Another way local fur buyers make a return is by having contacts with specific orders. Furriers place orders for certain pelts and establish a price they are willing to pay. The fur buyer then actively seeks out those types of pelts and does his best to fill the order. If the buyer produces quality merchandise, his customer is happy. Keeping contacts and customers happy is necessary for success in any business, and the fur industry is no exception.

The advantage of trappers selling to local fur buyers is they get their money immediately. Trappers can send their fur to an International auction house but may not get paid for several weeks or months. Additionally, there is always the chance that the local buyer will pay more for pelts than he receives. By selling to a middle man, trappers know what they are going to get and get paid immediately.

Lonnie would write us a check on the spot, and that was it. The money Tony and Mike received helped put food on the table. For me, I used the extra cash to pay for gas or buy clothes. Having that money was a significant help to my family then and is still essential for many families in Montana and across the country today.

After graduating high school, I decided to go to college. I went to the North Country Community College in Saranac Lake, New York. My major was wilderness recreation. I absolutely loved going to college there, except I didn't have any place to trap or put up my fur. During winter break, I did one thing when I was home. I went trapping.

Part of my curriculum for my degree was a public speaking class. On one occasion, we were asked to speak about an issue of our choice. I chose trapping. I brought in traps and fleshing tools and a beaver pelt. I gave a demonstration and talked about the benefits trapping provides to wildlife and the economic and social positives. One student in the class named Marnee refused to touch the beaver hide as it was passed around. Several weeks later, I was standing in front of a vending machine in the student lounge and was a quarter short. I openly asked if anyone had a spare quarter I could borrow. Marnee said, "I wouldn't give you a quarter if you were the last person on earth!" before storming off down the corridor. I was confused.

I asked another student what her problem was, and he said, "You're so archaic, man." I hadn't even considered that anyone would be so upset.

As the year progressed, I met my future wife, Katie. We became friends and shared a lot of time together. Just before spring break, she asked what I was doing over the holiday. I told her I was going to go home and trap beavers with Dad and couldn't wait. "Is that even legal?" she asked.

"Legal!" I exclaimed. "Yeah, it's legal. Are you kidding me?" I asked. She wasn't kidding. I had heard and read about anti-everything environmentalists but didn't realize that the general public didn't know anything about trapping. *How could this be?* I thought. Trapping had been such a big part of my life. Could it really be so unknown?

I went home and trapped with Dad. We caught several beavers and muskrats and had a great time being outdoors together. Those days spent with Dad on a trapline were special. I had no idea how short our time would be together. The tables had begun to turn, and it was I who was able to set the traps. Old age and arthritis prevented him from using his previous abilities which I remembered from my youth. When I was thirteen or fourteen, I couldn't get a number 3 long-spring set. Dad had to set them for me. Now he was the one unable to set them. He would try anyway, and on occasion, he would get one set. He'd remind me that he "wasn't dead yet" and then go about making a set. Those days are bittersweet and make my heart sink and pound with excitement at the same time. Those memories live on, and I'll cherish them forever.

After graduating from college with a degree in wilderness recreation, I decided to head south to see what the Carolinas had to offer. No particular reason or logic was involved in that decision. I jumped in a truck one day with a buddy and drove south until we found jobs. The summer was hot and humid, the work long and hard. I missed my mountains and cold air; and it didn't take long for me to miss trapping the rivers, streams, and muskrat marshes of the North Country. I left on a bus back to my beloved northern mountains and trapped beavers, fox, muskrats, mink, fishers, and otters. My sister lived far out in the mountains, and I often left her house for a twelve—to fifteen-mile trapline on foot. That adventurous season lives in my memory as the wildest of my life. Much of my line was in the high country, and I had a canoe stashed for trapping along the Oswegatchie River.

In the meantime, my future wife was only an hour and a half away and came to visit me and my fur shed on occasion. She also went on my trapline for the first time and really enjoyed it. I caught several muskrats, a mink, and one red fox that day. We skinned the animals, and she got a lesson in fur trapping. I remember asking her if she would stay to help put all the fur up, to which she replied, "Those muskrats aren't going to help me with my chemistry homework!"

I decided to go back to college at her request and enrolled in a state university for biology. I missed trapping so much. I left the wilds of the trapline for a studio apartment in town. What a drastic change! I studied hard and did well but couldn't wait to change majors and universities.

It was at this college in 1998 that I first began to use the Internet to post my protrapping views on various forums. My eyes were opened to the absolute hatred toward trappers and trapping. I really couldn't believe it. The "bubble" I grew up in popped.

I decided to get involved in trapper education to help teach responsible trapping. I knew more had to be done to improve the trappers' image, and I wanted to get involved. I applied to be a New York State trapping instructor. A game warden came to my apartment and interviewed me as part of a background check. He asked me about my experience and laughed when I told him my stories. I was in, and he set me up with two head instructors to begin teaching classes in the fall.

Katie and I enrolled in the State University of New York at Plattsburgh, located on the eastern fringe of the Adirondacks, not far from where she grew up. This area offered excellent access to marshes and beaver ponds with a short drive out of town. Even better was the availability of a makeshift fur shed in her parents' abandoned woodshed. I trapped two beavers and half a dozen muskrats that fall. It was great just to get out. I also managed to shoot a white-tailed buck while on my trapline. *Things aren't so bad here after all!* I thought, even as I longed to return to my wilderness trapline.

Chapter 3

Tools of the Trade

Give me six hours to chop down a tree and I will spend the first four sharpening the axe.

—Abraham Lincoln

Truly understanding the trapping culture requires learning about trappers and what they actually do. Trapping is physically challenging and commitment to the trapline is paramount to a trapper's success. So many would-be trappers quit after a few short weeks once they realize what it takes to manage a trapline. Taking a hard look at the hands-on aspects of trapping reveals the required knowledge and practical understanding of topography and the animals that inhabit the forests and waterways.

There is no room for laziness in trapping pursuits. Traps must be boiled, dyed, and waxed to withstand the elements; lures made or purchased; locations scouted; traps tagged; and weatherproof waxed dirt made by the barrel and traps boiled all weeks in advance of season. Then there are the physical demands of hauling, setting, maintaining, checking traps, and handling fur. Fur handling would be considered a full-time job for most people, but trappers just consider it part of a night's activity. When many people are sleeping after a long day's work, trappers make another pot of coffee and "get after it" in the fur shed. Good fur handling is an absolute must for trappers. Pelts must be skinned with fine attention to detail, combed, sometimes washed; all flesh must be removed from the hide through the act of rigorous scraping.

Stretching and drying methods that produce the best possible fur pelts require attention to detail and refined technique. It's no wonder there aren't more trappers, trapping is hard, requires extreme physical stamina, devotion to the trapline, and a high level of skill which must be developed over time. There are no shortcuts, no easy money, and the road to success is paved with challenges. So why would anyone put their self through this? Where does the relentless drive to succeed in such endeavors come from? Why do trappers trap? How do trappers trap?

Trapping fundamentals are based on two major types of trapping; land trapping and water trapping. Trapping on land targets furbearing or predator species who primarily make their living hunting or scavenging in the forests outside of the water. Water trapping involves setting traps for aquatic furbearers that spend a majority of their time in and around the water. There are key differences between land trapping and water trapping and the knowledge and skills are far different. Some trappers run a mixed species line that involves land and water sets while others choose one over the other.

A land trapper drives to a location on public or private land and after sorting through traps and trowels, lures and sifters, loads the items into a pack basket. Then the trapper hikes along the trail until he finds an area where the target species may travel. These areas could be where a steep ridge meets a creek bed or a tight draw works its way to the bottom of a canyon. It might be a saddle on a ridge top or a narrow spot in a bubbling brook, depending on the species and their habits. These locations may naturally funnel an animal to a location accessible to the trapper.

A walk of one hundred feet or more from the trail and a blown down tree or an exposed root is found that will make a perfect place for a cubby set. A few added sticks and branches piled just right form a small cave and bait made from glands, meat, urine, visual attractants like goose feathers or Christmas tree tinsel in any combination are placed in the back of the cubby. A foot trap of appropriate size, no greater than six inches in total width, is staked solidly to the ground and placed in a manner that will direct the bobcat, fisher, or fox to the two-inch diameter trap pan. Care is taken to get the trap in position and bedded solidly. Close attention to detail is paramount and more furbearers that approach the set are missed due to improper placement of traps than any other reason. If the trap is too close to the cubby, not bedded solidly, pan set too high, stepping sticks are inaccurate or any number of other mistakes can prevent the trap from being successful. Trapping is difficult, and it takes a keen level of understanding about animal behavior to be effective.

Not just anyone can trap with consistent success, and more often than not, a new trapper will fail. If they don't get proper instruction, they give up. Many trappers place forty traps or more on their traplines, and days, even weeks can go by without catching anything. It can be frustrating to check empty traps time and again. Trappers begin to think that they may have done something wrong; left too much human scent around the trap, used a poor bait or lure, and picked a poor location. They begin to question their trapping ability. Then the weather will change and suddenly three or four traps hold animals. With renewed confidence, the trapper checks his line with vigor, adds lure to each set, remakes sets thought to be frozen and moves traps to new locations—excited to have another successful day. It is a lot like hunting, day after day of near misses or nothing at all then one or two days that are exceptional; these are the days all outdoors people live for.

There are numerous ways to make set locations other than cubbies. Dirt hole sets, which are just as they sound, are made up of holes in the ground with bait or lure placed in the hole and a steel foothold trap buried in front and staked solid.

Pee post sets are made where urine is sprayed on a fence post or tree with a trap placed right where a wild animal will step when they stop to freshen the post. Sometimes the pee post is natural, and other times, the trapper creates one. Sets without any lure or bait, simply a prediction of where an animal will step when it passes through, are called blind sets.

Sets made for aquatic furbearers add a whole new dimension to trapping and far different challenges and subsequent approach. Water freezes and ice builds up on traps and snares. Deep mud and swift water all present unique challenges. Most water sets are made as blind sets, without lure. Observing tracks and underwater travel routes of the local furbearing species and placing a trap in that very location yields high numbers of catches throughout a season. Gland-and food-based lures can also be placed near travel routes to bring the furbearers into the trap.

Hundreds of books and videos are available to teach trapping techniques. Online trapping forums also provide a place for trappers to learn and share. Success in trapping takes years of practice, and every region in the world offers unique challenges. Trappers setting locations in the tidal marshes of Louisiana face far different conditions than a Montana Rocky Mountain trapper. Trappers adapt or fail.

A trapper can have one or two traps set along a single trail, or he can have ten canyons set with a dozen sets each. It depends on the trapper and his ability to set and maintain traps. Other trappers have access to miles of roads either on public or private grounds and make sets which are visible from their vehicle. These trappers then drive along two track roads in vehicles or ATVs while keeping an eye out for good locations to set and check each already made set for caught furbearers.

Although this may sound easier than the wilderness trapline, ten to twelve hours a day spent driving, getting out, walking several hundred feet, sorting traps, reluring and remaking sets after a storm, dealing with heavy mud and snow takes its physical toll. Sometimes traps are sprung and empty either from a false mechanical release or by an animal which tripped the trap but did not get caught.

Regardless of the number of traps or method of travel, the sets a trapper make become "a trapline." The reality of the trapline is misunderstood by the general public. The average person, not well versed in the signs of nature, can't discern a one-pound marten track from a thirty pound wolverine let alone fathom what managing a trapline with a hundred or so traps might be like.

The question is often asked by novice trappers: "How many animals can I catch in one season?" That is like asking how many fish a new angler can catch or how many mountains a new climber can climb. Depending on the population of the animal a trapper intends to trap in the area, how many quality sets are made, weather, location, lure, technique . . . so many factors contribute to the success or failure of trappers. Some trappers focus on one species like marten and run long hard traplines deep into the wilderness and may catch forty marten in one season. In some parts of the country, two hundred marten might not be unheard of. But most trappers are closer to six or eight.

A long liner, a term used to describe a trapper who drives 50-350 miles a day tending traps in several counties or across state lines may collect upwards of five hundred fox where their numbers are high, but again, that is spread out over hundreds of miles and takes an extreme level of dedication and competency. Most trappers running multispecies lines close to home are happy with four or five fox over two or three months of trapping.

While it is difficult to make a statement about an average trapper's catch, if there is such a thing, most trappers target different species throughout each season. They may start with coyotes, fox, and bobcats then switch to marten during the winter, and in spring, focus on beavers and mink. It all depends on the animals that fascinate the trapper the most. Some trappers are strictly coyote trappers while others only trap beavers, otters, and muskrats. A lot depends on the availability of the furbearers and the trapper's preference. Some hunters like to hunt white-tailed deer; others like to hunt mountain lions or both. It really can't be explained, trappers and hunters develop a love for one thing over another, and that is it.

Hollywood and political propaganda make up the vast majority of our nontrapping public's knowledge of traps and trapping. Images of huge bear traps with steel teeth and animals suffering for days are infused in the minds of those who never listened to the trappers' side of the story. The fact is that most trappers have a high level of respect and admiration for the animals they trap and use the most modern and humane traps possible to ensure the least amount of distress.

Although trap modifications have advanced over the last three decades, it has been a difficult road for trappers to find and use the best methods for trapping. Humane methods and equipment are widely available to trappers today, and the improvements have been significant.

The leghold trap, more appropriately referred to as a foothold trap because of where the device holds an animal, was the first steel trap commercially manufactured. The Peck Stow and Wilcox Co. was making traps with cut springs and cast jaws in 1831. However, S. Newhouse, has been credited with making the first commercially available traps in the U.S. mostly due to his good advertising sense. Regardless of who first started manufacturing these traps, the basic design concept of steel traps hasn't changed all that much since the first one.

Foot hold traps commonly employed by trappers range in size from traps with jaw spreads three inches wide to just over nine inches. The jaw spread is the distance between the jaws when the trap is set. A pan located roughly in the center of the jaws is the part of the trap that the animal must step on in order to cause the trap jaws to close. Trap sizes have developed as changes in specificity for each type of furbearing animal have been found. The trap sizes traditionally have been seemingly arbitrary but have been designated as number 0, number 1, number 1.5 and so on up to number 5. Similarly large traps have been given other designations such as number 9 or 44. The largest jaw spread used for fur trapping is about 9 inches. While dimensions for sizes vary somewhat depending on manufacturer specifications the common number 1.5 used for a variety of species has about a four inch jaw spread and a number 5 is much closer to nine inches. Other manufacturers have determined their own trap size designations such as Minnesota Brands 550, 650 and 750. The MB 450's have a jaw spread of about 4.5 inches and by comparison the MB 750 is about eight inches.

The humungous bear traps shown on television dramas are still manufactured for novelty and certainly draw attention as cabin décor but bear traps such as these are no longer used by fur trappers. Under very specific and unique circumstances regulations may allow a trapper to use a large bear trap following strict protocol. Most states do not allow their use at all. In cases where bears are trapped for relocation or depredation foot snares are used instead. A major improvement for the bears and the safety of the trappers who once had to pry those huge jaws open by using a stout pole wedged under a tree root to press the levers down and using a sturdy rope and cautious approach set the trap, there was no room for inattentiveness.

Traps are chosen based on the animal the trapper is trapping the bigger the animal, the bigger the trap. In order to keep small animals from getting caught in a trap too large to be humane a pan tension screw is tightened so that only heavier animals can trip the trap. As for the small traps, if a larger animal steps on it, the trap fires and the animal simply pulls its foot out a little warier but no worse for the wear. Trappers targeting bob cats where mountain lions frequent the area may choose to use coil spring traps with just two springs instead of four. Two springs have the same jaw spread but less holding power. It's a tough balance but trappers have developed effective ways to be selective and avoid non target catches on their traplines. Regardless of which animals are targeted the general concept is to conceal the foothold trap in a location where the animal will naturally step or place bait or lure a short distance from the trap so that the animal will step on the trap pan as it investigates the scent. In the cold months of trapping season the ground freezes, and so will a trap set in damp soil. Trappers either mix an antifreeze component such as salt in with the soil covering the trap or used dirt coated with wax to prevent freezing. It is frustrating for a trapper after weeks afield to see a fresh track on the pan, bait dug up and eaten with the trap still set and frozen solidly in place.

Improvements in trap design such as jaw thickness chains with swivels, tension springs and many others have greatly improved the efficiency, selectivity, and humane aspects of the foothold trap, but the basic concept has remained the same. The animal must step on the pan and the jaws close on the foot. The animal is held until the trapper arrives to dispatch or release it. While trappers and manufacturers have gone to great lengths to improve trap design, staking systems and speed of closure, nothing has impacted trapping more than state and federal trapping regulations in regard to the use of foot traps except for one thoughtful Canadian.

In the early 1960s, a Canadian man named Frank Conibear invented a trap that closes with great force over furbearing animals' chest and neck which ensures a quick and humane death. This trap, known as the Conibear body gripping trap, earned him honors. The design principle is similar in nature to the common mouse trap purchased regularly by the American public to trap the pesky rodents before they pillage the bread cupboard. This excerpt from Bevington 1983 [1] depicts the impact of Conibear's trap design:

The Association for the Protection of Fur Bearing Animals financed the manufacture of 50 traps, and Fric Collier, President of The Trappers' Association of British Columbia, both supported their field testing and advocated them in Outdoor Life. Success at last—a trap that was light, could be built in various sizes, and could be set on land or in water. Frank contacted the Woodstream Corporation of Pennsylvania, and within a year the Victor-Conibear trap was on the market. To introduce this product, the Canadian Association of Humane Trapping, working with the Canadian Provincial Wild Life Services, encouraged trappers to exchange their leg-hold traps for the Conibears—free. The trap became popular and recognition followed. In 1961 Frank Conibear was presented the first Certificate of Merit by the American Humane Association, acknowledging his achievement. In 1981 he shared a first prize of $24,000 with two others for his ideas submitted to the Humane Trapping Committee, an award made by the B.C. Government for "outstanding creativity in the development of more humane animal traps. In 1970, during Queen Elizabeth II's tour of the North, Frank Conibear was invited back to Fort Smith to meet Her Majesty in recognition of his outstanding contributions. Conibear Park, located in the center of .Fort Smith, was created on land donated by the Conibears. It provides a pleasant, relaxing spot for travellers and local residents, and a large plaque honours the donor.

The success of this new trap was exceptional and spread across Canada and the U.S. As time went on, it became clear that the conibear body gripping trap was both effective and humane. Any animal that entered a conibear body gripping trap was dead in seconds, the issue of animals being held alive in traps for extended periods was seemingly eliminated. The conibear body gripping trap, commonly referred to as a body gripping trap, is now widely used in every trapping country in the world. But this trap with all of its excellent features also has limitations. Canine species such as the fox and coyote rarely, if ever, will enter such a device, and some set locations are just better suited for a foothold trap.

Trap-shy animals, which recognize the unnatural square trap in their path, will avoid it and the aspect that makes the trap so effective is also a deterrent for the modern-day trapper. The fact that the trap kills instantly is a key to humane harvest, just as a hunters gunshot is intended to put an animal down quickly. However, place a body gripping trap where a family pet can get to it, and the trap no longer seems so humane.

Body gripping traps range in sizes much like the foot hold traps and have a similarly arbitrary number designation. Trap sizes are typically designated by number 55, 110, 160, 220, 330 with other variations available each with a specific use. A number 110 has a jaw spread of about 4 inches and by comparison a number 330 is ten inches. If a number 110 has two springs instead of just one it is commonly called a number 120. In areas where coyotes and fox are abundant, but pets also roam, the foot trap is clearly a better alternative. A trapper can let a dog out of a well modified foot trap unharmed and return it to its rightful owner, but if that same dog goes for bait guarded by a conibear trap, the outcome is not good for the family pet or the trapper's reputation. Regulated restrictions on the use of body gripping traps have alleviated conflicts and improvements in foot trap design ensure minimal injury to animals that are trapped.

Occasionally, trappers legally trapping on private ground inadvertently catch free roaming domestic dogs. Pet owners are responsible for their pets and are often bound by leash laws, but that does not prevent them from getting angry when their pet trespasses onto neighboring lands, and gets caught in a trap.

This poses quite the quandary for trappers who want to be as selective as possible. If all pet owners followed leash laws, the incidence of this happening would decrease to near zero.

In many states, it is now illegal to set body gripping traps large enough to injure dogs on land. Montana is one of those states. In order to use a body gripping trap on land in Montana, the trap must be placed inside a wood or plastic enclosure, recessed 7 inches with an opening not to exceed 52 square inches [2]. This severely restricts the animals a trapper can effectively trap but also eliminates the possibility of catching a nontarget animal.

While the body gripping trap is limited for many species on land, aquatic furbearers such as the beaver, mink, muskrat, and river otter can be selectively harvested without issue. Skilled trappers can take these animals by placing body gripping traps under water, eliminating nontarget catches and humanely killing the often troublesome animals instantly. In winter these traps must be completely submerged otherwise fresh ice forms around the trap preventing it from firing, much like the foothold traps set on land at the same time of year.

Perhaps the most effective and lethal trap used by trappers is the snare. Snares are essentially a loop of cable with a locking mechanism. When an animal passes through the snare loop the cable squeezes around the animal's neck, and with appropriate use, the animal succumbs in seconds. Several locking mechanisms on the market are designed to relax when any animal caught relaxes in the snare and often holds animals alive. A domesticated dog inadvertently caught in a snare that is leash trained will be held as if on a leash in these types of snares. Any pet owner who allows their pet to run free, whether against the law or not, should ensure that their dog is leash trained. This simple task will go a long way in creating resolution between trappers and nontrappers, and it is part of responsible pet ownership.

Snares may be placed in known travel routes or funnel areas such as on a creek bed where a log forces the traveling animals around the end of it. Other uses include bait stations made of dead domestic animals such as mules or horses. In late winter, many predator species can be taken by setting snares in the trails coming to and from the bait. Old time trappers made the mistake of setting it too close and spooked would-be feeders or captured nontarget birds of prey. Trappers in the modern age know better and won't set closer than 100 feet. This technique also completely eliminates nontarget catches, and in many states, restrictions in regard to distances snares may be placed from exposed bait ensure target catches as well.

Snares are arguably the most effective tool trappers have to manage predator species because they are light, easy to set, and inexpensive. The preparation work is minimal, and trappers are able to catch high numbers of animals in certain areas. Furthermore snares keep working all through winter and are less likely to freeze so hard that they fail to work than other types of traps. However, snares are not appropriate for many situations.

Because of this, the steel-jawed foothold trap is the most humane, effective, and user-friendly tool available to trappers.

Predator calling with calls which mimic injured rabbits, whining pups, or howls are often used by trappers to increase their catch as well. Predator-hunting is another difficult skill to master, but the best predator callers have great success and can add another hunting element to their outdoor experience, along with beautiful furs.

Hundreds of trapping-related products are available to trappers and predator callers for fur-shed work like skinning, fleshing, and sewing hides. Trappers also need a good basket to carry hammers for pounding stakes, trowels and shovels for digging trap beds, manufactured lures and baits, and knives and fleshing beams. Cold weather gear and gear for trapping in deep water complement boats and motors for trapping in rivers and lakes.

Trappers develop certain techniques for their trade depending on where they live. Trap modification is an important aspect of trapping and it often requires that a trapper owns a welder and knows how to use it. Simple modifications include things like welding a piece of 9 gauge wire to the top of trap jaws to increase jaw thickness or moving the chain connection area from the outside edge of the trap to the center. Additional baseplate material can be added to stiffen and strengthen the traps, and modifications to the trap will prevent the jaws from closing completely, which eliminates damage to the animal's feet. This modification is known as offset jaws. Knowing how to modify traps the right way is as much a part of trapping as setting traps. Having appropriately modified traps eliminates injury to trapped animals and allows animals to be released or relocated if that is the trapper's intent. It also benefits the fur trapper because a pain-free animal is a calm animal. It eliminates fur damage and is far more ethical.

Snares, body gripping and foothold traps all have a place in fur trapping and are the identical equipment used by wildlife managers and biologists to catch, radio collar and/or monitor multiple species of wildlife. Live trap and relocation programs rely on the expertise of fur trappers and the appropriate use of snares and foothold traps to improve or increase the population of various species. There are no differences in the types of traps, and often, neither is there a difference in the types of trappers.

Cage and box traps are often referred to as live traps and certainly have their place on fur trappers' traplines. Many urban and suburban areas across the U.S. support high numbers of wild species such as the raccoon, opossum, skunk, and marmot. These species aren't necessarily welcome in residential areas, and traditional foothold and body gripping traps aren't appropriate because of the high potential for trapping domestic animals. In these cases, trappers may choose to use a trap where the animal is trapped upon entering a box or cage. The animal trips the pan and the doors close behind it. These traps are effective, fairly selective, and safe to use around high concentrations of neighborhood dogs and cats. Specialized cage traps are often used to capture beavers and have been effective for use in wildlife capture and relocation programs around the U.S.

In some areas with high human use and high bobcat populations, specialized cage traps are the best way for people to trap without conflict with dogs. Cage and box traps have their limitations though. Many species such as the fox and coyote will rarely enter a cage or box, making them a poor solution for suburban-coyote removal. They are also not easily hidden and pose live transport challenges. These traps are not easily concealed either and traps and/or wild animals caught in them can be stolen.

Dog-proof traps are also an excellent modern invention. These traps are small and require an animal to reach into a tube and pull on a baited trigger. It is impossible for any canine to become trapped in these traps, making them an excellent alternative to the foothold trap when trapping species such as raccoons in areas where their population densities need to be thinned and dogs roam.

Other specialized traps are used around the world to trap animals such as bats, rats, mice, moles, and birds. Every situation poses new challenges, and no single trap is appropriate for every situation. Trappers must remain flexible and embrace technology and maintain skills with traps, old and new. As traps and trappers evolve, so too will the techniques and abilities to manage wildlife with the many trappers' tools of the trade.

Chapter 4

New Trappers

Distrust any enterprise that requires new clothes.

—Henry David Thoreau

I had learned that the farm boy hunting, trapping, and fishing types were few and far in between, especially at a university. Lost in a sea of students and searching for others who had a similar back ground as I did, I found a few friends and we spent time fishing the local rivers and hunting deer and waterfowl. We wanted to take it a step further so we started a sportsman's club on campus. It was here that I made several lifelong friends. No one seemed to know how to trap, so our club held a trapper education class on campus. I certified twelve students that day and held the field portion of the class along the banks of the river right in the middle of campus. I often wonder how many times that has been done?

Spring break had always been a time for me to trap, and this would be no different with one exception; I would be building a primitive shelter in the woods and trapping beaver for the week with three others. My nephew, Tony, came along as did my friends, Andy and Dustin, from the sportsman's club. We drove about a hundred miles to a place where I grew up trapping and set up a lean-to shelter frame and covered it with a tarp. We would all sleep under this structure for the coming week. We were about a mile off the road and camped on a rocky bench overlooking prime beaver waters, and the snow was deep.

We set out each day on snowshoes with traps and enthusiasm but by the end of the week hadn't caught much. It seemed that another trapper had been there recently and already took his share of beavers. Tony and I helped show the new trappers how to do things right. We had a campfire every night and life was good. Stars filled the clear night sky, and we sat around the fire ring talking about whatever came to mind. The air was crisp and cold, but the fire and camaraderie kept us warm. Snow melted from the fire ring's edge and dried our socks and boots propped up on the edge, at times a little too close. The fire light shimmered off the blue tarp tied securely to the lean-to frame. We didn't have alcohol or drugs. We didn't need it. The wilderness feel of this trip was real. We were miles from the nearest house and many more from any town. A mile from the road, our little camp warmed our hearts and set our adventurous spirits on fire! The ice was still about a foot thick on the large flows and the temperatures dipped into single digits at night. Dustin and Andy each caught their first beavers on this trip, making it well worth the effort.

Most college students come back from spring break with photos far different than their first beaver and primitive shelters in the snow. We had a great time and continued this annual trip for three more years. Even after I graduated college, members who remained in the sportsman's club and I set out on similar expeditions. Several of those participants are my closest friends even now. I wouldn't trade those experiences or my trapping friends for anything.

We set up primitive shelters, started our fires with bow drills, and set deadfalls and steel traps. For one week each year, we lived like mountain men. I wore a handmade muskrat fur hat and my older brother even joined on one trip. The last time we had a weeklong spring trapping trip, I had to work second shift and couldn't get time off. I would hike out at about 2:00 p.m., work until 11:00 p.m., drive forty-five minutes to the trailhead and hike into camp alone, find my bed roll, and curl up to sleep. I didn't want to miss any more than I absolutely had to.

Dustin and I teamed up to run a trapline together one season. My mother had died a week before college final exams the previous December. I passed my exams but floundered the following spring semester. We were very close, and her passing was devastating for me.

Kate and I lived in rural upstate, New York, and I found excellent trapping not far from home in the Adirondack Mountain country. She had landed a great job as a bench chemist at Wyeth Pharmaceuticals in Rouses Point, New York, and I had found work as a carpenter during the summer and decided that three months of trapping in the fall would be good medicine.

The solitude of the trapline was refreshing. I had missed it more than I realized. I drove to the top of a nearby mountain each day and checked traps set for fishers and raccoon then drove down the mountain to a huge flow with plenty of beavers, mink, and muskrats to keep me busy. Dustin would check his traps and stop by my house to put up fur in the evenings and on weekends. On more than one occasion, I would open the bulk head door and follow the wood stairs into the basement where my feet would find the dirt floor. I would turn the corner and find several animals on the skinning table. When this happened, I knew Dustin would be returning for a late night of skinning.

He was still in college and had a small studio apartment with his wife, Theresa, where he still managed to skin, flesh, and dry muskrats; but bigger furbearers like raccoons and beavers were handled at my place. Dustin stood about six feet, six inches tall and wore a reddish beard. His skinny frame and light complexion resembled the mountain men of years gone by. Seeing him hunched over my three-foot-tall makeshift table in a five-and-a-half-foot tall basement skinning animals was like seeing a homeless man in a cardboard box. We had many a good laugh and long conversation in that small confining basement.

I chewed tobacco then, and one night, I had a fisher hanging from a gambrel in the basement. I made the first few cuts with my knife between the hind legs and across the anal vent, split the tail, and began pulling on the hide to peel it off the carcass. As I did, urine from the fisher squirted out and hit me directly in the mouth! The mixture of wintergreen tobacco and fisher pee was unbearable. I began spitting and gagging with tears in my eyes. Dustin was laughing so hard he couldn't speak, and my lips were numb. I spit my chew out and continued spitting for five minutes before going upstairs to rinse it out. When I came back Dustin was still laughing. I finally agreed that it was funny after another twenty minutes of ridicule.

We had a lot of great memories on the line too. We checked our line together when we could, and one day, we paddled down the river to an island where muskrats burrowed holes into the banks. Dustin made a set where he attached a number 110 body grip trap on a stick four feet long and pushed it into the river bed with a white piece of potato on the triggers. The set was good, but with the deep water and slight current, it was hard to see into the water and therefore hard to tell if anything was in the trap. Dustin leaned over the bank hanging on a tree trunk to steady himself and put his face close to the water. Just as he did, a muskrat popped up a half inch from his nose and splashed the water. He screamed like a girl and pulled his lanky frame up on the bank and ran thirty feet at full speed, screaming the whole time. At first I thought he was hurt then he said, "A muskrat just came up and tried to bite my nose!" I laughed so hard I thought my waders would bust. A twelve-inch muskrat just sent a six-and-a-half-foot man running for his life!

Dustin and I continued to trap together on occasions for several more years until he and his wife moved away. He was one of the best trapline companions I ever had.

Several seasons went on, and I was hired on at a research facility as a laboratory technician in Chazy, New York, not far from Plattsburgh. Kate and I bought a house closer to our jobs and got married. I had some good trapping areas established and met a guy at work named Matt who loved the outdoors and wanted to come along my trapline with me just to learn. Matt was a longtime angler and had spent several years guiding fly fishermen. He had also spent countless hours pheasant hunting and even more on the water but had never trapped.

I pulled up to a large frozen-over muskrat marsh in my GMC Jimmy and began walking across the ice for several hundred feet to a muskrat push-up set I had made two days earlier. Muskrats will create a hole in the ice when it first freezes in early winter. Throughout the winter, they continue to stuff grass into the hole and create small mounds of grass about a foot wide and just as tall on the ice surface. These push-ups are great locations for a foot trap. All it takes is a two-foot long piece of wire and a solid stick wide enough to prevent it from being pulled down the hole. I cut the top off the push-up with my hatchet, removed the grass from the shelf in the ice, and placed a number 1 ½ foot trap there. I then put the frozen top back over the hole and left.

Matt was with me on the trapline and had no idea what I was doing. I grabbed on to the top of the push-up and saw the extra wire had been pulled down the hole. I tugged on the wire bringing the trap chain up through the hole. A muskrat was held securely in the trap by the front foot and had died quickly after stepping in it. As I pulled the wet muskrat out of the push-up, Matt was exhilarated. He began celebrating on the ice, shouting, "Yeah! Hell, yeah!" He had never seen anything like it.

Later on the line, we traveled to the river and I showed him muskrat feed beds tucked up under the grassy banks, the green tops of local grasses piled up in secret under root wads and six-inch wide holes in the banks under water. Matt couldn't believe it and told me it was like a whole new world just opened to him that he never knew existed. And he has a biology degree from Syracuse University.

Matt took up trapping for a time and had some successes. He was present on one of the spring break trips and is the man who first introduced me to bow drilling and primitive living skills—skills which I would hone to a sharp point later.

One season, I had a trapping partner named Jessie. My story about a trappers life wouldn't be, or should I say couldn't be complete without a crazy trapping partner. I think every trapper has had one, and I am no different. I met Jessie while fishing one day, and somehow, we became friends and started trapping together. I think he invited himself on my line, I'm not sure. What I am sure about is that Jessie was out of his mind. He was well-spoken but poorly educated. He had an eighth grade education, and in hindsight, probably would have qualified for Ritalin. He was fun and didn't care about much. But when I began showing him how to trap, he really got into it.

One day in mid-November, we were hiking along a river and I had sets on an island about thirty yards from the bank. I was wearing waders and Jessie had on a pair of blue jeans and sneakers. I made the mistake of telling him that he would have to wait for me to check those sets because he needed waders to get across the river. He looked at me for about three seconds before running as fast as he could toward the water. He jumped in, feet flailing and made it about halfway before the freezing cold water surrounded his waist and slowed his feet. He kept churning until he reached the other side. He climbed up on the bank and said, "I don't need any damn waders!" Well, Jessie was right, he didn't need waders. I walked to the island and Jessie realized that he had gone about twenty yards too far, past the island. I had already grown accustomed to Jessie's episodes, but I will never forget the day he invested in a pair of neoprene waders.

The area I lived in while trapping with Jessie was made up of dairy farms and hayfields. Large white oak and sugar maple stands met with balsam fir, blue and red spruce, red cedar, and goosefoot maple. Throw in a few thousand raspberry bushes, and you pretty well sum up the local vegetation. It was thick and dense, at times impenetrable.

The dairy farmers who first inhabited the area had to clear the land and remove stones from the soil to make it tillable. The stones were stacked along the edge of the fields as they were cleared a hundred or so years ago. These stone walls designated property boundaries and separated the crop fields from grazing pastures. Two track roads lead to short breaks in the stone walls where the next section of cleared lands open up once again. The result is a lot of edge cover. Edge cover makes excellent habitat for wildlife.

These broken lands are complemented with huge barns and outbuildings. Next to these barns are tall silos, small houses, a pickup truck and a tractor in the driveway, and some type of lawn ornament. The smell of cow manure sweetens the air and lets a visitor know he's in dairy country.

One day in early fall, Jessie and I stopped at a farmer's house to ask permission to trap. The farmer was outside when we pulled up and we started talking with the man about trapping, and the usual questions came up about the fur prices and what we were after. The farmer never looked at us, he just kept working and made his way into the barn and kept talking. We followed him in and the conversation changed from fur trapping to hunting and farming as he shared a few stories. The old farmer continued about his work shoveling stalls and spreading wood chips as he talked. Finally, he said we could trap so long as we kept the gates shut and didn't shoot near his cows. With that Jessie thanked him and extended his arm to shake the farmer's hand. The farmer hesitated, and then took his glove off revealing a hand with no fingers save his thumb. Jessie stared at the man's hand, looked at me briefly, grabbed the farmers thumb, shook it and turned around. He walked straight out of the barn without saying a word. I nodded to the farmer and thanked him then went out to the truck. When I got in, Jessie said, "I didn't know what to do, I couldn't shake his hand, so I grabbed the only digit he had." I laughed for the entire ride home.

The local farm lands produced a lot of fur. The fisher and raccoon population on these foothill locations was surprising. We weren't far from the Adirondack Mountains, a place with a very high population of fishers. But the lowland farm country isn't known for high fisher numbers. Our intention at the start of season was to trap raccoons. So we went to the town of Rouses Point and picked up the head and bones from filleted Champlain perch. Champlain perch are fished heavily in local shallow bays through the ice by fishermen and sold to local fish markets. Like trappers, these hardy anglers catch as many fish in a day as they can and sell them to local buyers. The local buyers then sell fresh fillets all over the country. The markets pay by the pound based on the size, and they fillet hundreds of fish per day. The bones and skulls of those fish are stored in barrels. This made the best raccoon bait and as we were learning, fisher bait too.

We set traps into the woods just off the two track road and checked traps every day. I had to be at work by 7:00 a.m. so Jessie and I would leave at 4:00 a.m. We'd drive along the two tracks with a spotlight pointed out the window. When we had one, we knew it and Jessie would let me know with his crazy screams of excitement—every single time.

On some days, we would catch several raccoons and fishers. The routine was, Jessie yelled, I stopped the truck, we would both get out, dispatch the animal if needed, remake the set, lay the prized animal in the bed, and move on. We worked fast and efficiently. I always drove fast, even in the fields. We had a lot of traps to run, and I had to be at work on time. By week 3, our catches started slowing down, and we decided it was time to pull traps and reorganize on different farms.

We spent all morning one Saturday pulling our traps and got to the last farmers' house much later than usual. We had agreed to stay on the two track roads and never wavered on that promise. I drove along the two track roads with only three traps left to pull out of nearly one hundred. Suddenly, I heard an odd sound, and from inside the vehicle, it sounded sort of like running over a bunch of plastic pop bottles. I got out taking a look at what I had run over. I could hear the hissing as soon as I jumped out. "What the hell did I hit?" I asked out loud. Then Jessie said there was hissing on his side too. I looked at the back tire which was also hissing. I ran back up the road to see what I had run over. There in the tires path laid two—two by fours, eight feet long nails had been driven through the boards along the entire length and intentionally laid in our way covered up with grass.

I was furious. I threw the boards in the bed of my truck and jumped in, saying everything but Jesus, and drove to the farmer's house. I jumped out and said, "What the hell are these boards doing on your road?"

"Huh. I sold a five-acre piece to my neighbor a few years back. That must a' been the piece you were on. I guess I forgot to tell you about that," he said with a worried look on his face.

The posted signs on the land still had the farmer's name on them, and there was no indication that anyone owned it besides the farmer whom I had written permission from. I said nothing and drove to Jessie's house as fast as I could. The air was gushing out of my tires and I had no time to spare. We made it, barely. We went inside and tried to figure out what just happened.

A state trooper showed up about fifteen minutes later and started asking questions. Here was a brand new Chevy Silverado sitting in front of a trailer park with four flat tires. As he walked up to the truck, there were four dead raccoons in the back along with three dozen traps. Apparently, the owner of that five-acre piece had seen us drive into his field every morning around 4:30 with our spotlight pointed out the window. On occasion, he heard a gunshot or two and then we left—always in a hurry. His only thought was that we were illegally spotlighting deer. He decided he would put a stop to it by blowing my tires up. I showed the police officer my written permission and explained that I am an ethical trapper and that if this guy had his own posted signs on his land instead of the farmer's name—whom I had permission from—this wouldn't have happened.

I threatened a lawsuit in my angered state of mind and could have won, but the landowner countered with a property damage claim if I sued. I spoke with him over the phone and dropped the whole thing. Needless to say, I didn't make a dime on that trapline and I was so upset that I never went back there.

As time went on, I forgot about the $500 tire bill and the animosity I had accrued, although it still makes me angry to this day on occasion. There were a million different ways that land owner could have handled that situation. We were there at the same time every day for twenty-one consecutive days. How many deer did he think we were jacking? Blowing up my tires . . . really? That was his solution? Enough said.

I kept trapping, but Jessie and I eventually parted ways. I loved trapping beavers, and I contacted the New York State Department of Environmental Conservation to get put on a list for nuisance beaver. When I called, I found out about a nuisance trappers permit that could be obtained by taking a course and passing a test. The test was held four times a year in different locations.

The DEC sent me a binder titled "Best Practices for Nuisance Wildlife Control Operators." The training manual was produced by the Cornell Cooperative Extension, the New York State Department of Environmental Conservation, and the New York State Integrated Pest Management Program. The book was filled with pages of how-to techniques, laws, ethics, safety, professionalism, and wildlife terms and species biology information. We had several weeks to read through the book and study. The test was held at the regional DEC headquarters in the town of Ray Brook, New York.

The certification allowed me to accept money from private homeowners for removing nuisance wildlife. It also allowed me to transport live wild animals provided that I didn't release them on public lands—alive. Every animal had to be documented on official trap logs and mailed to the department monthly. My first job was in a residential area plagued with groundhogs—aka woodchucks. A family of woodchucks moved into a wealthy neighborhood on the shores of Lake Champlain and spread into a nearby historical building where the expensive plants were disappearing at an alarming rate. When I arrived, there were woodchucks everywhere as were intricate networks of tunnels. The tunnels were dug from the edge of the lake to inside one home owner's basement. Droppings were piled up under the historical barns and neighborhood sheds. The area was infested, and it was costing hundreds of dollars a day. Enough was enough. But one of the neighbors came up to me and asked what I was doing. I told him that a landowner had called the DEC with problem woodchucks, and I was sent to remove them. "Ah, don't kill the beast," he said. "There's got to be a way to remove them but don't kill the beast."

I explained that no one could legally transplant wildlife from one area to another due to the potential to spread disease, and the only good alternative was to trap and kill them. He didn't like it. I knew that the burrowing rodents would just continue to overrun the area if I couldn't trap them from all the neighbors' houses, but at least, I could remove the ones that ended up inside the houses of the paying homeowners. I trapped this population of rodents for a substantial fee each summer for three consecutive years. By late August, nature's biorhythm caused the few remaining woodchucks to burrow ever deeper, and by September, they were gone—until the following June when they wreaked havoc once again. I moved to Montana after the third year. It would take an all-out assault and full cooperation with the entire neighborhood to allow trapping to rid the area completely of the troublesome creatures.

During that same time period, I received a phone call from a Redevelopment Corporation to help them with a beaver problem. The man I spoke to was a down-to-earth groundskeeper who asked me to meet him at the main office building in the afternoon. I arrived wearing rubber boots, wool shirt and pants, and a big warm hat. It was December in Northern New York, and the snow was deep. I had been trapping beaver for two nearly two months already that fall season and was happy to get permission to trap a new area close to home. I walked into the building and was greeted by a secretary and offered coffee, which I took. About ten minutes later, I was escorted into a room with seven environmental planners wearing collared buttoned-up shirts and ties and matching shiny shoes. I suddenly felt severely underdressed!

On a long square table lay maps of the base rolled up, and all eyes were on me. "Hello, Toby, we understand that you're a trapper," said a clean-cut professional looking man of about forty, dressed like his counterparts.

"Yes, that's right," I said.

"Well, tell us about your experience," he replied.

I hadn't ever really thought about my experience and certainly hadn't prepared for an interview. I was there to trap beavers because I like to trap beavers. "Well, I've been trapping beaver since I was a kid and have trapped just about everything you can trap. I am a licensed nuisance control operator and a trapper educator . . . ," I said with confidence, trying to read the looks on their faces to see if they were convinced. I could see they weren't ready to commit to me yet, and I really wanted permission to trap.

It took some convincing, but finally, they rolled out the maps and began showing me where the beaver were and explained that they needed them out by the first of the year. They had permits to trap the beaver, and it was clearly communicated just how serious this was for them. "This permit allows you to use any method short of stinger missiles," they joked. Followed by, "Go, take a look, and see if it's something you can take care of. If it is, write up a proposal and send it to us as soon as you can."

I followed the groundskeeper in my truck to the area, and he just pointed me in the general direction. He knew that I didn't need a map, but he handed it to me anyway. He said, "Now, Toby, don't be afraid to charge these guys, they are a big company, like Wyeth."

He knew that I worked in research at a local division of a major pharmaceutical company. After Looking around for a couple of hours, I returned home and wrote a proposal for the removal of all the beaver in the specified section of land prior to January 1 for a fee, and I also wanted permission to continue trapping for muskrats and mink throughout the remainder of season. The area was filled with cattails and muskrat houses piled high with grasses. Beaver ponds flooded the otherwise tiny creek running through the property and mink tracks crossed every beaver dam.

After six days of trapping, I had trapped about ten beavers. On January 2, a bulldozer came in and ripped out all the dams. Several beavers that I had trapped were piled up with all the debris. It took a while for me to sort it all out and find my traps and beavers. The company meant business. They needed to have the area drained and devoid of beaver to avoid having the land considered wetlands. Wetland is a bad word for builders in the Northeast. As the season went on, a large building went up a few hundred feet from where I had trapped the beavers. It turned out to be a really productive piece of ground to trap, and I had officially made more money trapping beaver that week than any other week in my life!

As time went on, I was promoted to staff scientist at work but continued to rid neighborhoods of skunks, woodchucks, and beavers, in addition to trapping an average of about two dozen beavers, a few dozen muskrats, a few mink and raccoons, coyotes and fox each year. I would spend every free minute trapping and also began a small business on the side doing taxidermy, a skill I had learned from my mother and improved upon over the years. It seemed to fit into my interests, and I was good at it.

After several years of having my trapping time eroded by big business, I quit and began working for a wilderness therapeutic program where I took troubled youth into the wilderness for eight consecutive days at a time. The program was designed to keep students for a minimum of twenty-eight days. One thing that really appealed to me was the primitive living skills taught to the students. Students had to learn how to spark a fire with flint and steel before gradually mastering the art of bow drilling. Students built cordage, made deadfall traps, and lived in primitive shelters. The instructors were there to provide support and encourage student s to use their newly acquired skills to draw metaphors for life.

The Paiute Deadfall trap is built of natural materials, consisting of cordage, a trigger, a deadfall, and a post. Students would create a metaphor about the trap like:

"The post represents my family; the rope represents me, connected to the trigger which is drugs and alcohol. The rock represents what happens when I trip the trigger, everything crashes down destroying me and my relationship with my family."

The traps were only used metaphorically in the program, but many of the male students who ranged in age from thirteen to eighteen asked if we could trap a real animal. For those interested students, I wished that we could, but it was not allowed. I instead told stories of trapping and hunting. Having native roots in the mountains, I was connected to the land. I knew every type of tree, could decipher animal tracks and scat, knew when it was going to rain, and how to navigate in thick forests.

The students who took an interest in trapping and hunting would ask how I tracked down deer. One group of about seven boys asked if I could show them what I do when I am hunting. I got on a deer track and followed it. I explained what the deer was doing and what I would be doing in response if I were hunting. Then I slowed down to a near stop, turning my head side to side before quietly stepping forward. I turned around to find every student stepping slowly and looking at the environment, really *looking*. It was one of the best days I ever had while working there.

The connection to the land is not something that is easy to teach, and I had done it. Not very many suburban kids ever get the chance in their lives to truly experience nature; the same can be said for suburban adults. That tears me up inside.

One student named Mike sent me a letter after graduating from the program I taught in. He had been sent to another program in Utah where he found a rabbit freshly killed by a coyote. He cut the fur from the rabbit, washed it and dried it before sending it to me along with his letter. He apologized for not trapping it himself but wanted to give me the fur he had found to repay me for a raccoon tail that I had given him. The tail had adorned my walking stick for years prior and I gave it to him in exchange for a handcrafted item he had made for me.

It may be hard to comprehend the connection one feels after living in the forest for weeks on end unless you have experienced it firsthand. Animals and trees are no longer there for human amusement. You realize that people are meant to be part of the environment, not casual observers. It becomes less "us and them" and more "us." This young student, on a cold morning in the rolling sage desert somewhere in Utah, found the connection. I didn't teach it to him, he found it. Just as trappers do who peel away the layers of nature and really see. There is no closer connection, and it can't be taught.

Chapter 5

Not Just about the Traps

We need to help students and parents cherish and preserve the ethnic and cultural diversity that nourishes and strengthens this community—and this nation.

—Cesar Chavez

The number of new products made and sold each year to recreational trappers in the U.S. and Canada is staggering, and it's not just traps either. There are hundreds of trapping and hunting supply stores providing everything fur takers need to pursue their passion—tools to modify traps and build snares, and trap setters of various designs and manufacturers. Lures manufactured and bottled by independent lure makers are made with the glands, and meat sold along with pelts. Urine from these animals is bottled and sold not just in trap supply centers, but also in sporting goods stores for cover scents and dog training.

Millions of dollars are spent every year on gear to aid fur harvesters' like headlamps, GPS and radio-tracking collars for hounds, clothing, and boots. An enormous number of how-to books are sold on trapping just about everything—from moles and mice to fox and coyote. Videos on fur handling, trapping, and hunting are produced and sold by the thousands every year. Trapping is a big industry and impacts far more than a few fur trappers in rural America. While many fur trappers make a substantial portion of their household income by fur sales, the world retail fur trade alone exceeds $14 billion annually.

The people who work and live within the American trapping culture have a huge positive impact on the local and global economy. ATVs, snowmobiles, and automobiles are also purchased for the trapline, and they need gas and repairs. It would be tough to estimate with any accuracy just how much trappers and other fur takers contribute to the economy, but it doesn't take long to realize the significance.

With the number of animal damage complaints on the rise, fur-trappers-turned-animal-damage-control-operators are having a hard time keeping up, and state game agencies' funding for animal damage control is often limited. Right now, they turn to local trappers to handle the removal of these animals, but what would happen when if the knowledge base created and maintained by trappers was no longer available?

While there are certainly fur trappers and animal damage control operators who do more harm than good with poor ethical choices and irresponsible behavior, I think it is fair to say that those types of individuals plague every organized group, regardless of their affiliations.

When suburban Americans pound their fists to bring an end to trapping, it is doubtful they really have any idea what it would mean financially to local businesses and wildlife management agencies. It is even more doubtful that they realize the impact to tens of thousands of people dependent on sustained yield trapping and hunting.

Urban people who aren't connected to the land may have no idea how isolated they are from the natural world—how could they know? A few trips to the countryside each year spent camping and hiking along trails and exploring the wilderness through car windows may be their only experience with a concrete free outdoors. Getting out and observing nature on occasion is a wonderful opportunity to get back to their wild human roots but it will never achieve the intimacy and acceptance of nature's harsh realities. Wild animals must be controlled in some way and nature's way doesn't involve humane treatment. It involves nature's law. Disease and starvation are just as likely to be the demise of any wild animal as predation or accidental death.

Their gauge for wildlife and wildlife impact comes in the form of thirty-minute TV shows and short tours in-between theme park visits and restaurants. Urban Americans are treating wildlife and wild places more and more as something to go see, a visual attraction with trails and hand rails, interpretive signs, and recreational maps. One trip to any major National Park verifies this point in dramatic fashion. Thousands of cars and tourists with cameras and binoculars hardly equates to a wilderness or natural experience for people who live their lives in rural areas. For that reason, congested National parks are often avoided by local residents, especially at the height of tourist season.

The people who live among the wildlife and wild places are the ones who love nature for what it really is, not what they perceive it to be during brief stints traveling along nature trails riddled with signs and arrows to point the way. These outdoorsy people who rightfully consider themselves part of the cycle of life are the same people who are being forced away from the very thing they desire more than anything in the world.

The trapping culture is imbedded into rural Americana as a unique blend of significant American history and modern-day necessity. Born out of wild men with a desire to taste wildness first hand as they reached ever more deeply into the west, trappers have evolved into entrepreneurs with roots ever more steeped in wild tradition. Modern-day mountain men are not romanticized as were the buckskin-clad fur producers of years past, but the spirit and desire to understand intimately the natural world through active participation has remained unchanged.

As cultures are destroyed around the world by unrelenting consumers, so too are the natural skills humans relied on for their very existence—cast into the tumultuous modernization and separation of man with his natural instincts. Can the world stand to lose cultures dependent on primitive skills?

The Amazon rainforest currently houses two hundred tribes of indigenous people with one hundred and eighty different languages, and each with their own unique cultural heritage. Reporters from civilized society record the daily lives of these primitive people. Some are captivated by the continuation of mini-societies where hunting and gathering are necessary for tribal and cultural survival, while others scoff at the barbaric practices of these indigenous tribes.

In areas of Africa, hundreds more tribesmen gather spears and bows, and create poison darts and prepare to spend the day hunting. When a wild animal is killed, they carry it back to their village and use the hides and meat to feed and clothe the hungry and naked. There are "modern" people who scathe these cultures because they are not evolving, not expanding their human horizons to get past the need for meat.

Should these native people give up their culture—their heritage spanning ten thousand years—just to placate a movement forty years in the making? A movement which hasn't had time to realize the potential impacts of removing a fundamental humanistic attribute critical to human survival?

How can an individual form a negative opinion about a native culture when their own civilized heritage is rooted in capitalistic ideals? Is it wrong to run through the forest chasing wild pigs because the option of living in a city sipping wine and eating a vegan diet is available? Civilized societies wage war over oil, kill in the name of religion, and destroy natural ecosystems to extract minerals from the earth's core. As an American living on American soil, I receive the benefits of oil, religious freedom, and plentiful unnatural man-made works of modern construction. But it would be hypocritical of me to espouse critical judgment on cultures which arrange marriages, chase down wild animals using poisons, and battle with other tribes, when people in my own society have disregard for so many natural things. Is my culture better because mine is civilized? On the other hand, is their culture better because it is not?

Certainly, trappers don't have a halo floating over their heads. Trappers can be as crass and judgmental as any group can be anywhere. It's the viewpoint, the place of humans in nature, and the hierarchy of animals that separates trappers from their opponents.

It seems that the loss of cultures and cultural diversity has left enough room for trappers to continue in their pursuit of wildlife in wild places, so long as the wild populations continue to flourish. Connectivity to one's cultural heritage and traditional skills is important, and the continuation of those skills must be ensured, in order to have skills to pass along. Take away the ability to pass along cultural knowledge, and no culture will continue.

In the late 1800s and early 1900s, the Inuit tribes of North America were forced to conform to Western ideals as their children were shipped to "white" schools and were not allowed to return home for weeks. Slowly, the native ways were washed out of their culture. This was the start of a very sad loss of cultural diversity. The same happened to Native Americans across the U.S. to a point that a once proud and extensive network of unique peoples has been reduced to a civilized American melting pot.

It may be too late to revive America's native people and their cultural heritage to its original beautiful uniqueness of natural symbiotic cohesiveness, although the native people are working to preserve their cultural identity.

The loss of native traditions imparts a loss of genetic biodiversity and drains the human interconnectivity present in so many nature-dependent cultures. The separation from man and nature has never improved the world environments. Perhaps the only improvement may have been to the world economy, at the price of natural human instincts and the destruction of beautiful places. The only direct link between humans and nature is through those who choose to be part of it. How can anyone or anything ever know another thing without intimacy? To only view nature from a distance would surely destroy the human spirit. Man needs to participate in his natural surroundings.

The sanctity of cultures and cultural uniqueness are crushed with monomaniacal ideals, which strive for a monoculture society. The belief that one culture is better or worse than another dismantles the essence of being uniquely human. The world network of people relies on cultural diversity. Cultures within cultures require acceptance to achieve a balanced state, where new ideas can be generated and shared freely. Compromise is paramount to the success of any human relationship and is surely the fulcrum of societal consortia.

That is not to say that certain social attributes in one culture or another can't be wrong just because they are the norm. However, forcing one culture's idea of right onto another culture's perceived wrong eliminates compromise and therefore destroys cultural integrity and articulation.

Trappers are part of a hunting culture, possibly the smallest and least represented among people of the land. Ranchers and farmers, hunters and anglers, loggers and guides, and other members of America's nature-sustained cultures are at odds with an urban anthropomorphic ideal. Ironically, those most disconnected with nature are the most likely to condemn those whose lives depend on nature for survival—all in the name of "saving nature." So what is it about trapping that separates it from all other forms of the American animal based subcultures? Nothing.

Fur trappers are of the smallest populace of individuals and are therefore the easiest to isolate, and by using basic statistical analyses, trapping is a logical place for anti-nature users to start. Why not start with the elimination of fishing? Since one of the goals of HSUS is to ban all sport hunting and fishing. Perhaps there are far too many roadblocks, and the number of anglers throughout the world is staggering. It is far easier to chip slowly away at the cultures that use animals, species by species, until there is only one culture, one set of ideals—no diversity.

All hunting organizations need to sit up when trapping comes under fire by special interest groups. Just as anti-animal use groups have clearly stated, they will chip away at every group of people who consume meat state by state until they have eliminated hunting. Trapping is the starting block, the first domino that ultimately ends in the elimination of hunting, fishing, and trapping. And if the leaders of anti-nature users get their way, nature will still be there, but only for observation at a distance.

It is important that trappers continue to trap, while improving their methods and equipment. Improvements are made every year to trap design and trapping techniques. Hunting groups cannot support the actions of irresponsible sportsmen, and trappers owe it to the outdoor community to do everything they can to improve and maintain a positive public image. There is no room for apathy and even less room for anti-trapping sentiment to be allowed to continue. Trappers and hunters must hang together or they will hang separately.

The trapping culture in America is as much a part of the history and wildlife legacy as the wild animals themselves. The knowledge possessed by trappers is not an outdated and unnecessary skill that can simply be discarded. There are very few Americans who truly understand how nature works, what holds it together, and how precious it really is. When you live so much of your life in the wilds, it is impossible not to appreciate it, inconceivable to separate yourself from it, and one cannot imagine a life without it.

Trappers are rough around the edges, wild and wooly and like a fawn barely escaping the hungry intentions of a coyote, tattered and torn. It's rare for a trapper to speak publicly about controversial issues, they would rather go to the mountain forests, step up on a boulder to get a good view, and watch nature unfold its eternal symphony of raw and natural wildness.

Chapter 6

Wild Adirondack Trapline

The last thing I did in New York was fulfill a dream of a month trapping in the wilderness. I wrote the following story titled "Wild Adirondack Trapline" originally published in July 2010 in *Fur-Fish-Game Magazine*, telling about that adventure.

The experience of solitude and freedom along creek banks and high mountain ridges was one I wished for since I laid my first trap along the muddy banks of the river flowing through my town. I dreamed of a remote cabin in the wilderness where I could put up fur as I warmed myself by the woodstove and boiled water for hot tea. Where I could reminisce about each day's adventure with a trapping partner, or read a good book by the lantern's glow. My brother, Bud, and I shared the same dream but realized our responsibilities at home would keep us from going. But what if we could experience the wilderness trapline a little closer to home? The Adirondack Mountains were right out our backdoor and offered solitude and beauty in prime fur country. We were certain no one had trapped there for years, and we could stay for a month, which is plenty of time to run a trapline and attain a true wilderness feel.

We decided to find a place where we would have the mountains and lakes to ourselves. New York State has millions of prime trapping acres open to the public. The Adirondack Mountains provide some of the best trapping opportunities in the country, especially for beavers and otters.

With thousands of lakes, rivers, and marshy areas, we decided to use these waterways to navigate through the thick forested mountains. The largest unbroken wilderness in the state is the five ponds wilderness area, named for a chain of lakes in the middle of a vast wilderness. The

Oswegatchie River meanders through the boreal woodlands, providing for excellent trapping. Being adventurous and overly ambitious, we decided to canoe twelve miles to a trail head, carry our supplies two and one-half miles over a steep moraine then paddle across Big Five Lake where we would establish camp.

In hindsight, we could have had a great experience without all the extra overland hauling of gear. The river is the best mode of transportation in the area. But we wanted solitude, and the Oswegatchie River is a popular travel corridor for hunters. After a three-day scouting trip during summer, we decided on the remote and trail less Big Five lake. A call to the local forest ranger secured a permit for establishing a temporary camp for our month-long adventure in the coming fall. Permission is required for any stay in the Adirondacks lasting longer than two weeks.

With our campsite chosen, we began buying food. This chore was more complex than we thought and more difficult than it should have been. After this experience, it is clear that potato flakes, pasta, minute-rice and freeze dried veggies should go at the top of the list, and whole grain rice, canned foods, and cheese should go at the bottom, or be eliminated altogether. Just think light and easy when choosing food. By easy, I mean it's done when you add hot water. This will save considerable time preparing food.

The final consideration was the traps we would need. Our targeted species were primarily fisher, beaver, and otter. We had also received permits to trap six marten each. Although the marten numbers are not high, the chance to catch marten pulled us deeper into the backcountry. I chose to bring two dozen traps including number 330, number 220, and number 110 body grippers, number 1 1/2 coil springs, and number 4 double long springs.

With trapping comes fur handling, and we decided to bring half a dozen beaver hoops, another dozen wire stretchers of various sizes, and fleshing tools including a single hardwood fleshing beam. We could have made a fleshing beam by peeling a six-inch diameter log, but my brother was willing to carry it in, so I let him.

We set up camp along the shores of Big Five Lake using a wood frame for our tarps. A lean-to style roof was placed over the door to keep our firewood dry and for fleshing our pelts out of the weather. Beds were constructed from small wood poles tightly wound together on frames secured with wire and penny nails. Shelves were built in similar fashion. A woodstove made from a twenty-gallon barrel was resurrected from an old hunter's camp of long ago. With a few new pieces of stove pipe and sand packed around the bottom, smoke was funneled out of camp. Our camp was two hundred feet from the lake on a flat, dry piece of ground that offered a slightly obstructed view of the lake. A latrine was dug away from camp and firewood put up. It would be a couple weeks before our adventure would begin, but we were ready.

The first day of my wilderness trapline finally came as I pushed off at the inlet in my seventeen-foot canoe. My brother would meet me at camp in a day or two. He had already spent several days at the camp and had returned home to get final supplies before settling in for a month. I paddled silently along the ever-winding Oswegatchie River, seventy-five feet at its widest point. I saw beavers and muskrats swimming in the water and listened to geese singing their unique songs. Several white-tailed deer jumped from the banks as I rounded a corner, splashing through the water-logged grass and tag alders. Slowly, the wilderness opened and everything else disappeared behind me. I was finally on a wilderness trapping adventure.

The 15-mile journey required an overnight stay since I didn't make it to our camp before nightfall. I made a simple camp with a tarp and parachute cord and settled into my sleeping bag, excited to get started. When I arrived the next day, I organized camp before paddling up the creek that feeds Big Five Lake. Several beaver lodges dotted the shoreline, and I spotted six river otters bobbing up and down in the lake.

I began stringing my line out, anticipating a camp filled with dried pelts. Shortly after returning to camp, a small pack canoe made its way across the lake. Bud unloaded his final supplies and went about organizing traps and splitting wood. He had been fortunate to stay at the camp for ten days, although the weather brought rain and wind the entire time.

We hoped for drier weather and talked about the possibility of the river freezing before we planned to leave. It was already November 1, and the Adirondacks have little sympathy for travelers. The only trail out follows the river for twelve miles but had not been cleared since a powerful windstorm swept through the area years before, leaving the route largely unusable. It was our only option, should we need it. But we would have to keep an eye on the weather. Neither one of us wanted to leave early, but we certainly weren't prepared to stay all winter.

Soon, our traplines began to produce fur. Bud came in with an otter, and I followed it up with a few beavers. One morning, I set out to check my line and found a beaver in a trap I had set in a feeder stream the day before. As I was removing the prime beaver from the trap, I noticed a number 330 I had set on a spillway was disturbed. I quickly paddled to the set and found a large otter in the trap. The next trap, located a few hundred feet up the creek, held another otter. What a great way to start a morning! As the furs piled up, so did our camp. Beaver hoops hung from the ceiling and stretchers, holding otter and muskrat pelts hung from a wire stretched across the corner. We didn't mind working around the pelts as we helped each other stretch our furs tightly while dinner cooked on the stove.

We fried slabs of fresh beaver meat in butter and added onions and spices. Mashed potatoes or noodles completed our meals. To add something different to our meal, we picked cranberries from the bogs in front of our camp. After softening the wild cranberries in water on our woodstove, we mashed them up and added sugar, producing the finest cranberry sauce. We ate like kings.

The temperature outside was unseasonably warm for the first two weeks before finally dropping. Ice formed along Big Five, and it became a challenge to get the canoes out to the open water. We continued to trap and explore the wild and scenic areas with our daily forays, returning in the evening to share stories and tend to camp chores before dark.

Our solitude was about to be broken as two friends made their way along the river toward our camp. We welcomed the visitors, as even the best of friends can wear on each other after a few weeks together. Eamonn and Jeff met me at one of three lean-tos on the way to our camp. We had planned for their arrival halfway through our trip to get a weather report, and so they could hunt deer for a week during the white-tail rut. It was truly enjoyable to have our friends arrive and take part in our wilderness experience.

Eamonn learned how to skin and flesh beaver and shot his first squirrel while at camp, and we all hunted deer together during the day. Early morning sits and deer drives filled our days while stories and laughter were shared late into the evening. On the final morning of his stay, Eamonn harvested his first buck, a mature eight point, along the banks of the Oswegatchie. As they rounded a corner, the buck stood still, just long enough for the .50 caliber muzzle loader to reach Eamonn's shoulder and fire. It was also his birthday, what a gift!

As the following week carried on, Bud and I began the bittersweet task of pulling our traplines and shuttling gear back to the river. On the final morning of our stay, we dug out the fire pit that had accrued under the stove and poured water over it to be sure it was out. We returned the natural vegetation to the area where our temporary home had been and scattered logs to cover it. Our latrine was filled in with dirt, and we respectfully left the area as we had found it. Ice was chopped to form a narrow path to get our canoes out into the open water of the lake, and we made our way back to the outlet then over the steep moraine to the trail leading back to the open river. My fur was placed in plastic garbage bags to keep them dry and fastened to the canoe with rope. Our journey would take us to a lean-to along the banks of the Oswegatchie an hour after dark. The following morning, our trip was over. It had truly been a memorable experience.

The wilderness trapline is the toughest adventure one can have. The work is hard, the days are long and tiresome. After hiking along the trapline all day, I put up fur as I warmed myself by the woodstove and boiled water for hot tea. I reminisced about each day's adventure with a trapping partner or read a good book by the lanterns glow each night, just as I had hoped. For my brother and me, a long season of trapping deep in the wilds is now a memory and no longer just a dream.

Chapter 7

Hello, Montana!

I went to the woods because I wished to live deliberately, to front only the essential facts of life, and see if I could not learn what it had to teach, and not, when I came to die, discover that I had not lived.

—Henry David Thoreau

The story of the trappers of Montana began with the mountain men who traveled west in search of beavers hundreds of years ago. But for me, the Montana trapper's story began in 2007, when, for the first time, I met trappers who had recently had to defend their trapping rights. They were united and fought fiercely to preserve their heritage in the "Last Best Place." Restrictive regulations had been pushed in legislature and a ballot initiative tore at trapper's rights to trap on two thirds of Montana lands. I began to learn what it meant to have my culture threatened. Nearby trappers in states such as Colorado, Washington, and California had been the recipients of a rash of animal rights ballot initiatives that resulted in severe restrictions on trapping, in large part due to the lack of unity with other sportsmen and agricultural groups. Hard lesson learned.

The trappers of Montana are dedicated to preventing the same thing from happening in their state and are fighting to preserve what they have. There is more work to do to unify sportsmen and ensure that the rural lifestyle Montanans enjoy isn't turned into the metropolitan cease-and-desist-all-uses mentality of the people who are rapidly leaving their hectic lives and bringing their failed views on wildlife and the environment to Montana.

The Montana's dedicated dyed-in-the-wool trappers are wildlife experts in their own right. They are sought after for their knowledge by novices, wildlife managers, and the agricultural community. The necessity of an experienced trapper's knowledge is irreplaceable, but nothing beats the excitement and enthusiasm of a young person learning something new for the first time. The enormity of a new prospect that includes impossible choices for tools and gear, places, and techniques overwhelms every novice faced with the newness of pursuit. Trapping is no different.

A chance encounter with a novice outdoorsman taught me to appreciate the total nature immersion upbringing and the mentors I had who gave so freely. Toni contacted the Montana Trappers Association and asked them how he could learn to trap. He attended a trapper education class, where I was one of the instructors, and we made plans to meet the following Friday morning, I taught him how to set a few sets along a creek for muskrats and mink. Muskrats and mink are great animals to begin trapping because they don't shy away from human scent, and the traps don't require much modification. The next day, Toni had his first mink and a muskrat. As he pulled the mink from the creek, with a number 1 ½ coil spring trap on its front foot, the look on his face told me what I already suspected—Toni had trapping in his heart.

There is a connectedness trapper's feel when they trap their first animal. Perhaps it has ancestral origin, a voice that speaks from ancient craftsmen or maybe it's man's natural instinct to hunt breaking free from the oppression of modernization. Or it could simply be a reuniting of the human spirit with its rightful place in the natural order of things. Whatever it is some people get it, some don't. Those who don't are the type of trappers that either trap for a while and move on, or trap only when prices are high. Those trappers never really become proficient and rarely ever develop the intimate relationship with nature that connected trappers do. It is impossible to explain, but when a trapper gets it, really gets it, the feeling is real, and it creates a solemn quietness that follows a trapper. Seeing that spark has relit my own trapping fire. It was, in part, that light in Toni's eyes that day that inspired me to write about trapping—to explain what a trapper knows and feels.

Toni was twenty-three when I met him. He had never hunted or trapped growing up but was an exceptional fly fisherman. He had been in Alaska, Florida, and everywhere in between fishing and working countless jobs. He settled in Montana and had shot his first deer and elk the previous fall. We attended the Montana Trappers Association Rendezvous together, and Toni bought quality used traps with an old government trapper's name stamped in them. Like most trappers, Toni loved old-style traps and the history they hold.

I trapped beavers starting in November and also managed to put an elk and a deer in the freezer before Thanksgiving Day. My trapline was slowly growing, and as December got closer, I began planning my marten line.

A few days before marten season, I trapped another big-blanket beaver, only this time, Toni was with me. We were in a remote drainage, accessible by vehicle, and it was dark. As I pulled the beaver out of the choppy ice just below a beaver dam, the beam from my headlamp showed Toni how effective a 330 body gripping trap really is. I rolled the prime beaver around in the snow to dry it off and Toni examined it, saying, "That is so cool!" I agreed and was reminded about my earlier years when I could spend an hour just looking at a day's catch before ever picking up my knife to start skinning. These animals fascinated him as they have fascinated me throughout my life. Toni's enthusiasm was growing, and so was mine.

On the first day of the marten trapping season, we set traps from daylight until after dark. A large plastic sled was attached to the back of the snowmobile by a rope fed through a piece of PVC pipe, three and a half feet long, which helped keep the sled directly behind us and prevented it from sliding into the track when we stopped. We were able to fit one dozen wooden boxes at a time, and as many number 120 body gripping traps—bait, feather attractors, and wire—on the sled at one time. After making several sets and showing Toni what to look for, we began to get an efficient system down. I attached a marten box about four feet up on a tree trunk or blow down and set the springs while Toni gathered boughs to camouflage the set. We set most boxes face down or horizontally to weather proof the sets. The boughs also helped collect snow for further concealment as the season went on. Toni scooped the bait out, added it to the box, and consequently ended up with scent all over him. When we attended a public FWP meeting during season, he smelled so bad, he was embarrassed. I considered it an initiation ceremony!

We set dirt-hole sets along brushy creeks in the low, flat sections of our line for winter-prime red fox. Having numerous fox to target, along with beavers and marten, was cause for anticipation. We also observed wolf tracks almost every day and tried calling them to within shooting distance on occasion but did not succeed. The opportunity to hunt for these giant canines added to our experience.

Toni's first marten set he ever made, and which he ever checked, held a big male marten. I hoped his luck would continue! On our next section of line, we picked up another marten. Things were getting good!

On one check at the highest point of our line, I stopped at a marten box, and it was about ten feet from where we had left it. Big tracks in the snow told the story of a wolverine who approached the box and apparently swatted it, knocking the bait out and devouring it before walking away. It was my first-ever encounter with a wolverine. On another check, Toni and I were driving along a winding road and spotted a mountain lion sitting along the edge. When it heard my truck, it ran into the woods, but then it paralleled us about a hundred feet away for several hundred feet before running up onto a ridge. Another encounter with a lion came when Toni was alone. This time, the lion ran up onto a cliff and peered down at him for several minutes.

As the season went on, the experiences we had continued to build. Toni is very inquisitive and had spent a day studying tracks in the snow by himself. After following a set of marten tracks for a while, he circled around to check a set. Just as he got there, he watched a marten run along the snow before peering into the box. Suddenly it darted into the trap! Toni couldn't believe he had just witnessed a marten getting caught! He was still excited when telling me about it later that evening. "That's why I love trapping so much! You never know what's going to happen. You can't get experiences like this anywhere—ever!" He exclaimed. It is rare for trappers to witness an animal step into a trap. The odds are quite small. I watched beavers on two occasions enter traps. Once, while observing beavers on a pond where I had several sets, and once while trapping with my father.

This trapline taught me to be thankful for my mentors and to never forget the basics. Without my mentors and friends to share my outdoor experiences with, I would not have had so many successful days trapping and hunting, nor would I have had the opportunity to take what I've learned and pass it on. Toni told me one day—while we were on our line—that he was grateful for me taking the time to teach him how to trap, and that he wished he could repay me. I'm not sure who learned more from whom. I, in return, was thankful for his enthusiasm and desire to succeed, and for paying attention.

The pieces of people I have shared time with throughout my life have shaped who I am and have added significance to my human economy. The human piece of the trapping culture is made up of trappers who have shared their time on the line and have impact one another the most. People who choose to spend a majority of their time in nature and truly understand how it works are the most passionate and concerned individuals about the environment—they love it because they get it. Trappers—real trappers—are true stewards of the land who seek to understand and make the natural environment a place to go, a place to breathe in, a place to recharge in. The serenity and peace that fills a trapper is unmistakable, yet often unexplainable. It is not the people who wish to be separated from nature or to be a viewer only from a distance, who will ever appreciate what it feels like to connect with something so powerful in such an intimate way. You can hear the call only if you get close enough to listen.

Chapter 8

Right for You, Rights for Me

Knowing what's right doesn't mean much unless you do what's right.

—Theodore Roosevelt

It was late December and the temperature was below freezing, a faint dusting of fresh snow on the ground. I parked my truck and made my way into a steep and narrow draw, made even narrower by fallen rocks and boulders. The sun had just begun to rise over the mountains but had several hours before its rays would reach the valley floor. I had a wooden marten box baited with beaver meat and guarded with a 120 body gripping trap setting on the rocks at the base of this draw. It was undisturbed, but as I made my way around the box, I heard the clinging of metal chain. I knew that I had something in a foot trap up the draw. As I peeked around the boulders, I saw it was red fox caught by the front foot. He had been walking by a hole in the rock where I had a beaver carcass tucked in the back and the trap bedded in the dry dirt in front of it. I shot the fox with a well-placed shot from a .22 caliber pistol and removed the prime thick furred fox from the trap and remade the set, taking care to avoid getting any human scent on the trap or around the set.

Back at my truck, I placed the fox in a grain bag to keep the fur from getting dirty and drove several miles along icy roads to the next stop. Here, I unloaded my snowmobile from the trailer and fired it up. I made my way along the forest service road and stopped periodically to check marten boxes and dirt hole sets in the thick forested mountain sides and draws.

About three miles down the road, I came to a cubby set I had made for a bobcat. I walked up the hill to the trap which held a prime Montana marten. All around the set were bobcat tracks, and I just had to put more foot traps nearby. I set three snares on bobcat trails coming in and circling the set then added two dirt hole sets and baited them with meat and bobcat lure. The remaining mile and half of line was made up of about half dozen marten boxes placed fifty feet from the road in narrow draws about four feet off the ground. There were no additional marten in any of them.

I made my way back to the truck and drove the sled up on the trailer, and about fifteen minutes later, I was on a plowed road where I stopped three times to check foot traps made for bobcats and fox. They were all set at least two hundred feet from the road on National Forest Service land. The snow was a couple of feet deep, but my tracks were frozen hard from numerous visits to my line, making the work easier. The second trap located about three hundred feet above the road was sprung, and the beaver meat gone. That was the second time in a row that trap was sprung and pulled out with nothing in it.

With no snow on the windswept hill side, there weren't any tracks to tell the story. I had made this set after hoofing straight up hill for about two hundred yards. From this set location, I could look down the steep hill and make out pieces of the road. I walked back to my truck to get bait and lure and remade the set. A couple more miles to the end of the plowed road, and it was time to get the sled off the trailer once again. I followed my previous days' snowmobile tracks along a creek dotted with beaver lodges and willows brush.

I had a few foot traps to check along the creek then made my way up the mountain road. I also had twenty-three marten sets over the course of about six miles, and I picked up three more marten from marten boxes guarded with number 120 body gripping traps. Every quarter mile or so, I had placed a hand built wood box about twelve inches long and just wide enough for a number 120 to fit. I had made a notch on either side of the box so the springs fit snug. In the back of the box, I had a chunk of red meat and a cotton ball with skunk essence on it, a proven lure for the Montana marten. The boxes were either wired directly to a tree or rested on an elevated stump or deadfall, each covered with boughs to camouflage the set.

When I got to my last marten box, it was about ten feet from where I had left it at the base of the tree. Tracks told the story of a wolverine that had walked down the ridge right to the box, knocked it over, and ate all the bait in the box before walking off, no doubt continuing its search for food. I took photos of his tracks and wished he had visited sooner. The wolverine season had just closed a few days before that. If it hadn't, I would have spent the whole day setting traps for that wolverine. I've wanted to catch one for years but never have. These majestic-looking creatures thrive at extreme elevations, making it rare for a trapper in navigable areas to encounter one.

I got back to my truck about an hour later and had to remake several bobcat cubbies on the way out to the main road. It was well after dark, and as I was driving along the snow and ice-covered road, I saw the glow of headlamps up high on the hillside in thick timber. It was odd to see people in this remote area of Montana, let alone coming off a mountain after dark. I stopped my truck and yelled into the darkness; "Hey! Do you need a ride?"

"Yeah!" a man yelled out of the darkness. I had so many coats, spotlights, water bottles, guns and ammo in my truck that it took me ten minutes to get it all cleared out and into the bed of the truck, which was about how long it took for the group of five to cross a flowing winter creek and make their way up to the bank. As they approached my truck, I asked, "Are you lion hunting?" My assumption was confirmed as two hounds suddenly ran up to me, followed by their party. "Did you get one?"

"Yup!" a young voice replied.

A scruffy man of about forty-five, wearing wool and a backpack full of lion hide introduced himself as Scott; another stepped out, and I knew him as Ben. We greeted each other with a handshake and typical, "Hey, how are things?" "Oh, good and you?"

"Oh, not bad, and yourself?"

Then the source of the young voice stepped into view. He too was wearing camouflage and carrying a rifle. It was Scott's fourteen-year-old son who had just shot his first lion. A young lady wearing warm yet colorful clothing about the same age as Scott's son, and another guy named John completed the party.

The excitement of the hunt was still present in the group. I listened as the story unfolded. The group had driven the roads most of the night looking for fresh lion tracks in impossibly tough conditions. It hadn't snowed much in eleven days, making it difficult to discern a fresh lion track from one three or more days old. A good hound is needed for these conditions to tell the hunters that this is indeed fresh and should be followed. With the level of excitement the hounds displayed with low deep bellows, the hunters put their faith in the dog's nose and turned them loose from the top of a mountain at 9:00 a.m. Using a GPS and tracking collar, they followed the hounds over extreme mountainous terrain until 1:00 p.m. where they had a big tom mountain lion in a tree. The youngster put a good shot on the tom with an old lever action rifle, and the cat leaped from the tree and fell dead shortly thereafter. After skinning the cat and taking photos, the party began making their way down the mountain toward the nearest road. Six hours later, I picked them up, heard their story, and drove them five miles back to their truck on a cold winter's night.

"Traffic's pretty scarce around here this time of day," I said.

"I know and there's not very many cars on the road either!" Scott exclaimed.

We shared hunting and trapping stories as Scott, an outfitter by trade, talked about his trapline in Idaho. He was trapping wolves with another outfitter in an effort to bring the suffering elk numbers of the Selway wilderness back up. So far, he hadn't trapped any, but his friend Tom had two, and they had no intentions of removing their traps and snares anytime soon.

The narrow forest service road gets some attention by locals because a handful of rustic cabins are tucked in the trees, off the beaten path. But there is no reason for anyone other than hunters and trappers to be driving along the ice-covered truck path. The remote area is nestled in against the Idaho border, far removed from any cell phone towers. The fact that I came along when I did was remarkable and saved Scott and Ben a considerable amount of walking back to their jacked-up pickup trucks with huge bubble tires, designed to navigate deep snow and rugged backcountry roads.

I said good-bye, and they thanked me again. Stopping to help a group of lion hunters and sharing in their camaraderie was one of the highlights of my 2011 trapping season. Where else in the world and what cultural group of people would ever have this kind of personal interaction? The outdoorsman, the true dyed-in-the-wool outdoorsman, made up of hunters and trappers, are the most generous, sharing, and helpful group of individuals the world has to offer. I can't imagine this subculture getting dismantled by urbanites disconnected from the natural world and who will never experience anything like this and will certainly never try to understand this lifestyle.

In Bud Moore's book, *The Lochsa Story* [3], Moore wrote about trappers at the turn of the twentieth century who lived and trapped in the wilderness along the Montana/Idaho border who would always leave fire materials on their cabin table whenever they were away so that if other trappers needed shelter and a warm fire, it was always available. That was part of the trapper's unwritten code. It was considered unethical for a man to leave his cabin without having it ready should another man show up in need. The same goes for a trapper in the mountains today, he is expected to leave fire wood in camp, always enough for the next user. And if an outdoorsman sees another person in the mountains who needs a hand, there is little hesitation, the offer is extended.

This small party of five turned two hound dogs on to a set of mountain lion tracks and followed the hounds as they chased the big tom cat. The cat ran from the sound of baying and when they got too close, he ran up a tree. The hounds made it to the tree and barked. They would not leave the tree. They were trained to follow tracks until they ended at a tree and stay put until their owners arrived. Years of training culminated into two hounds sitting at the bottom of a tree with a big tom perched high on a limb. The hunters arrived, having heard the sound of the hounds barking treed. With careful aim, the young hunter shot the cat out of the tree. After a short celebration of success, they made a camp fire and ate a hot lunch. The cat was skinned, choice meat saved, and the group hiked out of the woods where they met me.

Was what they did ethical? Were any moral lines crossed? This cat was taken after weeks of driving icy roads, searching for tracks. Their knowledge of lions and hunting was proven by the eventual outcome. But days like this are not the norm, not even close. Hours spent on dangerous roads in snowy conditions miles from civilization are required before finding tracks, and then more often than not, the lion wins and the hunters return home empty-handed. Is this ethical only because of the effort required? Is it unethical because they used hounds to tree the lion? What about the dozens of elk spared because this giant predator was removed from the forest—does that make it okay? Who can decide? And where do ethical lines of concern cross with irrational or unrealistic views of our natural ecosystem?

Trapping ethics are arguably the most important aspect of any trapper education class. How can it be that a trapper can love the animals and the landscape they inhabit, yet set out traps that will inevitably inflict harm? The same question may be asked of other outdoor users, like the waterfowl, upland game bird, deer and elk hunters; anglers; hikers; campers; and horsemen. Virtually, all outdoor recreation users have an impact on the land and animals they love; the extent of their impact can be minimized by applying good ethics but cannot be eliminated altogether.

While trappers may choose to release animals from their traps unharmed, the fact is that most animals trapped are not released. Animals are captured, killed, and pelts are skillfully prepared for the fur market and sold locally or on the international fur market. Glands and meat may be removed and stored for later use as well. But fur and glands are hardly the reason most trappers spend their days outdoors. It is difficult to explain how trapping, as mentally and physically demanding as it is, appeals to trappers.

When a rancher raises cattle for profit, several hundred acres of land or possibly thousands are fenced off in sections. Each fenced section can serve as isolation between breeds or bulls. It can be for rotating grazing lands or calving grounds. Regardless, it's hard work to maintain those fences. Year-round diligence is required to keep feed stored, fences mended, tractors in working order, crops growing, and herds protected. There's breeding season, calving season, branding season, sales . . . the list of things to do goes on. Cattle are left out to graze or corralled depending on what season it is. When it comes time to cash in on their investment, the cattle are herded into trucks and hauled away for sale. High bidders take the cows to slaughter where they are lined up and killed. The hides and meat removed and hung in cold storage. The meat goes to your butcher and the hides go to a tannery where shoes, gloves, belts, hats, and a covering for your couch or car seats are made. Is this practice much different than a ranched mink farm? Instead of meat, the glands and fats are removed for various products, and the hides removed to make garments too.

The same scenario can be made for fish farms, chickens, turkeys, rabbits, pigs, and whatever else you might eat. Even your local vegetable farm had to find some way to keep the raccoons and deer out of their crops. Chances are the animals were trapped or shot. That is reality.

People cannot live on the earth without impacting animals. And in order to feed the masses, we need to produce food.

Instead of tame or domesticated creatures, trappers target wild animals. The populations are not managed by fences or business needs. They are managed by regulations instituted by state and sometimes federal game agencies. When populations are high, quotas or limits are set higher, and when populations are low, so too are the quotas. Over the long term, trappers take the excess or surplus from local areas and move on. In a short time, higher density areas decrease as those animals move in to the now lowered density areas. This system has worked so well in the U.S. that there are more beavers inhabiting the country now than when Christopher Columbus landed here.

Is this different than the rancher with his livestock or the mink farmer with his mink? The populations of animals can be artificially raised or decreased without hurting the overall population of animals—domestic or wild. In fact, keeping populations within their carrying capacity is a key factor in maintaining overall population health, particularly in areas where high human densities overlap with high animal populations. The same goes for coyotes, deer, sheep or rodents. The management principles are different, but the concept is the same.

It may be easy to understand using a domestic animal for meat and hide. Like a child in a school program raising a calf to show at the county fair and then selling it to the beef industry at the end of the summer. That cow was raised with the utmost care, groomed every day, and fed the highest quality of grain and hay. These programs allow the studious youngster the opportunity to learn responsibility and to raise an animal for meat and leather. The cycle of life and death, of a relationship with another creature, and the separation of man and beast can only be learned through experience.

If animals, domestic or wild, are killed for their meat, skin, fats, glands, intestines, or whatever else may be used for human consumption, does it make a difference what the species is? Surely, a cow has no higher status than a muskrat or a sheep more so than a river otter.

So what is really the difference? What is it about trapping that drives extreme people to throw paint on fur coats or set fire to trapping supply stores? Maybe it's perception. Trapping is portrayed as a cruel way to harvest animals by animal rights groups. For those groups whose agenda is ultimately to end all uses of animals, trapping seems like an easy target to start with. Some people are willing to accept that a bullet was placed in the vitals of a deer or a bolt driven into the brain of a cow because it is quick and humane but are opposed to a body gripping trap or snare that kills just as quickly. A foothold trap is commonly used by biologists to monitor animal populations and for relocation programs, and those same biologists arrive at the trapper's call to radio collar and release wolves caught in sets intended for coyotes. Traps are clearly humane and practical tools used around the world for the benefit of mammalian research, so what is the real issue?

At an information session presented by the Montana Fish Wildlife and Parks in Missoula in 2012, the regional wildlife manager presented the fact that trapping was needed to manage wolves. Data tables and graphs demonstrated the predator and prey numbers in certain areas of the state, and it was clear that some deer and elk herds were at a critical low. He didn't say he wanted to add trapping to offer more opportunity for sportsmen. He said we need trapping.

The MFWP proposed the use of traps only and omitted the use of snares for their first-ever wolf-trapping season. Along with the omission of snares from the proposed regulations was the inclusion of a mandatory forty-eight-hour trap check requirement. The reason given for these critical changes were due to social considerations i.e., public acceptance. If snares are used poorly, the result can be a high risk of incidental or nontarget catches. Even though well-skilled trappers can easily avoid that from happening, the FWP wanted to avoid any chance of bad public relations.

The effectiveness of snares is exponentially higher than traps. Snares can be purchased for a fraction of the cost of a single trap, are easier to set, weigh a few ounces compared to a ten-pound wolf trap with number 5 chain and heavy drag. Still, the MFWP limited the potential success of trappers to avoid what they considered a potential to create negative public perception.

A forty-eight-hour trap check requirement is also a detriment for trappers. Wolves live in the rugged mountain country of Montana, and access is not easy. Trappers trying to make a living off the land trapping furbearers are not likely to invest their time and money into rigging, setting, and maintaining expensive traps for an animal that can be difficult to catch in any numbers. Additionally, without the ability to ship out of state and sell it on the world market—really isn't all that valuable on the world market. Even trappers who might enjoy the opportunity to trap wolves may not be able to afford the time and money required to do it.

The MFWP representatives who put together the proposal for wolf regulations decided that an appropriate time interval for checking wolf traps would be forty-eight hours, and since they had the power to put their views into action, that's the proposal that the public received.

In that one meeting, the viewpoints of ethics ranged from one person's plea who yelled at the crowd, "The killing of wolves is inhumane and unnecessary." In contrast, another yelled with equal vigor, "We should kill every wolf in the state using aerial shooting, poison, traps, guns, and explosives—whatever it takes."

Regardless of drastic decreases of ungulate populations in certain regions of Montana due to large predators, the best approach is likely somewhere in the middle of these two extremes. The job of a wildlife manager has got to be one of the toughest public positions there is. People on both sides of the extremes who don't have all the facts are screaming no matter what course of action is taken.

Hunters and trappers are viewed by some nonconsumptive users as unethical and ill-minded individuals, even though the track record of America's sportsman is one of tremendous success. It has brought both game and nongame back to exceptional and oft unprecedented numbers, but what about other groups of well-respected harvesters of wildlife?

Even a look at sport fishing shows extremes in philosophy. The spectrum covers the use of light fly fishing tackle to large fishing nets scraping the ocean floor. Both methods result in the capture of live fish. Both require specialized gear and knowledge. But there are obvious differences. It is easy to see that a single angler standing on a river bank casting a number 6 hook at wild trout has far less impact on the overall health of the population than say a net thirty feet wide with heavy weights dragged through seaweed and sand in critical oceanic habitats. If there is a difference between the two extremes, and one is found to be acceptable and one is not, then it is important for ethical reasons to understand why. It can be difficult to know where to start. This is a question of ethics and respect for the environment.

Anglers, and in particular fly fishermen, pride themselves in the catch and release of hungry Montana trout. Small flies are chosen from hundreds in their box and carefully laid on the water's surface with skill and grace. The beauty of the fly rod and fishing are often depicted in Hollywood films. Huge trout leap above the water and dance through river rocks, and the angler's excitement mounts as he plays the fish to exhaustion and scoops the trophy into a net.

Trout are treated with respect and care; the tackle used is chosen to minimize the damage on the fish. The happy angler returns the fish to the river after removing the hook and holding the fish by the tail, swishes it carefully back and forth to return water flow to its gills. A sudden kick of the fish's tail indicates recovery and the angler releases the tail and watches as his quarry swims back to the depths of the pool.

These same fly fishing enthusiasts turn their noses up at bait fishermen and fiercely charge them with killing the fish. The idea that bait fishermen cause damage to thriving trout fisheries is infused into fly fishermen and game agencies so much so that large sections of Montana rivers and creeks are artificial lure only, and angling stops when water temperatures reach unacceptable temperatures. A study titled "Effects of Catch-and-Release-Angling on Salmonids at Elevated Water Temperatures" used fly-fishing-only methods to catch trout on Montana rivers at various water temperatures in part to assess the mortality of fish caught, using typical angling techniques. The results were lethality rates that ranged from 0% to 28% depending on species, water temperature, and handling techniques, although the mortality rates were lower than predicted (<30%) based on other literature (Boyd, Guy, Horton, and Leathe, 2012) [4].

Another report titled "Catch and-release-angling: A Review with Guidelines for Proper Fish Handling Practices" states that "catch-and-release mortality can be reduced by using artificial bait." This data further strengthens the fly-anglers position but also goes on to say that "the location of hooking has been shown to affect catch-and-release mortality" and provides further recommendations for handling caught fish and equipment such as barbless circle hooks, appropriate line size to reduce playing time, and knotless landing nets made of soft rubber. (Castleman, S. J., 2005) [5]. So it is clear that in order for catch-and-release techniques to have minimal impact to individual fish, great care must be taken to use the right equipment at the right time of year with the best handling techniques. But the fact remains that sporting anglers do have an impact on the fish they catch, regardless of their fishing style.

Meanwhile, a bait fisherman will gladly tie a hook to his line and attach a sinking weight above it. A night crawler threaded to the hook and cast into a slow-moving section of river or stream is his way of fishing. The pools where fly fishermen just worked over with their light tackle and caught nothing suddenly come alive when hungry trout lying on the bottom attack the worm with voracious tenacity. The bait fishermen also counts success by the quality of the outdoor experience but his measure of success leans a little more on the number of fish landed. He may choose to return the fish to the water or place it in his creel to bring home for fine table fare. Fishermen who use spinning rods and reels to cast bait are called bait chuckers. These bait chuckers may be skilled anglers in their own right and scoff at the fly fishermen who play the fish too long and hardly ever catch anything. In the bait chucker's mind, the fly fishermen are detrimental to fisheries because they exhaust the fish to the point that it may not live once released, especially on extremely hot summer days. On the contrary, the bait chucker pulls the fish in quickly and has the option to release it with its full vigor.

Both parties are anglers, whether they agree or not—they are both there to catch fish, and they will often catch nontarget species. These die-hard anglers contribute thousands of dollars and man hours to habitat protection and restoration. Groups like Trout Unlimited tout their contributions to "conserving, protecting and restoring North America's cold water fisheries and their watersheds." Rightfully so, with millions of dollars in net assets, the organization puts its money where its mouth is. But even though dedicated anglers are clearly dedicated to their sport and continue to create viable habitat for their quarry, it doesn't make their resulting harvest acceptable to everyone. Animal rights groups around the world oppose sport fishing and are fighting to end it.

Sensitive species like Montana's bull trout are listed as threatened. While anglers are not allowed to target bull trout specifically, there is no good way to avoid catching them. The fishing tackle used to catch plentiful cutthroat and rainbow trout is the same tackle used to catch bull trout. While both sides of the fishing community can argue that they can release threatened species unharmed, it would be hard to imagine that same argument being used by a trapper who catches a lynx in Montana, where they are listed as a threatened species that must be released. Strict regulations apply to sets made in lynx habitat to avoid the inadvertent capture of a lynx. If a lynx were to be accidentally captured in a foot trap set on Montana soil, it must immediately be released per Montana Law; same for the Bull trout caught by an angler. The lynx could be in the trap for several hours. If unharmed, it is easy to let it go. The capture and release of animals is a part of trapping, just as it is with fishing. Anglers may argue that they catch their quarry and release it within several minutes, not hours, and that the fish is sure to survive, but several studies have proven that is not always the case.

Ethics are dynamic and impact human activities. What was acceptable by the general public ten years ago may not be the case today. But should the trapper who learned to trap thirty years ago be expected to stop because of a new public perception? One in which he had no part of. The ethical responsibility hasn't changed, but the perception of what is acceptable has. Many people remain neutral on the subject. Fur coats are just another animal product like shoes or gloves. It makes no difference to them which animal the garment came from. On the other hand, a relatively small percentage of people are adamantly opposed to fur, and an even smaller percentage refuses to wear leather because it was once the skin of an animal. They instead wear synthetic materials made from petroleum-based products or choose cotton or hemp. They believe that the artificial and chemically-treated materials are less impactful to the environment than leather goods or furs. At least they don't result in a direct killing of an animal. Fair enough. But what about the rubber soles of those shoes? Or the beaver castor used in perfumes? How far can they take it? Pretty far.

While the vast majority of people in the U.S. have no issues wearing the skins of cattle, fur is a different issue. Clearly the issue cannot be that an animal died to make the fur garment, and therefore, they won't wear it. Is the issue that the animal which the leather came from was also used for meat thereby making it okay to use? Some trappers eat what they catch; would the fur from that animal then be acceptable to wear?

The issue is that animal rights groups have made an impact on public perception. Their agenda is clear, to eliminate the use of animals in *any* way.

Constant media and celebrity support of the animal rights agenda have also swayed public opinion. Fur fashion in the U.S. has diminished significantly since the late 70s. Foreign markets are the primary demand for furs today, and countries like China, Russia, and Korea wear fur garments and feed a willing U.S. industry and vice versa.

Are trappers in a different class of consumptive users than say Big game hunters or bait chuckers? How about pheasant hunters or fly fishermen? The big game hunting industry is huge in the U.S. as is commercial fishing. Anglers are paying to catch fish. Is a river guide any less impactful on his animal of choice than a trapper? It's hard to say. But if trout were cute and cuddly and beavers were scaly and slimy, the tables might be turned.

Humans use animals. We use them for food, research, clothing, companionship, for utility in acts like retrieving ducks, pulling us along snow-covered trails, sports, medicine, and as symbols of freedom and fear. Animals are utilized in so many capacities, it is impossible to list them all. Are all animals treated well by every animal user group that exists? Are all pet owners kind and firm with their training and handling? Is every research facility spotless and humane in the treatment of their test subjects? Is every farmer committed to the best treatment of his stock from birth until slaughter? Is every musher appreciative of their huskies? The simple answer is—no.

When the owner of an animal, whether in the capacity of pet ownership, livestock, or any other facet of animal use doesn't treat their animal appropriately, they are subject to the laws pertaining to that animal. If an animal research facility raises animals, feeds them, provides them with all the amenities that a pet might receive from a caring owner—yet terminates and necropsies the animal for scientific or pharmaceutical advancement, that is acceptable. It is acceptable because the operators of the facility followed the rules governing the treatment of those animals and behaved in the best interest of science. If one research facility is found to be deficient, does that mean that *all* research facilities should be shut down?

How about pet owners? If ten pet owners a year are found to be abusive in a given city, should *all* pet owners be required to relinquish their pets to the authorities?

Trappers who use the best equipment available, go the extra mile to avoid nontarget catches, and refuse to trap in areas where other uses may be a conflict are not dissimilar to other users of animals. But when one trapper makes the news for his lack of responsibility, animal rights groups jump at the chance to publicize his mistake and claim that all trapping is barbaric and unethical and should therefore be stopped. By that logic, when a vehicle inadvertently strikes and kills a family pet, shouldn't we then stop all vehicular travel in neighborhoods that house pets?

In thousands of towns around the U.S., populations of animals like the white-tailed deer and raccoons are inadvertently managed by vehicular traffic. Thousands of animals are killed or maimed and suffer for days. Is that acceptable? Would it be better if the animals were hunted or trapped? Hunting and trapping would be controlled, bring license revenues to small cities, and feed families. Animal/vehicle collisions waste the animal, damage vehicles, raise insurance rates, and cost communities thousands of dollars each year. And as an added benefit, those animals crushed and maimed by vehicles could be humanely trapped and removed.

Photos of anglers dressed in $500 waders holding a 6 lb. brown trout is a nice photo. Yet the same photo of a trapper with a river otter may be used as propaganda by those opposed to animal use. Is that trout any more important to the ecosystem than a river otter? It depends who you ask. There are different standards for wildlife depending on the reaction achieved by photos. A rare insect smeared on a windshield won't get any environmentalist very far. But show an extremely prolific animal like a raccoon in a foot trap, caught by both front feet and you can almost hear the checks being written to support a local trapping ban. Even though the raccoon is not endangered, not even close, the emotional reaction of nature-starved people is powerful and helps line the pockets of activists involved in the lucrative protest industry.

The protest industry is growing, and for good reason. By using the Equal Access to Justice Act (EAJA, 1980) any nonprofit group can sue the federal government and get their legal fees back. These groups then raise money to "recoup costs" in fundraising campaigns. When money is the driver for activism, is it really activism or is it simply just fraud?

With so many different viewpoints on what is right and what is wrong, how can an ethical person choose? For example, a conscientious consumer decides that she is not going to buy commercial fish caught in dredge nets. That is her choice. She decided that she will not support commercial fishing because there are too many nontarget fish caught, and the impact on ocean environments are well documented as detrimental to healthy fish populations. However, she will eat red meat that is certified free-range-organic. The ability of the animals she consumes to have unrestricted movement and pesticide-free food is natural and therefore good. She has established her values and is controlling, to some extent, her impact on the world.

Another consumer decides that it is wrong to eat meat. He has decided that animals have basic sentience (ability to reason) and have equal rights to humans, and he refuses to eat red meat. He will only eat meat from fish because fish do not have the ability to reason. He is a vegetarian who consumes fish. He has established his values and is controlling his impact on the world within his abilities. It doesn't matter where the fish comes from, only that the fish he consumes are fresh and complement his vegetarian lifestyle.

Another consumer decides that he is going to eat meat but only from wild animals that he harvested himself. He doesn't want to let someone else kill the animals where his protein is derived. He makes fur garments from the animal's fur he trapped and wears them when it's cold. It is important to him that the animals he catches are killed quickly, and he ensures that happens by using the best traps available, often making modifications for improved humane methods. Although the laws don't require him to check his land sets any more often than every seventy-two hours, he feels that a minimum of every forty-eight hours is his ethical standard.

He chooses to trap because animals fascinate him, just as fish and elk do. He enjoys the outdoors and has decided that he will gather his food and clothing from a natural renewable resource and not from chemical-ridden clothing or clothing that required hundreds of animals to be dispelled in order to clear and plow cotton or hemp fields. He wants nature to be left intact, takes only the surplus, and fits his ideals into a modern world by selling or trading his fur for other goods. He has established his values and is controlling to some extent, his impact on the world.

These three people have made a conscientious decision and have made sacrifices to limit their impact on the planet. They directly contradict each other. Who's right?

A fair argument could be made that all three are right because they chose the things that are important to them and stick to it, regardless of others' opinions. If this is true, and I commend them for thinking about how their personal behaviors affect other aspects of the planet, then how can it be that any of them are wrong? Are they all right?

Who decides what is moral and right? Good and bad? Is it society or the individual? If one argued that it was society then which society do we choose to listen to? If it is up to the individual then how can society decide what is right and wrong for the individual?

It is neither an easy topic nor one that can really be answered. Ethics are determined by the individual. Will a grizzly bear kill and eat me if it can? Yes. Does that mean that I have a right to give it the same rights to kill me that I have to kill him? Maybe. According to the laws in the lower 48, I cannot kill a grizzly bear. Why? Because wildlife officials have decided that there aren't yet enough to provide a sustained yield harvest, or the hunting seasons are tied up in litigation. So it is illegal and therefore unethical for me to kill it. But if that grizzly bear attacks me and I kill it in self-defense, I may not be charged with any crime.

What about a buffalo? Will he kill me if he can? Yes. Can I kill him? If I apply for a permit and I am successful then, yes. Is that ethical? Maybe, but I've got to decide for myself. But it is socially acceptable. It is the hunting and consumption of a wild animal, one of many animal uses. Where does the use of animals fall on the scale of socially acceptable uses?

Trapping is a choice, and it is a legal activity. I can trap according to the laws of the state and according to current society. It is not someone else's choice, it is mine. If I choose to eat beef, make omelets and sausage for breakfast or use animal research derived medicine to save my life that is also my choice. Catching and holding an animal alive in a foothold trap, catching a fish, or raising chickens for eggs and meat align with other animal uses like holding a dairy cow in a barn for milk, hunting ducks, or raising hounds. Animal uses are acceptable in our society and will continue to be acceptable.

If I choose to eat meat, wear leather or not, that is my choice. It will impact animals. Just as wearing cotton or leather, or eating fruit will in some way impact animals. The fact is that trapping has a direct and personal impact which may be hard for people who don't live by the laws of nature or those of the trapping culture to understand.

It doesn't mean that trapping is wrong or immoral. When a nontrapper, nonhunter, or nonangler impacts a wild animal, they don't have to look; they don't have to see their impact. They choose not to. Trappers know what their impact is. They see it first hand and know what it means. It is their own ethic, their decision, and for hunters, anglers, and trappers, it is right.

The rules you write for your own code of ethics may not align with someone who also takes their ethics very seriously. They may think you're wrong and accuse you of ignorance. They have no idea what your thought process was to get you to the point where you made a decision. They weren't there when you saw the options and picked the one that suited you. And you weren't there when they made their decision. Does that mean that we shouldn't question our own ethics constantly? That we shouldn't strive to be the best humans we can even if that means we must change? Of course not, but neither can we criticize others for the decisions they have made. Not everyone can agree—so what is the solution?

There are baseline rules that must be followed in the United States and around the world for any and all uses of animals. Clear-cut laws with specific regulations are used to regulate trapping just as in virtually every natural consumptive practice whether it is trapping, hunting, fishing, logging, mining, mushroom gathering and berry picking, farming, circuses, zoos or countless other activities.

Since the 1800s, wildlife conservation has been a priority in the U.S., and the reasons for the wildlife and wild lands that Americans enjoy today are the result of wise use, not total preservation. If the millions of acres of wilderness were set aside only for viewing at a distance, how could people appreciate the wilderness, fall in love with it and accept that it is untouchable? Can a person who has never experienced a wild place truly love it?

Our land ethic stems from individuals such as Aldo Leopold, Theodore Roosevelt, and George Bird Grinnell—avid outdoorsmen and consumptive wildlife users who, by virtue of natural participation, gained real appreciation for wilderness and everything about it. They fought to preserve not only the land, water, and animals, but also the lifestyle and the heritage of living *in* the wild and participating as their human nature led them to. Without the ability to live with and among the wildlife, they could not have developed their passion for wild places.

The result of setting aside wild lands was the gain of responsibility. The people of the United States changed from dominator of wild lands to wilderness stewards. The concept of land use ethics began to emerge and with it a call by hunters and sportsmen to protect North America's wildlife.

In 1878, the state of Iowa instituted the nation's first regulated hunting seasons, and so the conservation model that developed into the greatest wildlife legacy in the world began. The North American model of wildlife conservation was developed and used with unprecedented success. Now, every state in the U.S. and every province in Canada have regulations to sustain healthy populations of wild animals forever—the results have been second to none in the world. Great care has been taken to ensure that North America maintains an abundance of wildlife for all. The legacy of America's wildlife is one which sportsmen are rightfully proud of.

Other nonconsumptive uses are also heavily regulated in areas where people are "loving the wilderness to death" for activities such as hiking, biking, camping, horseback riding, and videoing. Restrictions on how many people may travel in one hiking group or how long a campsite may be occupied by the same person exist to protect the safety of our wild lands. Permit systems have been instituted throughout the U.S. in an effort to regulate commercial industry and keep trail erosion and human impact to a minimum.

A "Leave No Trace" philosophy has emerged with a basic premise to leave no sign of human activity when recreating in wild places. Before setting up camp, all natural forest debris such as sticks and rocks are to be removed and saved aside, fire rings are not allowed; instead a fire pit is to be dug or campfires avoided altogether. Hikers are to stay on trails and avoid scuffing moss as they travel. When they move camp, all forest debris is scattered back over the area where they slept and fire pits are filled in. This land-use philosophy, which has developed over the last twenty or so years, is a far cry from the "Bury Your Trash" philosophy widely used in the 1970s and 1980s. To ensure adherence to the laws for recreational land use, forest rangers, conservation officers, and other law enforcement personnel are employed to enforce the rules.

For hunting and trapping furbearers, regulations are published by governing wildlife agencies and overseen by state authorities. Regulations vary in every state for trapping just as they do for other regulated uses. Laws about the number of each species allowed for harvest, size of traps, where and how they may be placed, season dates, and harvest reporting all apply just as they do in the North American model of wildlife conservation. It is the trapper's responsibility to adhere to the laws and his or her own personal ethics just as it is for all other recreational users who choose to venture out of doors in our modern-day regulated natural environment.

In order to appropriately define the acceptable actions of any group, there must be a standard baseline guide. For engineers, doctors, and lawyers must follow their respective code of ethics, so too do sportsmen and women. Regulations or guidelines do not always have to be formal industry-specific guidance to be effective. Many religions also have guidelines which they refer to when faced with matters of moral or ethical consideration. For Christians, it is the Holy Bible, for Muslims the Quran, and Buddhists use sutras meant to inspire and provoke thought. So what guides a trapper's moral and ethical considerations other than his own conscience?

In 1996, the Association of Fish and Wildlife Agencies began a program to test all types of commonly used traps under varied conditions and with every furbearer species in all fifty states. The idea was to develop the most humane, effective, and appropriate traps and trapping techniques to enhance and improve furbearer trapping in the U.S. The project mimics solutions for other wildlife challenges for things such as water quality and forest management. These standards are called better management practices (BMPs) [6] and have been developed for nineteen furbearing species in the U.S. The ultimate goal is to compile data for all species and provide a world standard for other countries to use in their wildlife management programs.

This guidance has been produced to provide fur trappers and wildlife professionals clear information based on scientific research. The information in each BMP includes basic biology and very detailed specifications for trap design, modifications, pan tension specifications, snare cable dimensionality, lock types and uses, and the lists go on. All traps that meet the specifications determined to be the best "listed in the BMP have been tested and meet performance standards for animal welfare, efficiency, selectivity, practicality, and safety."

Additional information includes details about the study data such as "Chain attachment used in trap testing: 6 inch center-mounted with two swivels and anchored with a stake" and "Selectivity features: Brass pan tension machine screw; pan tension set so four pounds of pressure triggered the trap, and checked and readjusted as needed after every capture."

There are thirteen pages of detailed information for eastern coyotes alone and another twelve for western coyotes. The list includes nineteen species, and they aren't done. The BMPs send a clear message that as new technology emerges, it will be considered and added that "BMPs are the product of on-going work that may be updated as additional traps are identified through future scientific testing."

The BMPs are trappers' standard for trap selection, and as time goes on, it will be important to continue developing and utilizing the best possible practices. Trapping opponents scoff at the work done by the Association of Fish and Wildlife Agencies, while their argument that trappers haven't done anything to improve their tools since the last century is weakened by the emergence of a decade and a half of continuing scientific improvement.

With every improvement in trapper technology come criticisms that the traps don't kill quickly enough or aren't humane enough. All the while, millions of domestic animals across the country are euthanized with anal electrocution, lethal gas chambers, or poison. In the spectrum of all animal uses in the U.S., trapping furbearers is among the most humane, not the least. If a trapper killed animals the way many animal shelters do and then tossed the entire animal into a garbage dumpster they would be arrested for wanton waste.

Not that all animal shelters use these methods to kill and dispose of their ever-growing domestic animal population, but many do. Trappers capture free-ranging animals and either hold them temporarily or use traps which kill them instantly. Trapping is used as a management tool for wild animals, just as electrocution and gas chambers are used to manage domestic animal populations. The difference is trappers use part or all of the animals they are responsible for killing, what do animal shelters do with the millions of domestic animals the kill every year in the U.S.? Are dumpsters and incinerators a respectful end to the lives of domestic animals with no owners?

A comparison between managing domestic animal populations in and around urban America vs. managing wild animal populations in and around rural and suburban America does not show that the methods used for domestic animals are more humane than those used for wild animals. Fur trapping tools and techniques are used by wildlife professionals for a reason.

Trap modification requirements are taught in trapper education classes, rendezvous, trapper camps, and in general discussions among trappers. Trappers are absolutely catching on to the benefits of proper trap modification. As the traps, snares, and techniques used by trappers continue to improve, so too does the distance between the levels of humane treatment of animals between the socially acceptable euthanizing of domestic animals and trapping of wild animals.

Well-funded animal rights groups have made millions of dollars by collecting domestic animals then raising money by showing videos of animals confined in shelters and then killing them. They don't use the word killing, rather it is euthanize, put down, or some other sensitive words to separate death from the termination of the animals which they kill to make more room for more animals and raise more money. Is this common and well-known practice ethical? Whether it is or not, it continues under the guise of protecting and sheltering animals.

Ethics can be defined by doing what's right, even when no one else is looking. Trapping is a perfect example of this. Often, there is no one looking, no audience to please, or accolades for doing the right thing. Early mornings or late nights, heavy snows and freezing temperatures can wear a trapper out. None of that can matter; there are traps to check, long summers, and a million things to do. None of that can matter; there are traps to modify, jaws to laminate, springs to attach, and swivels to clean to keep traps in good working order.

Everything a trapper does must be done to showcase his respect for wildlife, passion for the outdoors, enjoyment of the trapline—everything . . . from the type of traps and equipment purchased to when and where they will be set and how often they are checked. Trappers need to step up their game; there is no room among trappers' ranks for unethical behavior or irresponsible trapping.

While ethics in regards to any earthly creature may always be more a matter of social-emotional perception resulting from propaganda than factual information regarding necessity and ecological health, one thing is for certain. There is no room for trappers to error when it comes to ethics. Trappers must stand up for their culture and fight politically with everything they have in order to maintain the privilege to trap. Trapping is woven into the cultural fabric of American history, it is necessary for wildlife management and as much a part of the human—nature connection as other forms of hunting and gathering.

All sportsmen must remain united; there can be no division among these like-minded groups if the outdoor lifestyle is to remain the integral part of our wild lands and wildlife-loving society. Every consumptive user needs the other, and without one of them, none can continue.

Trappers especially have a responsibility to hold high ethical standards; to treat animals and people with respect; to represent all trappers, hunters, anglers, and outdoorsman as responsible stewards of the land; and never ever compromise their integrity. If you are a trapper, be proud of who you are, know your limits, work hard, and trap smart. Represent trappers not by screaming to the world that you have arrived, but by quietly, thoughtfully coalescing with nature and man, the way people are meant to. Only a few members of society are lucky enough to see nature through a trapper's eyes. If you know what that means, trap ethically or quit trapping now and forever. The future of America's trapping culture is the cost of ethical irresponsibility.

A contestant in the Women's trap setting contest sets one of five traps at the Montana Trappers Association Rendezvous held in Lewistown, Montana in 2012.

A marten box being re-set by a trapper after taking a Marten.

A typical dirt-hole set with the trap bedded under sifted dirt in the fore-ground. The hay bale is placed so a fox or coyote will approach the set on the same side as the trap. Bait or gland lure are placed in the hole.

A well-crafted sign welcomes participants at Montana's annual Youth Trapper Camp.

A variety of furs are looked over by fur buyers at a Montana fur sale. Greased furs in the fore ground include pelts from beaver, muskrat, mink and river otter. Long haired furs in the back ground are from fox, coyote and bobcat.

A young trapper receives instruction about trap setting at the annual Youth Trapper Camp held in Montana in 2012. The YTC is a cooperative effort between the Montana Fish Wildlife and Parks, 4 H and the Montana Trappers Association.

Marten Tracks in Rocky Mountain snow. Studying tracks is a favorite past time of many fur trappers. Tracks will teach the studious observer a great deal about wildlife.

Montgomery No. 4 traps. Traps on the left are unmodified. Traps on the right were laminated. Notice the difference in thickness achieved by welding a piece of 9 gauge wire onto the trap jaws shown lower left of photo.

Fur sales generate thousands of dollars for trapper's families around the country. Like this one held in Montana in 2012.

Snowmobiles and tow behind sleds are important tools for trappers in the North Country. This photo was taken on a Rocky Mountain trap line in 2011.

Various grades and quantities of furs are found in regions around North America. Coyote pelts make up the majority of fur at fur sales in the western U.S. like this sale in Montana.

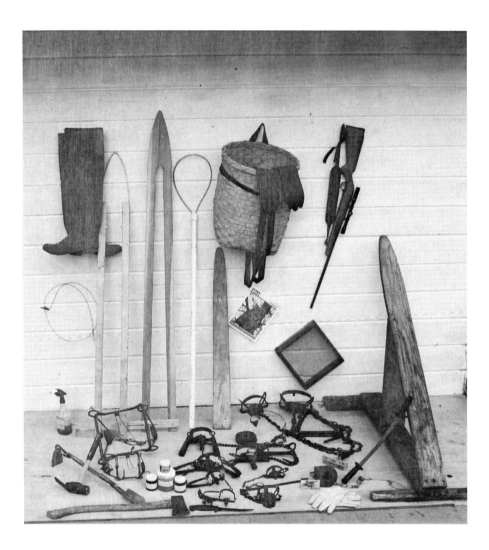

Tools of the trapping trade are varied. From mice to wolves, traps and assorted equipment have specific functions to ensure selectivity, effectiveness, and humane capture.

Well-handled furs commonly trapped in Montana and stretchers. Pelts are fleshed of all fat and then dried on specific types of stretchers. From left to right; coyote, bobcat, red fox, river otter, marten and beaver.

A Montana Pine Marten captured in a cage trap by biologists in 2013. Trappers often assist biologists with their knowledge of furbearer habitats and trapping techniques.

A Montana Trapper removing a muskrat from a trap placed along the banks of a creek. Trappers spend countless hours in the field learning the habits of animals so they know where to place traps.

Chapter 9

Protecting People, Pets, and Wildlife One Trap at a Time

The problem, then, is how to bring about a striving for harmony with land among a people many of whom have forgotten there is any such thing as land, among whom education and culture have become almost synonymous with landlessness. This is the problem of conservation education.

—Aldo Leopold, *A Sand County Almanac*

In 2012, I stood in a room filled with people from the Devil's Kitchen working group with a fellow trapper. He and I were presenting information to the conservation group in Montana about trapping, the equipment, ethics, the responsibility of trappers, and our role in effective wildlife conservation.

"How many people in this room own traps?" I asked.

About five people out of forty raised their hand. I counted them out loud before reaching into my pocket and removing a mouse trap. "How many people own one of these?" I asked pointedly.

The room roared with laughter as everyone raised their hands. "Wait a minute, I thought only five people owned traps in here!" I said with a smile. I had just made a point, one which no one could deny. They were all trappers and didn't know it. They had the option to use poison or could have laid in wait with a pellet gun to remove the mouse invading their kitchen, but had chosen to use traps. Obviously, an animal inherently larger requires a larger trap. And by choosing traps, the mouse trappers eliminated the possibility of missing or wounding the animal or accidentally poisoning their family pet. The same is true with other much larger wildlife in far more wild places. I emphasized that fact and then asked if they would use a trap of the same size for mice as they would for rats?

Home owners manage wildlife based on human need and human perception as to the value and plentitude of that animal. As the animals in need of management become larger in size like raccoons for instance, the trap used to remove that animal must become larger too, but there are other differences in the management of those species—some more subtle than others.

A body gripping mouse trap is designed to kill quickly and efficiently as is the body gripping trap so widely used by trappers. But unlike the mouse trap routinely used by home owners, there is little threat posed by the use of these small killing devices. A large body gripping trap, large enough to kill a raccoon quickly, can also kill a house cat or medium-sized dog. Because of this threat to domestic animals, home owners may choose to use a cage trap instead. This seems like a good alternative on the surface.

The problem with this alternative is homeowners cannot legally relocate wild animals in most states. Professional wildlife managers are the only people who have authority to do so. The reasons for this are that the animal live trapped, transported, and relocated may have a disease or ornery disposition, and the habitat suitable for that species is often complicated and may not be understood by your average home owner. Releasing a problem from one area into another especially at the wrong time of the year can result in starvation, sickness, and death for an animal released into unfamiliar territory. It takes time for wild animals to find food sources and acclimate to a new environment, and any move must be done correctly.

In Scott McMillion's book *Mark of the Grizzly*, [7] he recounts in 1981 a female Yellowstone grizzly bear with two cubs locally known as number 59 that became habituated to humans and their food. The rangers in the area decided in September to use trapping to relocate the three bears twenty-two miles away to prevent them from human contact after too many human conflicts. September is just several weeks before hibernation time for bears which become hyperphagic and are trying to pack on weight for their long winter slumber. Within two weeks, she returned to the area that she was removed from but had abandoned her cubs. It was a poor year for food availability, and she was hungry. The cubs likely starved to death, and number 59 was killed after killing and eating a photographer who got too close, even though the man had violated all the rules when dealing with wild bears.

Situations like that may be the extreme, but it certainly illustrates a point that relocation of animals is not always a viable solution as there are too many considerations to take into account. The same goes for all wildlife, and like it or not, the displacement of wild animals occurs to make room for human habitat whether it's for human crops or houses, it is unavoidable.

Mice and rats are not the only rodents that cause damage to human homes. While a few chewed-up bags of cookies in Grandma's kitchen is a nuisance, irrigation ditches and dams with burrows large enough to sink a tractor tire or break the legs of livestock create significant safety and financial impact. Muskrats frequently highlight human-wildlife conflict. It isn't just to ranchers and farmers either; waterfowl production areas often rely on the control of water levels at various times of the year. There is an ideal water depth needed for puddle ducks and other types of water fowl to reach aquatic vegetation and other food sources along the bottom of marshes and ponds.

When muskrats poke holes in and around the dams used to maintain or alter the water levels, the impact is more than monetary. Such disturbances create challenges to Waterfowl Production Area (WPA) managers. These waterfowl production areas are essential to create and maintain waterfowl habitat. According to the United States Geological Survey Water Supply Paper 2425[8] there were about 221 million acres of wetlands in the U.S., but only 103 million remained as of the mid-1980s. Six states lost 85% of their original wetlands and twenty-two lost 50% or more. What's more, the effects of this substantial loss may not be fully realized.

Because of this drastic decline in America's wetlands, artificial wetlands must be created to keep wetland-dependent species high—including muskrats. Wetlands restoration is beneficial to people as well due to a plethora of benefits resulting from the existence of wetlands. Some easy examples of these benefits are the processing of human waste and wastewater, capturing and filtering soil erosion, and of course, creating wildlife-watching areas. Hundreds of waterfowl production areas and wildlife refuges and parks across the U.S. are shining examples of the benefits of having wetlands. These multiuse areas rely on both consumptive and nonconsumptive users to work in concert with one another for the greater good. Such is balanced wildlife management—whether overseen by humans or Mother Nature—balance for the greater good is the fundamental principle for the existence of multiple species, including humans.

Beavers also impact critical habitat areas as they chew down trees to build food caches and lodges. In areas where beavers dam small creeks, they create wetland habitat. The water flow is impeded and backs up into dry-land vegetation. Over time, the vegetation types in the flooded areas change just as soil conditions do. The shoreline vegetation is reduced and new edge cover is created. This new habitat offers a food and cover source for birds, furbearing animals, ungulates, and other nongame wildlife such as frogs and salamanders. The benefits and biodiversity created by beavers and muskrats can also be their undoing. With no real consistent natural predator, beaver populations will explode in a relatively short period of time just as their distant relatives—mice and rats will in a low predator-food rich environment. Muskrat populations are very susceptible to disease and well documented boom and bust population fluctuations are common, but so is human conflict.

Naturally created wetlands in remote areas, far from human habitat are often maintained over time without human interference; however, when management objectives created by biologists are impeded or dismantled due to large rodent activity, trappers get a call. Beavers chew down trees that stabilize riverbanks, dig holes in those same banks, plug culvert pipes designed to allow water flow from one area to another, which floods critical waterfowl habitat beyond usable levels. Muskrats thrive in areas dammed by beavers, and when their numbers are high, they can overeat the aquatic vegetation and destroy levees. Further complications occur when the wetland habitat is being used for waste treatment or potable water. Beavers and muskrats are rodents and carry numerous human transposable diseases. The most widely known of which are diseases like tularemia and giardia commonly known as beaver fever.

At the turn of the last century, beaver numbers were at an all-time low in the United States. So much so that beaver trapping was eliminated or severely restricted in many parts of the country. Reintroduction programs were implemented by state agencies through the first half of the century. Today, beaver numbers are at all-time highs and have reached nuisance status. By following a surplus harvest, it keeps beaver numbers in check without depleting those numbers below the carrying capacity.

Wildlife management has come a long way, and the learning curve has been steep in some cases. Today's wildlife solutions rely on new techniques, population surveys, and strictly regulated seasons. In order to prevent the destruction of suitable habitat and human sickness, the best solution is often found through sustained yield trapping. By keeping beaver and muskrat numbers in check through trapping, ideal habitat conditions for multiple species can be maintained.

Even the ballot box initiative I-160 drafted in 2010, which called for an end to trapping on Montana's public lands, admits that trapping is necessary. The wording of the initiative as documented by the Montana Secretary of State[9] would allow "trapping for scientific purposes and for breeding of migratory game birds" and "also allows trapping by public employees to protect public health and safety . . ." While the individuals who crafted the wording for that failed initiative clearly have no idea that the public employees rely heavily on the citizen trappers for wildlife control, it is also clear that trapping is necessary to protect public safety. Wildlife management, not only for furbearing animals but so many other species benefit as a result of appropriate trapping methods—methods that take years to master.

In addition to the ecological and health benefits of trapping in these types of situations, there is the opportunity for financial gain for the trapper. What better way to benefit wildlife, public safety, and perpetuate the cultural and necessary significance of trappers?

Trappers truly are conservationists; even the opponents to trappers support trapping and acknowledge that it is necessary. It's rather ironic to say the least, especially when the opposing groups demonstrate their acknowledgement in a public document designed to eliminate trapping.

If some trapping is needed on public lands to control wildlife populations then how could anyone rationalize the banning of all trapping on public lands?

While human-managed wetlands rely heavily on trappers for their continuation, numerous other situations require trapping as a means of human-wildlife conflict resolution. The agricultural industry has employed the use of traps and snares for years. Herds of sheep and cattle grazing on large tracks of land throughout the west are susceptible to predation by coyotes, fox, and wolves. These predators often hunt at night and are difficult to catch in the act. There are certainly cases where wild predators have lived in close proximity to livestock and have not caused any conflicts; however, when the instances do occur, and they occur frequently, trapping is the most widely used and effective means of removing those populations, just like the mice in Grandma's kitchen.

According the United States Department of Agriculture (USDA) Predator Damage Management Report[10] provided by the National Wildlife Research Center (NWRC) in 2010, "Livestock predation costs producers approximately $127 million each year. For the sheep and lamb industry alone, predators account for approximately 36% of the total losses from all causes. Concerns for public health and safety, as well as animal welfare, have also pressured wildlife managers to seek immediate solutions when predators cause conflicts."

The need for predator management is evident, just imagine if your paycheck were decreased by 36% each year, it would be difficult to ignore that there is a problem. Alternative methods for reducing predator impact to wild pronghorn populations were examined in that same study, which reported, "Current techniques used to manage coyote predation on wildlife species generally focus on lethal control methods, as there are few effective nonlethal methods available. However, NWRC scientists have demonstrated that coyote sterilization can be effective in reducing sheep predation. Sterilization reduces the energetic need for parents to provision coyote pups, which may decrease predation on fawns by sterile coyotes."

While the concept of coyote sterilization is feasible, practical application is virtually impossible for the tens of thousands of coyotes spread out across millions of agricultural lands across the U.S. Researchers also evaluated the use of various designs of cable restraint devices in contrast to modified foothold traps in an effort to find the most humane and cost-effective device to use for predator control. They concluded that "All three restraints tested had lower injury scores than unpadded steel-jaw traps but only the chain cable restraint had a lower mean injury score (though only slightly) than the padded steel-jaw trap. Scientists note that the padded foot-hold trap may cause less injury to the coyotes when captured than either the standard or chain cable restraints, serving as a more humane method for capturing coyotes."

As time goes on and new advancements in trapping equipment are developed, trappers may very well find themselves using modifications to their equipment. But until that time, it is clear that the traps currently employed by conscientious trappers are the most humane and viable tools

available. Until something better can be developed, the best traps are the
ones currently on the market.

Human-wildlife conflict is in virtually every aspect of human life
and always has been. History shows man in constant competition with
large predators like cougars, bears, and wolves. Near-extermination of
America's largest meat eaters was the result of unregulated hunting and
trapping. Through the 1940s, landowners and government agencies used
unrestricted poison, aerial gunning, baiting and shooting, bounties, and
traps to eliminate these unappreciated animals on America's landscape.
Other unregulated wildlife destruction came when people were allowed
the wasteful shooting of the bison and passenger pigeons—prime
examples of our nation's greatest losses which were a combination of
habitat loss and zero resource management.

It was from these incredible losses to our wildlife that
conservation-minded sportsmen pushed for wildlife management. Since
those early years in U.S. history, Americas' wildlife management has
become the gold standard for every country in the world. Nowhere else
is wildlife so plentiful and so protected from overabundance or overuse.
Nowhere else in the world are wildlife and wild lands used as a resource
and so wisely conserved. But it took a lot of learning to get where we are.

On a much smaller scale, home owners deal with wildlife conflicts
in their houses and on their property. Suburban America has sprung up
and landed exactly between urban and rural America. Currently one of
the fastest-growing small businesses in the U.S. is animal damage control
(ADC). ADC work is performed by a mix of former fur trappers looking
for alternative ways to trap and earn a living and also by new trappers
who have never set a trap for the sole purpose of fur. Courses are widely
available to entrepreneurs interested in the wildlife-urban interface that
demands wildlife control. Like fur trapping, the wildlife damage control
industry is often criticized for its practices. Removing wild animals from
overpopulated areas is scrutinized regardless of whether it occurs in the
wilds of Alaska or the suburbs of New York City.

The National Wildlife Control Operators Association (NWCOA),
a nonprofit, professional trade association "devoted to professional
development of the Wildlife Damage Management Industry through
the individual development of well educated, experienced, and dedicated
wildlife control operators" [11] has attempted to create industry standards
and protect the industry through education, not unlike fur trapping
organizations. The focus of the association is also on public image,

professional behavior and socially acceptable techniques and tools. Every industry needs a set of rules to operate by, and as time goes on, wildlife nuisance control operators will have to live up to higher standards—a phenomenon that is good for wildlife, human residents, and trappers. The NWCOA may have high tech equipment and exceptional skills in dealing with wildlife in human residences, but their impact on balancing nature with human interests serves the same function as trappers in more wild areas.

Even in rural Montana, nuisance wildlife finds its way onto private property and finds the habitat suitable for their existence. Garage roofs, basements, wood sheds, chimneys all make great places to get out of the weather and raise young of the year.

In 2012, I received a call from a resident in Montana for the third year in a row. The first year she called was because a beaver had plugged a culvert which allowed water to flow under the county road from her property to a neighboring property. The water backed up for several hundred feet and over a foot of water covered her driveway and saturated her lawn and threatened the integrity of the public highway. I trapped those animals under state permit issued by a game warden. The following year, marmots overtook her lawn, dug under her house, and managed to get inside her living room. That was the final straw.

She called me once again to remove the problem wild animals. I showed her the body gripping traps and explained how they worked. She was a bit concerned about killing these creatures, but there was no alternative—she had tried everything. By allowing these animals to prosper on her property, they became habituated to the outbuildings and horse barns on her land. Although cute and harmless in appearance, these animals can dig networks of underground tunnels and leave scat behind in unbelievable proportions.

The deck built off the backside of Suzy's house was covered with rodent scat just like the crawl space under her living room. The odor was appalling. Horse barn floors were also covered in scat and holes were dug all over her yard, under her house, and through expensive shrubbery. I trapped eleven marmots in a few days, and she wanted to leave a few because she enjoyed wildlife, and as a self-professed animal lover, didn't want them all killed. The following year I received the following message:

"Hi, this is Suzy. I'm here for a couple days . . . I noticed that there are marmots, the big one is still under the house to the right there because we never sealed off the den, there's one there. And she doesn't seem to have babies, but she's a big girl, and there are two nests in the yard with varying marmots out there, and I know where they are. If you are around over the next couple of days, I need for you to trap these marmots. If you're still interested in doing this work for me, there is marmot poop everywhere, and I am interested in having you trap these. These marmots are everywhere, and I just can't live here given the way things are, and I need especially to get the marmots out from under the house before we seal up the house because otherwise, she'll just die under there and it smells bad and it's not a good death and I care actually . . . let me know if you can come after work or during the day and if not, we'll just let the marmots be, and next time I come, we'll go after them . . ." The message was long and desperate and was followed the next morning with another plea for help.

Her perception of these animals changed dramatically once they began to overrun her property. Suzy had hired a contractor to remove her front porch, seal up the base of her house by digging up the earth and pouring concrete imbedded with wire mesh, and had a landscaper manipulate the shrubbery to prevent these large rodents from their damaging ways—the final and only solution was trapping.

It is not too far a stretch to say that if this local population could get to such an elevated level under these conditions that the same thing could occur in localized wild populations with other species, and since that is the case, then it stands to reason that it could occur on a much larger scale. That is wildlife management in a nutshell; keeping numbers at healthy and sustainable levels while also considering the impact to humans and human tolerance.

Cases like these are not at all uncommon. In fact, a high number of calls by landowners come into the Montana Fish Wildlife and Parks (MFWP) each year, and these calls are often referred to local trappers.

Another time, I received a call from landowners who had recently received a sales offer on their house. Beavers had moved in and were destroying the trees, the very trees that the new home owners had cooed over just weeks before. The home owners were afraid that if the property were damaged before the sale date, the buyers might change their minds.

They had put up wire mesh around the bases of every tree on the property and ripped out the dam several times, but the beaver just found a way to eat around the mesh and rebuild the dam. The creek flowing through the property was dammed up and a rather large food cache was built out of the expensive trees planted along the banks of the creek. I removed two large beavers out of the creek, using powerful body gripping traps set under three feet of water, and the problem was ended.

Calls are often made to the Montana Trappers Association as well by people looking for trappers to alleviate nuisance wildlife impacts to their property. Without the skills of trappers who often do the work for little to no cost, these issues would be exacerbated to extreme levels like states with trap restrictions.

A referendum was pushed in Massachusetts by a coalition of animal rights groups called Pro-PAW (Protection of Pets and Wildlife) in 1996 to ban the use of foothold or body gripping traps anywhere in the state. The law was called the Wildlife Protection Act. When the beaver and muskrat population quadrupled in less than four years, legislation was passed to allow a "10 day emergency permit" to be obtained by landowners which enabled them to use body gripping traps to control property damage. The permit application must be filed by the landowner and assessed by the "city and towns Board of Health (BOH) which have the authority to determine whether a complaint is caused by beaver or muskrat and whether the situation constitutes a threat to public health and/or safety, as defined in M.G.L. c.131, s.80a." according to *Beavers and the Law: A Citizen's Guide to Addressing Beaver Conflicts,* [12] a publication written by the Massachusetts Division of Fish and Wildlife.

If the permit is approved, the landowner or an agent may use body gripping traps for ten days in addition to cage or box traps. If the issue is not remedied within the ten-day period, an extension may be filed for an additional thirty days. If the application is denied, the applicant then has ten days to appeal the decision by contacting the Department of Public Health. In addition to this complicated permit system, the permit holder must take a trapper's education class and purchase a trapping license. Prior to 1996 when fur trappers were allowed to trap like most other states in the country, there were isolated issues but not anywhere near the extremes the state is faced with now. The fur trappers were providing a public service—and paying to do it.

The impact on public health due to the trapping restriction in Massachusetts has been a significant drain on state agencies. There is an open trapping season for beaver using cage or box traps, but the effectiveness of trappers without foothold or body gripping traps has left them hamstrung. It seems to defy logic that fur trappers be restricted to the use of inferior tools, only to let nontrapping landowners be the only public citizen allowed to use traps that work.

Trapping and relocating live beavers is also prohibited by Massachusetts's law. Animal damage control businesses have been able to reap the rewards of public need evidenced by the sheer number of ADC companies in Massachusetts. Extreme flooding in the last decade caused by beaver has resulted in incredible costs to taxpayers. Septic systems, public water sources, highway damage, and other public safety threats riddle the newspapers throughout the state.

The beaver and muskrat issue in Massachusetts is an unnecessary wildlife management challenge—one which could be easily remedied by allowing regulated trapping by fur trappers. Instead of costing the state money, the overabundant beaver could generate revenue and alleviate extreme damage to public and private lands as well as human health. Without lethal means of take available to skilled fur trappers, the state of Massachusetts continues to battle beaver and muskrat infestations.

In a letter to the editor in a Montana newspaper, retired wildlife biologist Paul Fielder stated, "Licensed trappers help control wildlife populations before they become major problems. My collection of newspaper headlines from states that banned trapping include: 'Eliminating trapping escalates beaver complaints and cost to the public,' 'Coyotes blamed for killing 22 pets in Lakewood (WA),' 'Skunk and raccoon rabies in the eastern US,' 'Coyote drags toddler from front yard,' 'Wildlife officials feel consequences of trapping ban,' to list just a few." . . . "Regulated trapping, similar to regulated hunting, is a biologically sustainable, safe, effective and ecologically sound method of capturing individual animals without impairing the survival of furbearer populations or damaging the environment. Trapping is part of our cultural heritage and provides income, recreation and an outdoor lifestyle for many citizens through the use of a renewable natural resource. Trapping is important in animal damage control, wildlife research and in suppressing some wildlife diseases."

A quick search for newspaper articles across the country that are the result of trapping bans or restrictions yield hundreds of examples where removing trapping from the wildlife management toolbox has been detrimental to the health of wild populations, public health and safety, and a financial drain on wildlife agencies. The negative impact to wildlife and the resultant unnecessary waste is undeniable. Who picks up the tab when wild populations increase beyond socially acceptable levels? Taxpayers—whether they agree with the crippling restrictions or not.

But there are other costs incurred by residents which aren't necessarily monetary. When predator numbers are allowed to reach a level not consistent with a balanced approach to wildlife, ungulate numbers may decrease to a point that is difficult or impossible to recover from. In 1995, gray wolves were reintroduced into the Yellowstone ecosystem in the Lamar Valley, an act that was carried out with much public opposition. The impacts to ungulate populations have been significant, and as wolf numbers continued to increase in areas of Montana, Idaho, and Wyoming, the numbers of deer and elk decreased.

While much has been written on the wolf recovery and wildlife impact of that effort in the western U.S., it wasn't until 2011 that the first wolf-trapping season was approved as a necessary management tool by the Idaho Fish and Game Department to be used in certain areas in Idaho. In July of 2012, the Montana Fish Wildlife and Parks Department approved wolf harvest regulations that include trapping for the first time in Montana.

Sportsmen's groups dissatisfied with the decrease in hunting opportunities, which they attribute to the presence of wolves in conjunction with high numbers of mountain lions and bears, support the taking of wolves with traps and snares (although the wolf-trapping regulations only allow for the use of foothold traps in Montana as of 2013). Regulated wolf trapping currently occurs across Alaska and Canada. It will be interesting to see the outcome of this large-scale wildlife management issue. But one thing is for sure, trapping will be a necessary tool in the wildlife manager's toolbox—as always.

At an informational meeting hosted by the Montana Fish Wildlife and Parks in 2012, one individual stood up and stated, "If you've got to get the wolf numbers down then go ahead and allow them to be hunted, but don't trap them!"

She was speaking to the Region 2 Wildlife Manager Mike Thompson who thanked her for her input before stating, "We are at a point in our large predator management where we need trapping."

The dynamics involved in predator management create more challenges facing professional wildlife managers. Not the least of which is balancing public perception with the needs of wildlife based on science. Trapping is certainly a useful and important aspect of wildlife management, whether used for the common mouse or gray wolves. The impacts to wildlife and people with the omission of trapping are well documented by wildlife agencies, newspapers, scientific journals, and research papers, and the list goes on. Trappers are a necessary part of a modern, healthy ecosystem, particularly at the point of the wildlife-human interface of the ever-growing suburban America.

The current wildlife management system in the U.S. is dependent on hunters who for seventy-five years have spent millions of dollars through the purchase of license sales and a self-imposed excise tax. The result of the Federal Aid in Wildlife Restoration Act of 1937, known by most as the Pittman Robertson Act, due to its sponsors. In return for their dollars spent, hunters and trappers expect increased recreational opportunities. And it's not just hunting and trapping that has improved; shed antler hunting, wildlife photography, fishing, mushroom and berry picking, and camping opportunities are also added to that list due to improved habitat and increased numbers of all wildlife.

Multiuse areas include corridors or buffer zones to reduce impact to the land or wildlife during certain times of the year. By preventing people from using motorized vehicles in areas where elk calve or rotating areas where people are allowed to camp to prevent soil erosion and tree degradation, the needs of wildlife and people are taken into consideration. Perhaps it will be this mentality and the sharing of the wilderness with all the users, skiers, hunters, trappers, and wildlife that will be required for everyone to get out of our natural resources; the things we wish to while maintaining the sanctity of our cherished natural resources. Certainly, multiuse areas are not a new concept, but one which must take all viewpoints into consideration lest we snuff out wild lands, wildlife, or wild people.

Driving along the highway for several miles virtually anywhere in rural America, it is common to see dozens of dead furbearing animals lying alongside the road in various stages of decay. These animals are not eaten, instead they are wasted as traffic wards off predatory birds and animals until the carcasses decay beyond any usefulness save blowflies and microbes. Dozens more make it beyond the roadside edges out of sight from passersby before they suffer and die. The wasteful act of motorized vehicles terminating an otherwise healthy animal is in itself a replacement for natural predators. Roadside crews make their rounds to pick up the wasted dead and transport them to county dumps, but the effect is essentially wildlife management by vehicle.

Trappers, on the other hand, would utilize those surplus animals and reduce the number of auto collisions and dispose of the carcasses where they become safe food for eagles, hawks, and other predatory species. To trappers, it makes no sense to allow surplus animals to be hit and killed when a viable alternative is readily available. One which creates revenue for people protects pets from disease and conflict and manages wildlife in a way that is sustainable.

In areas where people and wild animals clash, it is far easier to define surplus. If your attic is filled with guanos from three hundred bats, it is easy to say that is too many bats for that area. Likewise, in urban and suburban areas, there is no shortage of problem wildlife ranging from rats and mice to raccoons and deer.

There will always be challenges dealing with surplus, whether it is a human value judgment or not, trapping will likely be the most effective, humane, and necessary means of keeping the surpluses in balance—regardless of how our definition of balance is perceived.

Chapter 10

This Little Trapper Sold to Market,
This Little Trapper Sold at Home

You have brains in your head. You have feet in your shoes. You can steer yourself in any direction you choose. You're on your own, and you know what you know. And you are the guy who'll decide where to go.

—Dr. Seuss

When I was a young boy with my first lot of fur to bring to a fur buyer, I walked into the shop and stood there at the counter, amazed at the sheer amount of fur hanging from the ceiling. Beaver pelts were stretched on wire hoops hanging from the ceiling and on plywood boards leaned against the wall. Otter pelts on basswood stretchers with tails pinned wide open lined with shiny steel thumbtacks. They seemed huge, stretched out to almost five feet in length. Muskrats hung by the hundreds on wire stretchers spaced every two inches on a cable that ran from one wall to the other just over my head. Mink, raccoons, fox, and coyotes were hanging or were piled on tables. It was unbelievable to a youngster with a few pelts in his hands. The fur buyer spent some time looking at the fur I had worked hard to put up. He sorted them into piles based on size and grade then he began writing out numbers next to each pile; muskrat—7 $2.50, 3-$3.25, beaver 2-$22.00, mink—1 $12.50, coon 2-$15.00 1 $18.00." When he was done, he added up the total dollar amount. He then turned it around on the counter. "That's my offer, young man," he said. I couldn't believe it, I was looking at $149.75. For a poor country kid who just spent four weeks trapping and having fun, that seemed like a ton of money. "Thanks!" I said with a smile, not able to hold a poker face.

"So I take it that you accept," Lonnie said as he smiled back. What else was I going to do, say no? I had not yet learned the fine art of haggling.

As the years went by, I got better at handling my fur and learned as I went what it takes to have top-quality fur for the local fur buyer. Local fur buyers are called country buyers in current trapper lingo. Any fur market report generated in trapping magazines suggests the prices a trapper can expect to receive from country buyers in their region for prime well-handled fur.

I sold furs to Lonnie for years. When I moved several hours away from my childhood hometown, I began a new relationship with a buyer named Paul. Paul gave me advice about how and when to trap different species to maximize my profits. We established a special relationship that often turned my fur sale into hours' long conversations, ranging from trapping to politics. Paul explained to me that even if he bought furs that resulted in a loss for him at a national sale, he took the money and cut his losses. The longer he held on to devalued fur, the longer his bank account suffered. It was better to receive something back to be used for working capital than to sit on the fur he already bought and have nothing in reserve to generate more income later. The fur-buying business is dynamic and involves a lot more than just pelt sales and crusty old trappers.

Other fur-related articles include meat, porcupine quills, claws, and taxidermy. Another noteworthy product produced by fur trappers is animal glands. Beaver castors are one type of glands sold on the world market which doesn't specifically relate to fur sales. These glands are used in the world perfume market because of their desired qualities in absorbing and maintaining scent. As a result, prices paid for castors have recently exceeded $70 per pound. Three or four big beavers can produce one pound of glands. Other glands removed from furbearers are used in the manufacture of lures, another important and sizable market related to the fur industry. Glands have significant value, and the conscientious trapper takes full advantage. Like furs, the value of glands varies considerably from year to year. There are various grades and quality, and gland buyers use a similar approach to assessing the value and quality of goods as they do with furs.

Fur buyers have a business to run, and like any business, they need to make money. Many well-established country buyers run ads in magazines offering to pay top dollar for raw wild furs, in addition to waiting for local trappers to arrive at their door with furs and/or glands. The relationship between trappers and local buyers is important. Local buyers play a major part in keeping local trappers motivated and offer the convenience of immediate payment.

For years, I thought that country fur buyers took the fur they bought from local trappers and simply brought it to state or national fur sale where they sold it for a profit. While that is one way fur buyers make money on their investment, the stability of the international market is unpredictable due to a multitude of factors.

It is important that fur buyers have a good handle on current market trends; however, a large portion of the fur buyer's market comes from fur garment manufacturers called furriers. A good working relationship with established furriers is a key component to ensuring that the money spent by a country buyer yields a return. Fur garment manufacturers determine what they need for the coming year and place orders for fur in advance. Likewise, fur buyers buy fur based on the known needs of their customers.

This method of business ensures that buyers know exactly how many of any one species are needed. This takes the guess work out of buying goods because the country buyer can calculate profits even as he is writing the check. If a furrier requests thirty bobcats of a certain color and is willing to pay the fur buyer $500 apiece, the country fur buyer does whatever it takes to fill that order, while making a profit. If the buyer can fill those orders entirely from trappers coming into his shop, it can be easier to make a profit while keeping his primary customer happy. It's when the country buyer goes out to fur auctions that things get tough.

State auctions are the next level of sales in which trappers can sell fur and glands directly to fur buyers. Many of the buyers at state auctions are simply country buyers from anywhere in the state or nearby states, who have orders to fill and are looking for more fur. State auctions are often held by state trappers associations, and they charge a commission for placing furs in the sale. Fur trappers and country buyers arrive with their fur for registry with the sale. Stringent state and federal laws require trappers to fill out paperwork which includes the trapper's name, number of each species checked in, trapper's license number, and state association membership status. If the trapper is a member of his state association, she will usually get a break on the commission.

Each state has different requirements around reporting for furbearer species at the time of harvest. The reports are used to collect important data about the health and stability of local populations. This is especially important for species known to be sensitive to overharvest. Sound furbearer management relies heavily on fur harvest reports to ensure the sustainability of fur trapping. Without harvest data provided by trappers, it would be difficult to know where the highest and lowest concentrations of furbearers are. Trappers are conservationists by design.

In Montana, trappers must present the skulls from all bobcats and report the township, and range it was hunted or trapped in as well as the sex of each animal. Biologists use this information to locate population densities and age/sex ratios indicative of the overall health of a given population. When this data is extrapolated out and overlaid with annual harvest information from previous years, biologists can trend population fluctuations. In addition to this specific harvest data, a numbered tag must be placed on each pelt by a wildlife official before that pelt can be shipped, sold, or tanned.

Other species in Montana that must follow this process include marten, fishers, wolverines, swift fox, and otters. Species such as muskrats, raccoons, fox, coyotes, and beavers are not sensitive to overharvest with proper harvest management regulations, and therefore, it is not a requirement to have a numbered tag or seal placed on the pelts of those species.

Basically, species that aren't listed as sensitive are unlikely to be overharvested by trapping pressure. In some states such as New York, a tag must be filled out for each beaver and otter trapped and then presented to a wildlife official for tagging even though the numbers of each of these species are very high. Virtually, all state wildlife agencies collect data to trend harvests and for long-term monitoring of various species. This assures a sustained yield harvest of furbearers and keeps populations healthy. Most importantly, monitoring and tracking data provided by trappers keep furbearing animals on biologists' list of things to do. Because these animals have socioeconomic value in addition to their inherent value, wildlife agencies allocate funds specifically to overall population health.

Although trappers must report the harvest of certain species within twenty-four hours in many cases, trappers typically have until ten days after the close of season to get the fur properly tagged by a state official. This gives the trapper time to prepare the fur for sale and make arrangements to meet with local wildlife authorities. Additional requirements may include the presentation of carcasses. Biologists take measurements and biological samples for a clear understanding of the health of individual animals, eating habits, size, weight, and other indicators. Every state in the U.S. has stringent regulations for furs and fur sales which starts with the trappers reports. Every buyer must be licensed and is required to present documentation of all transactions.

It is virtually impossible for a fur trapper to sell a pelt that has not been properly tagged and accounted for by state agencies. There is not a fur sale in the country that will allow untagged fur from required species to enter—period. Fur buyers and organized fur sales make no exceptions to this. A trapper's fur is legal or it's out.

Trappers may place their fur in the sale by individual lots or altogether. A stack of muskrats that are over sixteen inches in length, perfectly prime, and well-handled may be given a grade of large number 1, but not all muskrats are created equal. Some muskrat pelts stretch out to fourteen inches while others only reach twelve. A trapper may have twenty-four muskrats and eight may be large, ten medium-large and the rest medium. The size of a muskrat may also vary based on region, age of the animal, and stretching techniques. An overstretched hide might make the hair appear thin, so trappers must use discretion when trying to attain that sixteen-inch mark. Furthermore, a muskrat caught in October will never have fur as thick as one caught in December or January and will therefore not grade as high. The same goes for all pelts regardless of species. Prime fur is always the goal for simple reasons; the fur looks better and is far more marketable.

At state fur sales, trappers may place minimums on their fur. If the minimums are not met, the trapper takes his fur back and may market it at some other venue. For example, a blanket beaver pelt is a pelt that measures over sixty-five inches, a measurement taken by measuring the length and width of the beaver pelt and adding the two values together. A beaver pelt which measures between sixty-five and seventy inches is called a blanket; if it is greater than seventy inches, it is called a super blanket. If a trapper brings ten blanket beaver pelts to a state fur sale, she may place a minimum bid on that lot of $25.00 each or $250.00 for an overall average of $25.00.

As more and more trappers check fur into the sale registry, the fur is sorted, tagged with the fur sales tag, and placed on grading tables in stacks according to the trappers' registered lots. The tables fill with pelts arranged by species and lot designation. Pelts in the sale are differentiated by basic type. Grease fur is just as it sounds. Beavers, muskrats, mink, raccoons, and otters are classified as such due to these pelts propensity to weep fats. Other furs are coyotes, fox, bobcats, marten, fishers, and wolverines which do not readily leach fats. The skin side of grease furs takes on a shiny appearance and diligent trappers constantly wipe the grease off and rub sawdust into the hide to keep the fat from matting the fur, or worse yet, causing grease burns. Furs are stacked in a manner to keep the fur side touching fur side and skin side touching skin side. Good trappers take an extreme level of pride in their fur handling, and usually, the most diligent trappers are compensated for their efforts.

If a fur buyer doesn't have to clean grease out of the fur, comb, and trim the pelt before delivery to his primary buyer, that is one less step in his busy trap-buying process that he can eliminate, so buyers pay more for the decreased work involved in marketing their fur. More money is lost due to improperly handled fur than any other reason.

Trappers are required to have their fur checked in by a specified time and then the registered fur buyers are the only people allowed to approach the tables. At the Montana state fur sale held in 2012, eight buyers of wild fur made their way around the tables stacked with fur. It is quite a sight to watch fur buyers look over pelts, lifting each one, brushing the hair back with their hands, all the while writing down and shaking the furs. They listen for the crinkly sound of fat-free, well-handled fur and sniff for the telltale aromas of poorly dried ears. Fur quality is assessed based on thickness, color, length of guard hairs, and other factors as well. The general appearance of the furs consistency of preparation can go a long way in increasing the prices offered for any individual lot. Good fur-handlers get better prices.

After examining a single lot of fur, buyers write down numbers just as country buyers do. Then they go to the next lot and repeat. This goes on for several hours until the allotted time is up. Although there are many formats used at fur sales, the Montana Trappers Association has recently adopted a sealed bid process where buyers had to submit their bids in a sealed envelope. The highest bidder gets the fur, provided that they met the sellers' minimum bid requirements. The total sales are tallied and when the buyer's checks clear, the state association organizers begin writing checks to each trapper, minus the commission of about 6 to 11%, depending on the sale.

Along with the fur check is a slip that shows the trapper who bought his fur, how much the buyer paid for each lot, and the commission removed from the check. State sales allow the trapper to refuse or accept the offer and have other benefits. Trappers are paid quickly for their sale. Not as quickly as selling to a country buyer, but often the prices paid are much higher because there are more buyers vying for the fur. The more buyers, the more competition and completion lead to higher pay checks.

While money is not the most important aspect of trapping, trappers compare the prices they received to the overall averages. It is a matter of pride. If the average muskrat pelt sold for $7 and a trapper averages $6, that may indicate that his fur was by comparison, substandard. This is unacceptable for most trappers, and he may refuse sale, or at the very least be motivated to try harder next year.

Most trappers know that there is potential to make much more money selling their fur in an International auction but they might choose to sell their furs and glands at a state sale to help raise money for their state association and to get returns more quickly. It is typical to receive payment within two to three weeks after a state sale.

By comparison, international auction houses are a different deal. There are several national fur auction events that take place around the world each year. These auctions take place at different times of the year and care is taken by event organizers to prevent overlapping dates. The reason is simple, auction houses don't want to force world-class fur buyers to choose one sale over the other and risk having fewer buyers.

The more buyers there are at any one auction, the more customers who put their trust in the auction house will receive for their furs. When a trapper has furs in the top lot at international sales, he is rewarded not only financially but he may also receive a plaque and a coveted hat that reads: "Top Lot Trapper." The top lot or lot of any given species that receives the highest price at the sale is referred to as a top Lot; this distinction in the quality of a trapper's fur is highly sought after. I know one trapper who has a goal of getting a top lot for every species he traps. It is a personal goal and a matter of pride.

But the advantages of selling directly to international markets don't end there. If the prices offered at the sale don't meet expectations, the auction house may refuse sale and return the pelts to storage for the next sale. This is a great benefit to the trappers; the auction house wants customers to receive the most for their product. The ability of the auction house to refuse sale is good but is also cause for concern for some trappers because it could potentially take years to receive a fur check in the mail. This loss of control has its pros and cons, but the difference in prices trappers receive can be substantial.

Large fur buyers register with international sales houses and show up ready to buy, moving huge volumes of fur and glands from auction floors to a ready market. It may seem odd to the casual American consumer that the demand for wild fur is high on the world market when many domestic clothing stores don't carry fur products and fur fashion hasn't been in for a couple of decades. But Parker Dozhier, an authority on the international fur market, reported in the November 2011 issue of *Trapper and Predator Caller Magazine* [13] that the retail fur trade is quite strong:

"There is little question our fur markets are expanding. The International Fur Trade Federation, which tracks fur trends and worldwide sales, reports that four out of five Russians own one or more fur articles. Internationally, the retail fur trade exceeds $14 Billion annually. Such growth is impressive considering consumers in North America and Western Europe are purchasing fewer fur garments."

Dozhier goes on to explain the other major markets that are opening up around the world:

"Beyond Russia and China, Korea is becoming increasingly important."

In this same article, Dozhier also mentioned another potential expanding market: "A viable Japanese retail fur market could very well be our next expanding outlet for wild furs."

A strong international fur market brings buyers with deep pockets to the table and there is no shortage of wild furs. Further demand for ranched furs attract buyers but for different reasons. Ranched furs, like domestic beef, is harvested at peak times when the product is worth the most. Ranched goods are always offered in prime condition and ranchers can offer what trappers can't: consistency. Ranched goods are developed from genetic lines just as fine merino wool is. Over time, ranchers breed their stock to produce desired qualities for the garment market. In comparison, trappers must take what nature provides, and that means different sizes, color variations, and different fur quality. There is a very short window for trappers to ascertain fur in a prime state which happens to be when the weather is the most foul.

With the strength of the world fur market well established, buyers attend fur auctions with specific goals in mind. They may be interested in beaver or bobcats or both. It depends on the current market which means the prices trappers receive for their hard work is equally variable and unpredictable. There are several advantages to trappers who place their fur directly on the world market through large auction houses. One of the advantages of using a large auction house such as the North American Fur Auction Inc. (NAFA) is that regional representatives will meet trappers as predetermined locations for pickup and delivery.

Trappers provide their trapping license number, and all pelts must be registered with the sale. Pelts are tagged appropriately according to state and federal regulations the same as furs sold to country buyers or state sales. The furs are hauled to a depot where they are checked in and sorted by species. The NAFA provides excellent fur storage facilities which are temperature and humidity controlled to optimize fur quality and prevent any damage due to heat or insects as do other reputable auction houses. On the date of the sale, the furs are displayed in the best possible manner and the fur buyer's grade, sort, and make a competitive offer. While commissions are often higher at these large auction houses, the higher prices received by trappers often offsets the small difference of a few percentage points.

Another major fur auction house, Fur Harvesters Auction Inc., sums up the international advantage quite well in an advertisement found in outdoor magazines: "You work hard for your Fur, Sell it to the World!"

So just how big is the world fur market? An excerpt from an article written by Serge Lariviere, a wildlife biologist from Quebec, Canada, published in the *Trapper and Predator Caller Magazine* [13] in December 2011, paints a clear picture:

> "In the past year, worldwide production of ranch mink was estimated at about 44 million pelts. The official production numbers by country are 14 million pelts from Denmark, 9 million from China, 4.5 million from the Netherlands, 3.7 million from Poland, 2.8 million from the United States, 2.3 million from Canada, 2.1 million from Finland, 2 million from the Baltic States, 1.3 million from Russia, 1.2 million from Sweden, 600,000 from Belarus and 500,000 from Norway. So, of the worldwide production of ranch mink, only about 11 percent come from Canada and the United States. Now, an ever-growing proportion

of ranch mink come from China—9 million mink in the past year. And there are rumors that China actually produces a lot more than this official figure—some claim upward of 20 million.

Want a bleak comparison? In numbers of pelts, all wild fur produced in Canada and the United States reaches less than 10 million skins annually, a very humble contribution in comparison. However, wild fur produces the most expensive pelts. If ranch mink usually sells for $50 per skin, wild fur might range from less than a dollar for squirrels all the way to several hundreds of dollars for bobcats, wolverines and wolves . . ."

With the high volumes of fur moving throughout the world and ever-expanding markets opening up, the fur industry is clearly not fading away into the annals of history. Quite the contrary, furs and their use for clothing, whether for fashion or utilitarian reasons, continues to be a valued commodity among humans. It is hard to imagine a more natural and renewable resource from which to derive materials for garments. For now, the fur trade is a healthy and viable market which demands attention on the world stage.

The impact to the local economy shouldn't be overlooked either. The MTA fur sale that took place in 2012 generated over $225,000 in sales. This is money that went straight into the pockets of local Montana trappers. This one fur sale, in one small town in Montana, generated significant income for local people, not to mention the economic impact on local businesses in the area which trappers and fur buyers patronized over the three-day period.

Another interesting thing about fur sales are the phone calls and conversations that happen when trappers get their results. Trappers have caught on to the benefits of technology, and as international fur sales results roll in, they are posted on the auction house's Web page. The information provided shows the number of pelts per lot, grade, and price offered. Most trappers focus on the averages over time, but individual pelts may bring the highest dollar, and it doesn't matter if it was a $9 muskrat or a $111 marten. There is a little friendly competition among trappers for who received the most for their fur.

The wild fur market, while much smaller in comparison to the volume of ranch furs, produces the highest valued pelts. For the trapper, the personal satisfaction of a job well done is reflected in both the quality of his pelts and the prices offered. These are far more important than market strategy, return on investment, and profit margins. It takes diligence and attention to detail to consistently produce top-quality furs. The amount of pride successful trappers take in their fur cannot be overstated. It is very important that their pelts are the best they can be. Hats that read "TOP LOT TRAPPER" are coveted among trappers for a reason.

As long as proper management of our natural resource is maintained through stringent science-based principles, the fur market will be continually renewed for years to come, and trappers will continue to produce high-quality fur. It's primarily a matter of pride and somewhere far down the list for most trappers is financial gain.

Chapter 11

Trappers by Association

A small body of determined spirits fired by an unquenchable
faith in their mission can alter the course of history.

—Mahatma Gandhi

In 1976, the first group of organized Montana trappers met and established themselves as the Montana Trappers Association. The MTA was formed by trappers who were decidedly "dedicated to the conservation and management of Montana's furbearing animals and the application of proper predator control methods."

The MTA evolved over time and established a good working relationship with the Montana Fish, Wildlife, and Parks (MFWP). This relationship has benefited the furbearers of Montana through the compilation of firsthand experience and on-the-ground data collection. Who better to inform biologists about the health of furbearers than trappers? The philosophy of the MTA is founded in conservation through wise use of natural resources, and it works.

Fifty-one state trapping affiliates make up the core of the National Trappers Association, representing thousands of fur takers from every part of the country. The MTA is one of the fifty-one very active state associations in the U.S. Almost every state in the continental U.S. has a trappers association similar to the MTA. Each state association promotes ethical trapping, publishes a newsletter, represents trappers on legal issues, and holds a state trappers rendezvous. The MTA is an active group of between eight hundred to one thousand members strong who do more for trapping in Montana than all other sportsman groups combined. Without the MTA, wildlife management, which utilizes trapping, might not be the same as it is today.

The MTA is broken up into seven basic districts. These seven districts correspond to the Montana Fish, Wildlife, and Parks (FWP) game management units. Each game management unit has a wildlife manager employed by the MFWP who oversees both game and nongame allowable harvest based on biological information. Every year, an MTA district meeting is held by each district director in their respective area to address MTA business and to provide a direct line of communication to wildlife managers and biologists. At the annual district 2 meeting held in Missoula in 2012, trappers voiced their concerns about public conflict, local opposition, and MTA business—all the usual things any nonprofit organization must endure to be successful. When that was done, trappers and biologists got down to wildlife management like they do year after year and looked over the hard data about wildlife health.

Data collected by fur trappers in Montana has allowed biologists to trend furbearer populations over time. The data collected for certain species include such details as age, sex, juvenile-adult ratios, township and range where the animals were trapped and total number. Additional information is obtained through trapper surveys, but that is just the tip of the iceberg.

The wildlife manager provided data on all species known to be sensitive to population cycles. Each trapper in attendance was handed a stack of data tables going back almost twenty years. Marten, fisher, otter, bobcat, and wolverine harvest information and trends were reviewed by about forty people in all. Every trapper spoke about their experience in the field with the number of each species harvested, seen, or evidenced of their population. These trappers know when populations are strong or in decline, and have a solid history of relaying that information to the FWP in district 2. Virtually every furbearing species open to trapping was discussed, including the nonsensitive rodent species and predators (which are not categorized as furbearers in Montana).

Based on age-sex ratios of bobcats taken by trappers and hunters during the 2009-2010 season, the bobcat quota was reduced from one hundred eighty to one hundred for the district 2010 and 2011 seasons. In 2011, the quota was filled in just twenty-five days, and the number of females to males, and juvenile harvest were indicative of a healthy bobcat population. Further input from trappers during the meeting reassured biologists that the quota could safely be raised to previous levels. Based on this valuable input, it was the recommendation of the FWP representatives to increase the quota. This recommendation was followed up with a letter written by the MTA district 2 director in favor of that decision. Furbearer management is not taken lightly by trappers or the FWP. The sustainability and overall health of wildlife is paramount in the continuation of trapping. The close relationship between the MTA and FWP is special, and important for wildlife. By working hand-in-hand, wildlife professionals ensure healthy populations of furbearers.

Wolverine trapping opportunities in the state of Montana has recently received a lot of attention. While the data from several studies show that the wolverine population has steadily increased over the past thirty years in a trapping and hunting environment, the allowable trapping of a few wolverines each year in Montana has been a matter of contention. While wolverines are abundant throughout Alaska and large parts of Canada, their overall numbers in the lower forty-eight states are small. This is due—in large part—to shrinking suitable habitats and the naturally occurring low numbers due to complex ecological and behavioral attributes. Even wolverines at maximum carrying capacity are low in comparison to other wildlife species.

The MTA has always supported increases and decreases in furbearer quotas based on the best interest of furbearers themselves. Opposing groups try desperately to convince the nontrapping public that trapping contributes to the decimation and extinction of wildlife, in direct contradiction to many intensive scientific studies.

As long as the overall health of Montana's furbearers and other wildlife is in the hands of well-informed trappers and conservationists who use proven scientific based data to continue our rich wildlife legacy, furbearer populations will remain safe. Abundant, healthy wildlife begins with sound wildlife principles. A philosophy the MTA has promoted and stood by since that first meeting in 1976.

Genuine concern for furbearers and other wildlife is not the only thing the MTA promotes. The continuation of Montana's trapping legacy is foremost in the MTA's agenda, as their slogan indicates, "Working Today for a Tomorrow in Trapping." The MTA doesn't just talk the talk, they walk the walk.

A Youth Trapper Camp is held in June every year which first began in partnership with 4-H, MTA, and FWP. This three-day camp—which is held annually in the beautiful Bear Paw Mountains—has been incorporated in Montana as a nonprofit educational organization. The camp is geared toward family participation as campers attend classes on trapping methods, ethics, regulations, fur handling, health, and safety. Camp instructors are made up of dedicated volunteers from the MTA education program, Montana 4-H, and MTFWP personnel.

The YTC is funded through various means, including camp fees, YTC membership gifts, individual and corporate donations, participation in the Albertsons Community Partners Program, and many more. In addition, the MTFWP offers a $20 scholarship to the first sixty youth, and YTC Inc. provides even more scholarships. The YTC is open to any youth under the age of eighteen years, and first year participants attend nine classes, dealing with trapping basics, conservation, regulations, ethics, furbearer ID, safety, and health. Returning students receive more intense hands-on training.

The purpose and goals of the YTC are to:

- Teach the proper care, management, preservation, and utilization of furbearers and other North American wildlife.
- Develop, promote, and support educational programs for the wise use, management, and conservation of furbearers.
- Inform and educate the public to more completely understand the problems of the wise use of furbearers.
- Stimulate public interest in furbearers.
- Promote environmental education, including the wise use and conservation of furbearers.
- Operate an annual camp which will fulfill the goals of YTC Inc. and benefit the general public.

I once spent some time working for an experiential education program focused on primitive living skills, metaphorically applied to life skills, for troubled youth. I left that program convinced that hands-on learning in an outdoor setting can do more to improve the self-confidence and mental well-being of a child than anything else on the planet. In June 2012, I drove to Havre, Montana, to participate in the thirteenth annual Youth Trapper Camp, and the experience reaffirmed everything I believed.

When I arrived, campers were stacked along the road like cordwood along with colorful tents, camp chairs, coolers, and children staked out along a creek. The encampment is nestled in fairly open country with steep grass-covered mountains charging up on either side of two-track dirt road. Springs emerging from high on the mountainside create long strips of aspen conspicuously on the open faces of the Bear Paws. The natural beauty of the area is a complement to the rich trapping history of the west. It is hard to imagine a more suitable location to educate youngsters about the ways of fur trapping.

Campfire smoke sweetened the air as volunteer trappers directed traffic and checked in campers and their families. Trailers filled with tents, tables, and chairs were lined up, waiting to be emptied. Many of the students arrive with family and friends, but for those who don't, the YTC provides chaperoned tents with cots for boys and girls. In true trapper fashion, the large tents were unloaded and went up with speed and relative efficiency. The work ethic trappers possess is apparent in everything they do. There is no milling around, no balking when anything needs to be done. Poles were grabbed, stakes pounded, and tent frames covered with canvas and tarps. The mess hall tent, large enough to accommodate up to a hundred and fifty people, went up with barely a hitch. Then tables and chairs emerged and too were placed in organized fashion quickly and without hesitation. The teamwork and dedication to the passing of the trappers' torch to the next generation is never taken lightly. Trappers know what needs to be done and they do it—gladly.

The first evening began with an introduction to the camp and camp rules under the mess hall tent. Campers were told to go to the mess hall whenever the siren sounded as the siren signaled meals, class changes, and important announcements. The outline of scheduled classes was given, and classes started right after dinner. The food was plentiful and hardy and followed by dessert. If anyone was going to go hungry at this camp, it would certainly not be the fault of the camp cooks.

John and Melody of J & M Furs had a trap supply venue on site for students to get trapping supplies. The prices were very reasonable to say the least, and both Melody and John could be seen at any time over the weekend, working with students to make sure they got the right traps and supplies. Several trappers also brought their fur pelts to sell to John, and the children received generous offerings for their fur. John's nicknames from his friends range from "Almost Honest John" to "Generous John." While dealing with young trappers, the latter is more fitting.

Older students followed instructors down the dirt road and up on a hillside to practice making sets with snares, foothold traps, and body gripping traps. In part, students were being assessed on their abilities and understanding of traps and sets. The twenty-four third-year students were broken into smaller groups and assigned to instructors for the most anticipated event of the weekend—trapping furbearers. Every year, YTC students—in cooperation with private landowners—are able to trap nuisance wildlife in the surrounding area. This aspect of the YTC is a win-win for students and landowners. Problem animals are removed at no cost to the landowners, and students have the opportunity to put the knowledge they have gained through several years of YTC participation to good use. The fact that they are also using their skills to help people is a significant added bonus.

First and second year students attended classes about various types of traps and equipment under the mess hall tent. The instructor explained how and where to use virtually every type of trap available and gave brief demonstrations with audience participation throughout the class. Instruction went until dark. Children under twelve were in their tents or with their families at nine thirty, while teenagers stayed up and poked the campfire until ten thirty. The first evening set the tone for two more action packed days of real-life, hands-on education.

The siren rang at six thirty on Saturday morning, and campers started rustling from their slumber—myself included. I had found a flat spot along the creek where I could hear the soothing water flow past my tent. It was great for sleeping, but I almost missed the sound of the siren. A flag raising ceremony took place, which included the pledge of allegiance and a rendition of a patriotic American song. Trappers are as patriotic as it gets, and I have never been to a trapper's event where this attribute wasn't represented.

Breakfast was well organized, and the offering of food was exceptional. Most campers gathered at the mess hall, while others ate at their own tent sites or in chairs positioned around the fire ring. The hour allotted for breakfast was used to catch up with old friends, reminisce, and prepare for the day. When the siren went off, so did students and their families. Classes were held all day, each lasting about an hour. Groups of students walked to various locations around camp and received instruction about all things trapping. Furbearer identification was taught by the Montana Fish, Wildlife, and Parks furbearer coordinator; ethics and the law was taught by two state biologists; and snare building was taught by the owner of a snare building expert.

Other students attended a class on predator call building, and a man who spent the better part of fifty years as a predator control specialist taught students how to use them correctly. Experienced trappers taught students to build wood stretchers for drying pelts. FWP employees also taught students about diseases, while MTA members taught safety and trap setting.

The quality and experience of the instructors would be hard to beat anywhere, but the cooperative efforts of these experts enhanced the experience to a level of the highest-quality education—regardless of the $40 cost per student for the entire weekend of hands-on practical application. And students walked away with snares, earth anchors, predator calls, stretchers, and more which they crafted themselves—the value of these items alone exceeds the cost of camp. The rewards of their efforts far outweigh any monetary savings; that's the first lesson of trapping these students learn.

Only third-year students were allowed to go off site with instructors and set a trapline. Pickup trucks loaded with students and traps created dust clouds as they made their way down the two-track out of camp. They came back for lunch and then headed immediately back out to set traps until dinnertime. Making and checking their own trapline would be all the instruction these students received for the long weekend, and there were no complaints.

Trapping instructors brought in various animals, including raccoons, badgers, and muskrats for skinning and fleshing demonstrations, along with trap preparation and appropriate use of body gripping traps. Students got to choose which demo they would attend, and many of the parents watched one demonstration while their children watched another, so they wouldn't miss anything. Parents were just as involved as the students at every class held at camp. They asked questions, built snares and calls, set traps, and got excited when they succeeded and frustrated when they did not. Experiential education works for parents too.

As the sun fell below the horizon, the demonstrations ended. Students asked if there would be more demonstrations for the night, and there was talk of rigging up a light source to continue into the night. But with tired children and another full day ahead, students and their families retreated to the warm glow of campfires and anticipation of the trapline check.

The following morning started again with a siren at six thirty and plentiful food at seven. The students who had set traps the day before were anxious to check their line, while first—and second-year students stayed in camp to learn about knife and gun safety, furbearer biology, and other topics of interest. On occasion, a "pack of coyotes" would sound off not too far from the tents. The source was from students learning to use the predator calls they had made the day before. Volunteers who were not teaching classes or performing other tasks sorted donated traps and awards.

Students returned from traplines with three beavers and a muskrat. On previous years, there has been three times that number. The aquatic furbearers were skinned and fleshed immediately by the proud young trappers. The work begins when the animal is on the table. Young trappers are not immune from this fact, and skinning skills are important for the development of knowledgeable trappers.

With the camp coming to a close, perhaps the most impressive part about Youth Trapper Camp was yet to come. Every student received a trapper education certificate documenting their participation. A single donation of over a hundred traps was divided into smaller groups of four to six, and names were drawn out of a hat one after the other until all the traps were gone, and twenty-six students in all received traps. Two brand-new guns were also won by students—one went to an eight-year-old girl, and the other to a young man about fourteen.

Buckets filled with trapping supplies, sifters, wire stretchers, and more were handed out for free to students by random drawing. The sheer amount of donations was staggering. And to ensure that no student left the awards ceremony empty handed, a box filled with brand-new 110 body gripping traps was placed at the end of the table. And as students walked by, they were asked to grab one. The pride and enjoyment on the young faces of those youngsters was worth the six-hour drive to get there, but knowing that I had a hand in providing that joy is enough to keep me coming back.

The educational involvement of Montana trappers is second to none in the country, but the MTA doesn't stop there. Clinics are held in every district of the state throughout the year to help improve trappers' abilities in fur handling and trapping. These clinics are most often held at a trapper's private residence or property. An open invite is made to any trapper, regardless of membership status. "It's about sharing what we know. It doesn't do any good for a trapper to keep what he knows inside his head. I'll tell any trapper anything he wants to know," says Ed, an active MTA member and a tireless volunteer. Ed has held fur sales, fur handling clinics, and trapping demonstrations on his property and on his own dime, simply to promote trapping and to improve a trapper's knowledge base. It is this kind of sharing and resolve by trappers in the MTA that make it such a special organization.

The fur-handling clinics are put on by MTA members with a desire to teach their skills of skinning, fleshing, and drying pelts—free of charge. The benefits of proper fur handling not only help trappers get more money for their effort, it also promotes a good image for the MTA and helps draw buyers at the MTA's annual fur sale. Once every year at about the same time, thirty or forty trappers from district 2 meet to exchange ideas and learn about fur handling and recently other districts have been holding fur handling clinics as well.

A handful of first-rate fur handlers bring fur for demonstrations and often receive other trappers' fur to put up during the clinic, and this isn't just for MTA members. On occasion, FWP employees show up to watch, or may even have animals they want trappers to skin and flesh in preparation for tanning. Tanned hides donated to or obtained by the FWP are the source of furs used in demonstrations for trapper education classes or other educational programs around the state. The MTA promotes the trappers' craft, a craft with both historic and current significance.

The MTA's dedication to education doesn't stop with trappers already in the know. The trapper's education program—funded in large part on MTA's dime and taught by their own volunteers—has been ongoing for over twenty years. The course is complete with high-quality instructors, excellent student manuals, and books for students to keep. All the instructors are volunteers, and the class is free to anyone who wants to learn about trapping. Each class lasts about eight hours minimum and follows a succinct curriculum, which includes topics such as ethics, politics and social concerns. Fur handling is always a student favorite during these classes and quality demonstrations are given outside on how to make sets appropriately for several species. When possible, law enforcement officers attend and answer any questions students may have.

A box of tanned furs, including every fur a trapper may harvest in Montana, are also used for demonstration. One by one, the tanned furs are removed from the box, a brief description of the furbearer biology is given, and then the fur is passed around to the students. Furs captivate the imagination of students, and when a trapper tells a tale of a trapping adventure with fur in his hands, the results are awesome. Students ask questions and listen to the answer intently. There is nothing more educational than hands-on experience. Students really learn about wildlife in these classes, as they will on their traplines, in a way that no other experience can ever compare.

The most interesting part for students seems to be the fur-handling demonstration. Instructors may bring any animal for demonstration. Instructors have skinned and fleshed muskrats, beavers, otters, skunks, and mink at the trapper's education classes over the years. Every time, students show keen interest and ask the most questions about this subject. It's like Biology 101 with a twist. Skinning, fleshing, and stretching a pelt is an art rarely used by the nontrapping public, but the traditional skills are kept intact through trappers. The interest in skinning by students most likely stems from their interest in the animals. Seeing a mink up close is not a common occurrence for most people, and peeling away the hide, cutting glands, and preserving the beautiful fur is a natural experience, one which up until just a few decades ago was quite common.

Interestingly, many of the attendees are nontrappers who show up just to learn about traps and trapping. One attendee at a class in 2012 was informed about the trapper's education class after raising concerns to the FWP about Montana's Bass Creek recreational area, an area she wanted to bring her dog. A meeting was called, in which six MTA members, two citizens, the area manager, a forest ranger, and two MTFWP employees attended to discuss the likelihood that traps were in the area. After a lengthy discussion, she was invited to an upcoming trapper's education class. While she may never set a trapline, she now has a greater appreciation for trappers and the trapping culture.

Trapping instructors take the class one step further and donate "prizes" for students. Annual memberships, traps, trapping equipment, and magazines are a few of the things dedicated instructors give away—in addition to their time in order to promote the trapping culture. While the course was not mandatory as a prerequisite for buying a Montana trapping license as of 2012, students who complete the course receive a certificate of completion.

Ethics are emphasized and reiterated over and over during the classes. The MTA doesn't just say they want trappers to be ethical, they prove it by offering a reward for un-lawful trapping. A link on the MTA's home page (*www.montanatrappers.org*) shows the MTA's dedication to this cause:

The Montana Trappers Association is a nonprofit organization incorporated in Montana in 1976 and is dedicated to the conservation and management of Montana's furbearing animals and the application of proper predator control methods. The MTA represents the organized trappers of Montana and through trapper and public education, maintains that trapping is a legitimate, desirable, ethical, and compatible enterprise of modern man. To this end, in 1988, the MTA Board of Directors established a reward for information leading to the arrest and conviction of person or persons responsible for illegal trapping or snaring in Montana. Most recently, the MTA Board reaffirmed this belief by increasing the reward to $300.00 per incident. If you have information of illegal trapping or snaring incidents, please contact the nearest MTFWP office.

Each incident is reviewed on a case-by-case basis to prevent fraudulence and is voted upon by the MTA board of directors. Not only does the MTA offer a reward, they also craft a letter to the illegal trapper and ask them to stop—and to join the MTA to get educated about responsible trapping.

The MTA continues to grow and promote ethical trapping techniques, public awareness, and education. But members also let their hair down a little each year at the annual trappers rendezvous, just as the mountain men met each year between 1820 and 1840—to buy, sell, swap, and trade; compete; share stories; and enjoy the camaraderie of like-minded people.

That tradition lives on at the annual MTA rendezvous. The rendezvous is held in the middle of Montana, literally. Lewistown, Montana, has been the rendezvous site for years. Trappers travel from all over the state to participate in trap setting, skillet toss, pistol shooting, and other contests. Demonstrations are held about fur handling, trapping, animal damage control techniques, trap modification, and other topics. Attendance is usually around three thousand people who have opportunities to buy products from over twenty vendors. Everything from new and used traps to fur crafts can be found at the rendezvous. While at the 2011 rendezvous, one trapper summed it up well. "There's nothing like living, eating, and breathing trapping for three days, man."

I went to the MTA Trappers Convention with a new trapper named Toni, whom I had taught to trap during the only two days I had free earlier that spring. We set a few traps on a Saturday afternoon, and in less than twenty-four hours, he trapped his first mink and muskrat. Now he was ready to buy traps, and he knew his best deals would come via used traps at the rendezvous.

We arrived at the fairgrounds late in the middle of the night and set up a rustic camp amid camp trailers and tents. A cot set up on the grass served me fine, while Toni preferred to set up a tent. At first light, trappers were stirring, and I went in search of fresh coffee. The building used by the MTA at the Fergusson fairgrounds is a large, white structure, set behind the grandstands and provides a relatively quiet setting for campers and events. Vendors filled the open room with tables displaying their goods, an MTA table showcased items, while a NAFA table was set up with various beaver hides for trappers to "grade" as part of a contest.

Snare men, trap supply companies dealing in new and used traps and equipment, hundreds of books, Montana trapper bags, and various lure manufacturers had wares displayed on tables and in crates organized on the floor. A stage stacked with donated items for the silent auction included things like beaver mittens, spurs, cakes and pies, traps, ammunition, clay pigeon throwers, spurs, videos, lures, and the like. Tables and chairs were set up in front of the stage, and concessions were offered.

The MTA sports a modest offering of traps and supplies in comparison to national rendezvous, but certainly sufficient for any trapper getting ready for the upcoming season. The list of events for the day included demonstrations on trapping various species and contests. Other mountain man rendezvous take place around country, celebrating the mountain man era. The Trappers Rendezvous is just as it sounds—a rendezvous specific to fur trapping. The spirit of the rendezvous hasn't changed since the days of the mountain men, but the venue certainly has.

There are contests held for trap setting, which involve five or six various-sized traps, which must be set as fast as possible. The timed event challenges trappers of all ages on their ability to get traps set fast. Another fun contest is the 330 Conibear setting contest, which is also timed. A plaque for first, second, and third place go to men and women divisions as well as boys and girls divisions.

I entered the trap setting contest, and it was enjoyable. I had no intention of competing in the event when I arrived, but it was nice to participate in a contest just as the mountain men from days long ago might have. Only I, like my competitors, was dressed in blue jeans and a flannel shirt instead of buckskins. But the spirit of the mountain man, of the western trapper, was no less present. The top three finishers got their photo taken with the Miss Teen Rodeo and Miss Rodeo Montana champions who participate in the rendezvous every year.

Miss Rodeo Montana winners have historically received a fur jacket or vest at the rendezvous, provided by a world-class furrier, courtesy of the MTA. They spent the weekend at the MTA rendezvous and participated in the trap setting contest and skillet toss.

The rendezvous isn't all fun and games. However, it is also the meeting place for one of three board of directors meetings, where elected members tend to organizational business. Food is piled high at the annual banquet, just before the much anticipated MTA auction. In true fund-raising fashion, bidders are generous with their money and donated items are excellent. Items range from fur mittens, ammo, and traps, to custom-made skinning tables and paintings. The quality of the items up for auction complements the raffle ticket items generated by the MTA every year. Winners are drawn for raffle tickets sold throughout the year, and even more money is raised. The MTA has an annual raffle with big prizes. First place is consistently an ATV, and numerous guns, custom knives, fur coats, and local artistry round out a very high-quality raffle—many donated by the Montana Trapper Association members.

The fur fashion show is a stand-out crowd favorite at the rendezvous as well. I didn't know what to expect the first time I attended the show. A fur garment maker asked several ladies from the audience, including the Rodeo Montana gals, to model his collection of fur garments. Each participant walked around the crowd, modeling the latest in fur fashion as the announcer described each piece. The ladies ranged in age—from adults to as young as ten or twelve—and they were all having a great time. Parents in the audience took photos and cheered their favorite models on. The collection was extensive and included long coats, vests, jackets, and hats of assorted furs. It is amazing to see a sheered beaver vest colorfully dyed with pockets, a zipper, and a collar. A casual observer might not even associate a fur article of clothing with fur. The look is modern and resembles fleece to the untrained eye, but with better warming properties and natural eye appeal. The collection was elegant, and the ladies modeling the furs enjoyed being runway models for an evening.

The MTA works hard to promote high standards and have found a way to have fun, earn money, and teach others about the benefits of trapping. Throw in a little competitive spirit, camping, food, and trappers—and you have all the makings of a modern-day mountain man rendezvous.

The efforts of individuals in the MTA to promote trapping cannot be overstated. Hundreds of man hours are donated each year for MTA events, and even more for representation at public meetings regarding wildlife and trapping. The MTA represents trappers at every turn and fights to preserve and protect the rights of trappers everywhere, regardless of the trapper's membership status.

State trappers associations across the country act in similar fashion—those affiliated with the NTA, and those who represent their own local trappers. Trappers are an independent breed and often choose not to join an association because they don't know what good it will do to spend a meager $25 for an annual membership.

As one trapper who attended the rendezvous puts it, "These trappers don't realize how close the battle to keep our trapping heritage alive really is. It is the few hardworking members of each state that is preserving every trapper's right to trap. Imagine the impact trapping associations could have if every trapper in the U.S. joined one association and committed to participating in just one event each year. The MTA is a shining example of working hard to preserve what they love. Every trapper in every state of the United States should join their state association and thank an active member every time they pound a stake and bed a trap on American soil."

Chapter 12

Wolves in Sheep's Clothing

Holding on to anger is like grasping a hot coal with the intent of throwing it at someone else; you are the one who gets burned.

—The Buddha

The wild and hardy trappers who spend days and weeks in the various elements of nature—even on days when bull moose are hiding from the weather—face their greatest adversary not in the mountains, but in the faces of groups opposed to trapping and hunting. Even with public support from professional wildlife and agriculture groups such as the Association of Fish and Wildlife Agencies, Furbearers Unlimited, USDA, and many agriculture-based groups, there is no shortage of attempts to destroy the cultures of people tied to the land—even in Montana. The agricultural community—including cattle ranchers, farmers and wool growers support and even endorse trapping as a necessary means of predator and rodent control. These groups are closely tied to the land and understand that nature can be harsh. These people live and make their living amid the wild lands and wildlife so foreign to urban and suburban dwellers.

The literature and information regarding the viewpoints of animal rights groups, specifically antitrapping groups, even in Montana, is overwhelming. The information is so overwhelming, in fact, that these animal rightists are likely doing their mission a disservice. There is a point of saturation in any movement where the public hears about an issue so much that they are turned off and desensitized. The difficulty in sifting through so much over-the-top disinformation in order to find the genuine concerns of people with legitimate criticisms to the trapping community is astounding.

There are numerous websites with "information" so outrageous and so disgusting that it is difficult to take any animal rights or animal welfare group seriously. One magazine geared toward children published a cover with the portrayal of an American mother preparing dinner by stabbing a rabbit to death, blood splattering all over kitchen walls, and another with a father dressed in fishing clothes with crazed bloodshot eyes, a knife in one hand, and a stringer of bleeding fish in the other. Another depiction is of a chicken holding a human baby in a turkey roasting pan, prepared and ready for the oven. It is hard for me to imagine the mind-set of people who would create these images for children.

Several antitrapping websites claim that trappers skin animals alive just to listen to them scream. Others claim that trappers in Montana are responsible for the extinction of endangered species, and at least one claim that trappers kill two nontarget species for every one target species. Other sites show grotesque photos of domestic dogs caught in traps that would be impossible to have occurred unless of course the laws of physics were altered first. These obvious fakes take advantage of an unknowing public.

Representatives of antitrapping groups in Montana have referenced "scientific studies" that report false data like "86% of lynx mortality in Montana is due to trapping." This is stealing data from a lynx study performed in Alaska where lynx are an abundant, regulated species—which are legally trapped—and erroneously applying that statistical data to a state 1,800 miles away. This particular claim erroneously references a study which took place in an area of Alaska, where trappers provided data about lynx trapped while maintaining their traplines. 86% of the lynx mortality occurred as a result of trappers because it was primarily trappers providing the data. None of the false data and gross exaggeration does much good for legitimizing their position.

Another website based out of Montana has a link to what they claim to be an "undercover video" that has caught trappers in the act for the first time ever. The video is nothing more than a trapping video, of which there are countless hundreds for sale to the general public. The twisted "data" used to evoke emotional response is either the result of poor data interpretation or fraud.

Given the incredibly high occurrence of misrepresented data, it would be difficult to believe that it was the result of honest errors in scientific review. It is difficult to separate radical enviro-terrorists from real grassroots organizations of concerned citizens. Perhaps the "separation" of these groups is much smaller than it outwardly appears.

On June 2, 2012, Theresa Manzella—founder of Willing Servants Inc.—held a public presentation in Victor, Montana, titled, "The Human Cost of the Animal Rights Movement." Here, Theresa told the story of starting Willing Servants Inc., which in her words, "was born out of the need to preserve the welfare of horses while assisting owners with temporary or permanent placement as an alternative to criminal neglect." When Theresa first started Willing Servants, she envisioned it as a horse rescue program that would encourage education to alleviate owner ignorance and indifference toward horse owners. Unknowingly, her mission was offensive to animal right groups.

She had thought for years that animal rights and animal welfare were one and the same—a thought that would change and eventually morph into an intensive research project that evaluated groups like HSUS and PETA. These groups scoffed at her when she spoke about horses, both in horse-reining events (which Theresa is a national champion) and horse processing. She couldn't understand why these animal rights advocates disapproved of her organization. Weren't they on the same team? She quickly learned that being a professional equestrian trainer pitted her against animal rights groups.

"Now, I am going to say things today and you will either agree or disagree . . . but I'd rather be hated for who I am than loved for whom I am not," Theresa said in her opening lines.

She showed a video of herself on a horse competing in a reining event. "I think this shows my abilities and legitimacy as a professional Reiner," she said. "Animal rights groups would have us believe that riding horses is wrong . . . animals are a big part of our lives." Her message was focused on the relationship she develops with each of her horses and how not all horses are suitable for use in competition. It takes a keen sense of horse breeding know-how and exceptional training skills, along with passion and commitment, to compete at the national level.

Theresa spoke for two hours about her horses and the animal rights movement. She talked about heritage, culture, and tradition—words that rang clear and resonated with trapping, hunting, fishing, as well as agriculture. When speaking about the relationship between sportsmen and the agriculture community, she said, "It is important to know that our interests are interdependent." Her common-sense approach to the use of animals was further demonstrated when she said that anytime you are dealing with animals, accidents will happen. I am emotional and passionate about my horses, but at some point, we have got to stop worrying about emotions and get down to the facts." Her message was so similar to my thoughts about trappers and trapping that I couldn't help but stay and listen to her other concerns.

In 2006, approximately 105,000 horses were processed by three USDA-regulated plants in operation, the last full year that horses were processed in the U.S. By 2007, the three plants were shut down via the efforts of animal rights groups, representing the loss of a $65 million-year industry. Now the only option to have old horses killed and processed requires that they be sent to either Canada or Mexico, where the industry regulations do not guarantee humane treatment as did the U.S. facilities. The exports to Mexico jumped from 18,673 in 2006 to 95,378 in 2012, and similar increases were seen with exports to Canada, from 25,625 to 59,693. The result has been devastating for horse owners in the U.S., and many horse owners who can no longer afford to care for their animals are forced to either neglect or turn them loose. That's where Willing Servants comes in, offering reprieve for horse owners caught between their love for horses and the lack of resources.

So how does this all fit in with fur trapping and hunting? Two things really stuck out to me in Theresa's presentation. One was a twenty-year-old quote from HSUS CEO Wayne Pacelle, when he was quoted by Theresa as saying, "We are going to use the ballot box and the democratic process to stop all hunting in the United States. We will take it species by species, until all hunting is stopped in California. Then we will take it state by state." The other thing that got my attention was a quote from Theresa herself, who said, "Animal rightists want people to think horse owners are mean, greedy, money-grubbing bad people, but that is not the case."

The same words used by PETA and HSUS to describe horse owners—mean, greedy, money-grubbing bad people—are essentially the same words used by antitrapping groups in Montana to describe trappers—also not true. Is this a mere coincidence or another clear indication of the marriage of two animal rights organizations?

The Willing Servants website (*www.willingservantsmt.org*) has detailed information about the differences between animal rights and animal welfare with links to eye-opening websites. The writing is on the wall; states that use ballot box initiatives have been the target of HSUS for the past twenty years and that trend is continuing. Any state that allows ballot box initiatives to drive political change has been impacted by groups associated with HSUS. The message similarities of local organized opposing groups and commercial antiagriculture and antihunting groups make it doubtful that the sole purpose of groups setting up shop in Montana is the result of genuine concern about traps.

The antitrapping movement in Montana and other ballot initiative states are not about traps, trapping, or trappers at all, it's about "taking it state by state." Theresa's message was that these groups are focused on destroying the agricultural, land-based society loved and cherished by so many. Hopefully, the legacy of the Montana mountain man and rugged cowboys will not fall victim to the deceitful tactics of these types of pseudo-animal welfare groups.

All consumptive users with ties to the land and a vested interest in wildlife populations are in danger of losing their heritage. Ranchers are criticized for taking up open spaces for cattle by animal rights groups who attack the beef industry. Anglers are harassed as they fish for salmon on their way to spawn. Recreational hunters—including big game, small game, and waterfowl hunters—have been fighting for years to keep the rich North American Wildlife Conservation Model in use. Gun restrictions and the U.S. citizen's Second Amendment rights are constantly challenged. Hounds men and bear hunters have to continuously defend their rights to hunt with dogs or lose their rights as several states have already seen. Rodeos are protested as are equestrian sport shows. Animal research facilities are bombed, and stores that carry fur products are torched. Fur, dairy, poultry, and swine family farms contend with the ill-conceived release of their animals to run wild. People wearing leather or furs are publically humiliated.

Acts of terrorism in the name of animal rights threaten the agricultural and outdoor cultures cherished by millions of Americans and countless others around the globe. Every attack on each subculture of American outdoorsmen is an attack on all of them. Groups cleverly disguise themselves as animal welfare groups, raising money for abandoned pets or as one-issue groups, such as antitrapping organizations. All the while, they are chipping away at rural lifestyles, piece by piece, and fattening the pockets of extreme animal rightists.

If the anticonsumptive users succeed at eliminating just one method available to consumptive users, they have succeeded at taking a piece of every consumptive user.

It is difficult also to imagine the mentality it takes for a person or a group of people to leave life-threatening messages on a hunter or trapper's vehicle. But in 2012, at the Montana Trappers Association district 2 meeting, I asked about forty trappers how many had been the recipient of a death threat. At least a dozen trappers raised their hands. It is harder still to fathom the manic mental state possessed by people that would cause them to burn down another human being's livelihood with total disregard to human life.

Such was the case in the early morning hours on September 26, 2011, in Caldwell, Idaho. The North Animal Liberation Press Office reported that a group who calls themselves the "Arson Unit," claimed responsibility for burning one of the buildings owned by Rocky Mountain Fur and Fireworks, a family run business that has been a part of the community for years. According to the *Trapper and Predator Caller Magazines,* November 2011 Issue[14], the group had never made any effort to approach the owners of the store. They carried out this terrorist act under the belief that "by oppressing innocent life, you have lost your rights." According to the press release received by the store owner that afternoon, the message continued. "We've come to take you down a notch. Stay in business, and we'll be back." This is terrorist mentality, not at all unlike the mentality that caused two planes to strike the World trade center on September 11, 2001. The tragic event in U.S. history that killed nearly three thousand people and destroyed the United States' tallest building among others is not reserved for mad jihadists. What's behind these acts that defy logic? It certainly isn't love for wild places, people, and wildlife.

There are countless acts of terrorism that occur throughout the world in the name of environmentalism and a plethora of other so-called "causes." It would seem counterintuitive that in a world with the ability to communicate in innumerable ways, these groups feel the need to resort to primitive and archaic ways to force their ideals. Perhaps the Montana values of a good conversation over a cup of coffee would behoove these radicals, but there is little chance that will ever happen. They seem to ignore established legal and social systems and follow their own rules, like so many supremacists and dictatorships in our world's history.

Attacks on cattle ranches, mink farms, chicken farms, dog kennels, logging operations, research facilities, storefronts, doctor's offices, and more occur every year in countries around the world. Further acts of terror continue in Arabic countries in the name of . . . what exactly? Is this time period in our world's history the terrorist age? If I don't like something someone is doing, do I have a right to burn down their livelihood? If I don't, who does? Do you? Or is it only animal liberators and martyrs? How long do we all have to live in fear? Until humans are completely severed from our natural environment and are no longer participants in our natural world? Or when every living human being on the planet agrees with the groups who will harass, threaten us, or worse—if we don't change our minds and blindly follow their radical agenda?

If you are a hunter, trapper, or angler in any state or any country in the world today and ignore the all-out fight trappers are in to protect their privilege to do what they love to do, you are also in danger of losing your right to do what you love to do.

Make no mistake. Groups that oppose trapping will soon turn their energy toward hunting. Many already have. If you spend any time following the major animal rights groups' agenda, sport fishing is not safe either. Agriculture, medical researchers, logging, or retailers carrying animal-based products are all being affected by animal rights groups, claiming to be concerned about animals while they rake in millions.

As consumptive users, we must all stand together and protect our heritage. We owe it to the thousands of conservationists who have worked to achieve the opportunities we have today—to hold high ethical standards and stick together.

As for the nontrappers who are genuinely concerned for their personal safety, the safety of their pets, livestock, and wildlife, trappers are thinking about ways to adapt to an ever-growing and ever-changing recreational public. Both sides need to educate themselves and listen. The answer to the conflict relies on good communication, acceptance, and education.

There is room for compromise and common ground. If trappers and nontrappers won't continue to work together, the joy we all experience while in wild places will begin to sour. We must find room for acceptance, or we all lose.

One such resolution occurred in February 2012 in western Montana when a woman and her friend called the FWP, asking if an area was safe for their pets. A meeting was called, and trappers, nontrapping citizens, a forest ranger, and MFWP managers were there on extremely short notice. After a couple hours of discussion, a resolution was made, and the group worked together to designate the heavily used Bass Creek area as trap-free. Through calm rational compromise, trappers, nontrappers, law enforcement officers, and game managers resolved a multiuse issue. That seems far more reasonable to me than death threats and cultural deconstruction.

Chapter 13

Montana Trappers

A fur trapper ... he calls himself.
Creatures wild he catches with traps cleverly devised.
Market for pelts good or almost nil, there he'll be, on the line.
Can hardly explain why, to self or others.
To satisfy a passion to kill? For some innate thrill?
He's sure it's none of this when in the forest deep, or wading a shallow marsh far from
sight and sound, or there by a busy highway where he follows his line.
A measure of skill keeps him there, but more an inner drive that brings him back,
year after year.
No reason to explain.

—Edwin A. Reid, *Hello, Adirondacker*

There is little that can be said which conveys the heart of the trapping culture like a good story. I was able to sit down with four Montana trappers who embody the spirit of the trapping community. My only regret is that I was not able to interview more or fit their stories into the pages of this book. So many trappers have a willingness to share and celebrate the great trapping heritage maintained in Montana. Both men and women trappers in Montana attend rendezvous, teach, advocate on a political level for trappers and hunters, and work hard to uphold a positive trapper image. I am thankful to have had the opportunity to hear the life story of so many nature lovers. I have done my best to capture their personalities and breathe life into these characters through words.

My hope is to show these people, as they are, who make up the trapping fraternity in Montana and around the country. These trappers are the epitome of trappers everywhere—some young, some old, educated, or not. These trappers have families and friends, careers and hobbies. They watch television, go to the grocery store, and celebrate American holidays. They value wild lands and stand their ground on matters of principle. This is the story of hardworking, down-to-earth individuals whom I am forever grateful to have met and come to know. Chug, Talks A lot, Walks A lot and the Drive By Trapper explain the reasons why trapping is so important to them. These four members of Montana's keystone subculture of American outdoorsmen tell their story in their own words. They are the true trappers of Montana.

"Chug"

Culture is made or destroyed—by its articulate voices.

—Ayn Rand

Wisconsin's nickname is officially the "Dairy State" due to its high production of butter, cheese, and a host of other fine dairy products. For a young boy named "Chug" in the 1980s, the local fields and streams around Madison were the source of hours of entertainment as he explored the wooded patches intermittently located between crop and hay fields. Meandering streams and rock outcroppings made the perfect place to grow up. Wildlife was everywhere, and opportunities to hunt small game and take in all the natural sights and sounds influenced his appreciation for nature. He always enjoyed being outside and playing in the woods.

One day, while out walking along a big row of pine trees that bordered sandy hillsides and dirt roads, he had a chance encounter with two men in a pickup truck that affected his life more than he could have imagined. With all the excitement of a ten-year-old boy, Chug told the story. "Here comes this truck driving down the trail, and these two guys jumped out, and I walked up to them and asked, 'What are you guys doing?' And they said. 'We are trapping red fox.' From that day, I thought that was the neatest thing, and they said, 'Do you want to see one?' I said, 'Yeah, I'd love to!' They took me around to the back of the truck, and they had six that morning. Back then, it was like 1979 or 80, somewhere around there. And they were worth like $80 bucks, and that was good money back then."

The two men showed Chug how to make a dirt-hole set for fox, and Chug later went home and begged his grandfather to take him trapping—his grandfather knew how to trap. But at that time, the minimum age for trapping was twelve years old, and young Chug was forced to wait. "The next fall, I turned twelve, and my grandfather bought me a number 1 long spring—just one—and we had a cave probably about a half mile out from our house," Chug explained. "I set it opening day of 'coon season, and I checked it every day for two weeks with a flashlight. And on the fifteenth day, I am looking under there for my trap and I couldn't see it. I looked under there, and there was a 'coon in my trap. I'll just never forget it, man. It was the most exciting time of my life!"

A family friend who was an avid hound's man came over that night and showed Chug how to skin his first raccoon. "The next night, we took it down to the fur buyer and got $35 for a skinned 'coon. Not fleshed, not dried. From that day on, I was hooked. I started buying traps. It was a way of life, the way I was brought up."

Chug's father was a doctor in a small town, and he encouraged Chug to go trapping with accomplished local trappers. The lessons learned while on these trappers lines have stuck with him through the years. He remembers one trapper who explained that if a beaver gets caught in a trap but is able to pull its foot out, it will be one of the hardest animals you will ever catch. "Beavers often don't get credit for being difficult to catch," the trapper explained. "But beavers can be very challenging." That same trapper who shared lessons on beaver trapping was a big believer in the Wisconsin Trappers Association (WTA). Because of his influence, Chug joined the WTA and began spending time every year at the annual WTA conventions. One of Chug's favorite smells is the ever-present mixture of skunk essence and gland lures, wafting from the tables of vendors at trapping shows. The aroma brings back fond childhood memories of trapper sport shows, demonstrations, and the trapping brotherhood found at those gatherings.

In 1985, Chug begged his mother to take him to the national convention, which was held in Illinois that year. National trapper conventions are held in a different state each year to allow trappers and hunters from all over the country the ability to attend. When the national convention is close to your home state, it may be the closest it will be for years to come. Trappers travel from miles around to participate. Going to a National Trappers Convention is like a rock concert for outdoorsmen. A typical convention may attract hundreds of vendors, selling everything from traps and attractants to videos and state-of-the-art camouflaged clothing. There are trap setting contests where the fastest trap setters in the country compete for trophies, and the camaraderie among the trapping fraternity is unmatched anywhere. Reminiscent of Trappers Rendezvous from the mountain man era, it's no wonder a young trapper from rural Wisconsin wanted to go so badly. Chug's favorite part about trapping conventions is the demos. "I love going to demos, you always learn something," Chug emphasized.

Since those first days, Chug has maintained membership to his state and national associations and feels that it is one of the most important things a trapper can do. "Even back in the 80s, there was a move to ban trapping, and the associations are the only thing we have to fight."

Some of Chug's favorite memories are with his grandfather. One day, they were walking along a meandering creek and saw a hole with mink tracks coming out of it in the mud. Chug set a trap there and caught his first mink. It took him until he was fifteen years old to catch his first red fox. "As a kid, I thought red fox were the hardest thing to trap." Chug would check his traps every morning before school with a flashlight. The year he caught his first red fox, he caught six more. He always liked to go to the traveling Groenewold Fur & Wool Co. early so he could see the furs other trappers brought in. He showed up that year with seven red fox, and other trappers were approaching him for the first time with questions about where he trapped them and how. "I was the man!" he joked. But at that time, it was a great accomplishment. "This year (2012), I got $90 for one [red fox], and that is what I got back then," Chug remembers.

That same year, Chug caught his first gray fox and more raccoons and muskrats. His thoughts were consumed by his traplines and what might lay in store on his next check. "I played football and I remember running out on the field, and I was thinking, *tomorrow is the opening day of 'coon season.* As a kid, I just kept getting more into it and kept learning more and more things. Back then, there were so many guys willing to show you how to do it. I can't imagine growing up any other way." Chug's childhood spent trapping and hunting influenced his life more than any other.

Fast forward about twenty years after catching that first raccoon. The lessons he learned about sticking to it, working hard, and persevering, have influenced everything he does. Chug owns and operates a successful business and lives with his wife and son in a beautiful home in the suburbs of Missoula, Montana. His daughter is pursuing higher education at a university. Her father graduated from the University of Montana with a business degree in 1992. Now a dark-haired, clean-cut man with calloused hands and broad shoulders—evidence of former football years—sits at his kitchen table with folded hands, sharing a lifetime of trapping and hunting adventures. The walls of his living room are adorned by taxidermy mounts of bobcats, deer, and elk antlers. Beautifully tanned pelts lay draped over his stairway. Each has a story. It is clear from the moment one walks into his home that Chug loves the outdoors. The rafters in his garage carry countless racks from elk and deer taken with the skillful hands of an archer. Every year during the elk rut, Chug sneaks away from his business for a week and is usually successful in bringing a bull elk home for the freezer. Like most trappers, Chug loves to hunt as well as trap, but his passion for trapping is far reaching.

When asked what it is about trapping he loves so much, he paused and stared for a moment into the past. "I guess it's the time of the year, the changing of the leaves, leaves falling off—I always feel like a kid again when I trap. I love putting up fur. I like to see it hanging, and I take pride in my fur."

Like many trappers, the quality of his pelts is a matter of pride. Hanging on a wall in a simple picture frame above a chest freezer in his garage is a letter from the North American Fur Auction (NAFA) for "Top Lot Trapper." Chug has received four such awards for his quality fur-handling abilities, and his goal is to eventually earn a top lot award for every species he traps for. So far, his fur-handling skills have earned him two "top lots" for beavers, one for mink, and another for bobcats. Top lot awards are given by NAFA for the very best pelts sold at auction on the world market each year. Receiving four is proof that this man knows how to handle fur.

The high-quality pelts Chug handles are the result of countless hours spent in remote backcountry areas and along public highways. Much of his trapping is done far from home to avoid conflict with other outdoor users. A typical trapping day for Chug begins with a cup of coffee at 6:00 a.m. before getting his son up and ready for school. When he drops him off at the bus stop, "That's always a great moment," he says. He races down the highway to get to his first bobcat set sixty-five miles one way from home. "A good day would obviously be catching a bobcat," he says.

But some years catching just one bobcat can take all his effort. He shook his head while rubbing his eyes. "Bobcats can be frustrating!"

"There's nothing more frustrating than seeing a cat track walking up to your set then seeing your trap and drag pulled ten feet away with nothing in it." Laminating trap jaws to increase the thickness makes a big difference in holding cats, according to Chug's experience. Proficient trappers don't happen by accident. It takes years of mentorship and practical application to gain the skills necessary, both in the field and at home on the work bench. "New trappers are overwhelmed with how much knowledge it takes and the equipment involved." The number of swivels, putting up fur . . . it's a complex sport, a lot more complex than hunting. With hunting, you can buy a rifle, throw a scope on it, and go out and shoot something. Trapping is like hunting elk with a bow, everything has to be right."

Trapping skills are demanding and are far more technical than hunting or fishing, in Chug's opinion. "You've got to have a lot of knowledge. You can go buy traps and set them out there, but you're not going to catch anything. There's a lot of time and investment. Like this year, spending money getting supplies, laminating, and four-coiling my traps, and you've got to know how to weld. I think a lot of people don't get into it because of the cost and the knowledge it takes."

Chug sets out about two dozen sets on the first day of bobcat season and adds several each day until he has about sixty sets out. "I check all my sets first then set out a few more each day." Chug checks his foot traps every forty-eight hours, and the total number he can set is limited because he has to race back home to meet his son at the bus stop at 3:15 p.m.

Chug's favorite trapping experiences these days come from his remote marten trapline, which he maintains via snowmobile. Because his line is strung out over many miles using small wooden boxes and 120 body gripping traps, Chug checks those traps once every week. The marten are dead almost instantly and freeze solid in the high country. On those checks, he drives in the opposite direction from where his bobcat sets were in December and instead drives over one hundred miles where he parks his truck and trailer. "My favorite animal to trap is marten just because of being in the mountains. No one is around, and you are usually catching something every time you check." Chug likes to set out about sixty marten boxes and hangs them vertically on tree bases. He makes his own bait by freezing meat in mesh bags and wires them inside homemade cedar boxes. Fish oil is applied to the base of the tree every time he checks to create a scent trail from the ground to the box located at least four feet from the ground.

Chug maintains about a hundred and twenty traps and an additional thirty snares at a time throughout the winter. When Chug grew up trapping, he had a twenty-four-hour trap check law, but things were different in rural Wisconsin. "Back there, it didn't seem to be an issue. You didn't need to go that far. Montana is so big." He adds that "the trappers who are good and care about trapping are going to check their traps religiously. They are going to fight through the mud, snow, rain—whatever." While Chug feels strongly about checking his foothold traps routinely every forty-eight hours, he doesn't like it for marten because there is absolutely no benefit to checking those traps frequently since the marten are dispatched quickly and are preserved by cold temperatures. Because of this, he says, "I don't like a trap check law, especially for marten."

In early March, when bobcat and marten trapping seasons are closed, Chug switches to beaver and muskrat trapping. Using dried castor glands and shells, he grinds them up with a coffee grinder and adds glycerin for preservative and antifreeze. A simple pile of mud to simulate a castor mound with a dash of his homemade beaver lure is enough to bring beaver in close. "Sometimes the simplest sets work the best," he said.

When asked about his thoughts on people who oppose trapping and are trying to stop it from use as a commercial and/or recreational activity, he said he feels sorry for them and wonders how often they will come home and say things like "I saw wolverine tracks today."

The subject sparked serious emotion, and he went into a long explanation of his thoughts and feelings on the animal rights movement in our country. "Well, my thoughts are that I actually feel sorry for people that are animal rights people. They don't get the way that I was raised and the way that I grew up, I feel sorry that they couldn't experience that. I don't think most of them have a clue about what we do—tree huggers or whatever you want to call them—they just want to jeopardize our way of life, and they want to shove it down our throats. It's really frustrating and it really bothers me, and that's why I am part of the MTA and fight for what we have," Chug explained.

"It's a sore subject. Just the thought of them taking away something we love so much is what bothers me the most. I think ultimately they want a completely natural ecosystem—they want to start by eliminating trapping first. If they are going to try to take trapping from us they are definitely going to go right down the line. The hunter the fisherman, it's all the same thing. You're shoving a hook in a fish's mouth and yanking it in . . . you're shooting an elk with a bow . . . ultimately they want a natural ecosystem and they don't want man to be a part of it. I think they just want to start with trapping. Why they want to start with trapping I'm just not sure, it's probably the easiest target for them. They can paint a picture in everybody's mind that it's cruel and inhumane. They just don't know what it's like to run a trapline or to be out in the mountains in winter checking traps, I mean to me it's the greatest thing that there is, I don't know what else I'd do.

"A lot of times, I think that I could take them with me and turn them into liking it, I really do. I'm not going to—some of those people are wacked out. I don't think they were raised right. I don't think they had the opportunities to experience wildlife or harvest it. We are at the top of the food chain and we are the main predator and we are smart, so we can use all different tools to harvest animals. It makes complete sense to me, but not to them. We are part of the food chain for sure. I am a strong believer in that. I think that's why we hunt and why we eat animals. I think they are trying to get us all out of the woods so they can go watch it from their car or whatever they want to do. It really bothers me that they spend their money and their time trying to stop us from trapping. It really, really irritates me. If they really want to practice what they are shoving down our throat, they should just not move and stay in a room all day. If you're going to live, man, you're going to kill animals . . . we can't take them lightly. They can brainwash a majority of the public who doesn't really care or know anything about it, and that's what worries me the most. They go after the emotions with their pets—that's their number one tool."

Chug is concerned about the future of trapping and trapper recruitment but says there are simple things trappers can do to help educate others and preserve the trapping and hunting way of life—things such as representing trappers well in everything we say and do. "Check your traps or don't set them. Trap ethically and use the right equipment," he said. "And don't have a dead beaver lying in the back of your truck . . . use common sense."

But perhaps the most important thing a new trapper can do is exactly what Chug's father arranged for him so many years ago. "Go with a mentor, especially young trappers." This may be the single most important piece of advice for anyone interested in learning how to trap. Veteran trappers love to share their knowledge, and it will make an incredible difference in a young or new trapper's success. By joining a trappers association and participating in trapper's education classes, everyone benefits.

Chug is the epitome of the modern-day trapper. When the season comes, he heads to the mountains to carry on his proud heritage with skilled hands and knowledge gained from years of mentorship and natural study. Tracks in the snow, the cold air on his face, and the success of a well-placed trap are enough to satisfy his trapper's heart. Through the season, his interests change from bobcat and marten to beaver and muskrat, but each animal brings with it something new. Prime fur and solace found only on his trapline draw him out each day until the season's end.

In his memories lay another year, another trapline set. He peers into a small cave made of rock. He laid a trap in there a short time ago. His flashlight illuminates the texture of the rock and dry soil protected from wind and rain. For a moment, he is twelve years old again, and he marvels at how well this lifestyle fits, and knows that any other couldn't. It's simple. He's a trapper, and always will be.

"Talks-a-Lot"

All great men are gifted with intuition. They know without reasoning or analysis, what they need to know.

—Alexis Carrel

Trappers are generally a solitary breed, hidden in forests or pickup trucks in all types of weather as they go about their own business. But some trappers stick out like a sore thumb, give input at every fur handling or educational gathering they can, and promote trapping ethics at virtually every turn they make. These rare individuals aren't afraid to take a stance. They wear their years on the trapline like a badge of honor and share the love of trapping to anyone who will listen. Although "Trapper Talks-a-Lot" is a first-rate trapper, it's the example he sets for all trappers that makes him stand out. Talks-a-Lot spends every free minute he has standing up for trappers, and is known by virtually every wildlife official in Montana. He works hard to articulate his message in a manner which reflects well on trappers everywhere. When I first approached Talks-a-Lot

about an interview, he told me there were at least a thousand trappers in
Montana alone who might be better to ask. After he agreed to do it, I
listened as a voice frequently heard by legislators, senators, fish and game
personnel, and students told a life-long trappers story.

The wilderness was home for Talks-a-Lot in the early seventies after
serving his country for two years in Vietnam. For four years, when
October came, it meant gathering up horses and packing in supplies for a
long winter, deep into the heart of the Bob Marshall Wilderness. Around
Thanksgiving time, the horses were brought out, and a single snowshoe
trip deep into the back country severed ties with the modern world until
April or May. Talks-a-Lot spent up to eleven months out of the year in
the remote backcountry trapping, hunting, and packing in camps for
outfitters. Throughout his life, Talks-a-Lot guided lion hunters and also
hunted lions in his free time. His outdoor pursuits included logging,
where he followed lumber camps across the Pacific Northwest and into
Alaska. Talks-a-Lot explained that in those days, a man with any work
ethic whatsoever could find a job at a lumber camp, and his stories of
those days are filled with adventure and crazy acts of bravery, remote
camps, and rugged men.

Talks-a-Lot has returned to his beloved Bob Marshall Wilderness year
after year to trap, hunt, and feel the wilderness as a participant in that
wild place. It was here that Talks-a-Lot caught his first wolverine while
running a beaver line along a remote creek. His ability to tell a story with
vigor and enthusiasm is reminiscent of the mountain men that preceded
him.

"I was snowshoeing through the wilderness. I was living in there and
I was trapping beaver down in the creeks and chopping a lot of ice, and
I only had to go three or four miles one way. And sometime during the
day, I just started getting a weird feeling and I thought, *I've been in the
mountains too long by myself.*

"That night, I was snowshoeing back and just got through a couple of
patches of real dark timber with a big old full moon out there, and I was
just spooked. I thought I must have just been reading too many stories
at night or something, and I came back over a little point and I looked
over. And out of that dark timber come a wolverine. He was following my
tracks. He seen me then. I jumped up and he seen me, and I never got a
shot at him." He said as if it happened yesterday.

"In them days, you didn't need a special tag or anything, and there
wasn't a limit on them. So the next day, I went out, and he had picked up

on me someplace. And he was following me all around, but he couldn't really do much with the beaver traps under the ice. So I went over to a little knoll and set a couple traps, and I thought, *I'll get that rascal.* A couple days later, I came back and crawled up on there—and it was ten or twelve feet up to this little bench and it overlooked this low ground for half to three quarters of a mile—and I came crawling up there and poked my head over, and this thing with all these teeth come up and snap! Looked like he was going to bite my nose off! Well, I flipped over backward and rolled down the hill without even knowing what it was. I just knew it was something with a lot of teeth! I'd caught that wolverine." After shooting it, he realized the wolverine was only caught by two toes. "It might have been pretty damned exciting. It was exciting enough as it was, but that always stands out in my mind."

Talks-a-Lot spent countless days in the far reaches of Montana's backcountry wilderness all through the winter for years. He would come out on snowshoes in the spring to gather mules to pack out furs and restock, only to return to guide for dude ranches all summer long and elk hunters through the autumn. During that time, Talks-a-Lot learned more about wildlife and wild animals than most people will ever dream of. His interest in wildlife led him to lay on beaver lodges for hours, where he listened to beavers communicate with various vocalizations. After months of doing this, he learned that beavers have five distinct vocalizations, which indicate what their behavior will be after exiting the lodge.

Years later, while working at an outfitters' camp, he met his future bride who was also working for the same outfitter. "She wouldn't talk to me for a year," he recalled. "They said I was a little wild after I got out of Vietnam, but I doubt if that were true." He laughed.

As time went on, Talks-a-Lot and his wife lived a wilderness lifestyle, as Talks-a-Lot recalled. "We were only living in an 8x30 camp trailer, okay, and you gotta put the beaver on the boards. And so, when you want to cook supper, you put all the beavers over by the kitchen table. And when you wanted to eat supper, you move all the beaver over by the stove, and then you put the food on the table! This is how we went through winter, coyotes on stretchers . . . you couldn't wiggle. It was a wreck to say the least." He laughed.

One day, his wife said, "You know, I never see you."

"Well, you knew what I did before we ever got married," Talks-a-Lot replied, thinking she was referring to all the months he spent in the backcountry.

"I expected that, but I figured I'd at least get to see you in the winter. And now all day long, you're gone from before daylight until after dark, and then you get back and you're skinning fur. And we're living in camp trailer—we are not doing this next year!" she demanded.

Talks-a-Lot built an addition onto the camp trailer, which gave them a wood stove and more room, but that didn't solve the time spent away from home. So Talks-a-Lot suggested that she come along with him.

"So I says, come along, and so she did, and mink prices was pretty good that winter. They was like forty bucks an average on my mink that winter. I sold them to Frazier, and he was the best buyer on the mink. At any rate, so I says, well come along, and so she did, and so I'm showing her what I'm doing. I'm explain this is why I'm doing it because the mink, he does this and he does that and he does the other, and here's his tracks and this that and the other. 'Well, you may as well have some hip boots so you can get in the water and see this stuff,' and so I got her hip boots and then pretty quick, 'You may as well carry some of this stuff too,' and so she's got a pack basket and hip boots, and I says there ain't no sense in both of us doing the same damn line! She got pretty good at catching those mink. She figured them out and got pretty darn good at them. So I made her a deal that every seventh muskrat or mink that she would skin and flesh and put up, one was to go to her for a fur coat. She wanted a fur coat. But in them days, 'rats was five bucks. It wasn't as good as it was back east, but for Montana, that was pretty good prices, and pretty much straight through them 'rats was five bucks, so no way was one of them five-dollar ones going back out of the pot, ya know it's what we were living off of. But I says, 'We'll get you one,' and when the 'rats went back down to 50¢ or 75¢, well then I caught a batch and she got her fur coat. So in essence, that muskrat fur coat she wears, she caught it. She earned it." He laughed.

His wife trapped for several years but didn't like to trap beavers because beavers are too big and the traps too strong. She also doesn't like coyotes because they have fleas.

These days, Trapper Talks-a-Lot still loves to run his trapline, and jokingly claims that he hangs around good trappers in hopes he'll gain knowledge through osmosis. His perspective on trapping, politics, and education are unique because of his direct involvement in all three aspects. When asked what he likes to trap for the most, he was quick to reply. "Anything with four feet and fur! Mostly coyotes and beaver. Beaver are a really good entryway to a place because they are a lot of work, but

I really like them. So when I trap the beaver, it opens up the ground for the rest of the stuff. Skunks are a good one for that too," Talks-a-Lot explained. "But I think beaver are the big game animal of the furbearer world, I think. They're a lot of work but, man, they are so cool!"

Talks-a-Lot has been fortunate to trap some of the same private ranches for years and attributes his success to using sound management principles. "If you're going to be a successful trapper, management is a prime thing. If you can't manage the animals to a certain degree, you're not going to be consistently successful. The more you learn, the more you know and the more you find out you don't know." Talks-a-Lot said.

The trapline is not the only place Talks-a-Lot has had to learn to manage. The growing political cloud has spread to Montana. New groups of nonconsumptive users are crowding the "Last Best Place" with foreign views. "What irritates me the most about the whole politics deal is that, in essence, what they're trying to do is that—they have, I'm going to call it a religion because I firmly believe that's where they're coming from. And they are trying to force their thoughts, their morals, their religion down my throat. Then trying to force me to follow that agenda, and I have a real problem with that. I feel that, between them and the media, they are infringing upon my own personal rights. I don't want to spend my time and money going to meetings dealing with legislators and senators, and fish and game people—it just ain't my bag. But somebody's got to do it. I believe if you are going to have something worth standing up for, it's worth fighting for, and you're going to have to put the effort forth. That's the reason I got into this education program. If you start educating people, it's going to involve you in the politics, because they're tied hand and glove. Instructors don't got to be a John Graham or a Ron Legget. They just got to be a trapper, and a trapper is simple. It's a fella that likes to trap and has spent some time doing it. That's all it takes."

Trapper education both in the classroom and in normal day-to-day life plays a key role in the advancement of the trapper's agenda. But it takes hard work and dedication. "Thirty years ago, you'd have played hell convincing me that I would've been in front of so many people as I have been talking about trapping, promoting trapping, and the aspects of it because I just wanted to do my trapping. I didn't like getting in front of groups—never did, still don't. I get a bad case of stage fright. I make up my mind, I'm going to try to get my point across in an articulate and lucid manner—I've had to work at this, believe me," he said.

Talks-a-Lot also shares trapping with fellow trappers and is eager to learn from others. "We have a fur handling clinic every year for our district. It's usually early in January. There's always something you can learn, people just bring what they've got. We've had fisher coyotes, otter, beaver, skunks, and marten all at once. And another time, it was strictly coyotes, because that's what everyone had. I think that's a really great thing, because I wish I had someone show me that when I was younger. Like Trapper Walks-a-Lot says, 'More money has been lost through mishandled fur than was ever lost by stolen traps or somebody shooting it.' If you're going to kill the animal, utilize it to the best of your ability. If I would have known all of this over the years, particularly back in the 70s and 80s, I would have literally made thousands of dollars just because I could have handled my fur so much better."

Talks-a-Lot's willingness to learn and share led him to Indiana, where he graduated from the Fur Takers of America Trappers College in 2005. "Just go! You will learn so much, all the instructors were just great," he urged.

Talks-a-Lot also urges new trappers to join an association, because as he says, "The old guys will help teach the youngsters how to handle fur. By joining an association, you get immediate and direct access to that, and I don't know any of them who won't help."

Talks-a-Lot shared how some members of the Association have hard feelings about the outcomes of meetings. Some have gotten mad and quit. Talks-a-Lot feels that trappers are some of the hardest-headed people there is, and he has had disagreements with other trappers, and it took looking at things from their perspective to change his mind. "A person can get stuck in one track. Especially when you spend time by yourself a lot, you start thinking that you're always right, well you find out you're not always right," he said emphatically. Considering things from another angle has changed his mind on a multitude of things, and he adds, "Maybe it works that way for other people too." He contends that if we had all the trappers in the state united instead of some that sit off to the side, trappers could be a powerful voice in Montana.

There is no reason to quit fighting for what you believe in. Quitting is not an option. With two exceptions, "For health reasons or if you die, those are the only reasons," Talks-a-Lot said, reaffirming his conviction.

One of the biggest concerns Talks-a-Lot has is when fur prices are on the rise. Trappers have told him on several occasions that they just bought a bunch of traps then ask, "So how do I catch a bobcat?"

"I hate to see high prices, I really like it in my fur check . . . but I hate to see the drain on the resource and the problems that are attributed to it." He said, speaking about the people who think they can just put traps out and make a lot of money.

"These trappers have never set a trap in their life, and now they are going to go out and scatter them around in the woods. They don't know anything about what they are doing. First off, they didn't learn anything about the biology of the animal, they're just looking at money, and that ain't the reason that I trap." Talks-a-Lot's sentiment rings true to most trappers, and although money is one objective for trappers, it is not the primary objective. "The trappers that I know, that ain't the reason that they trap either. It's definitely secondary," he said. Talks-a-Lot worries about new trappers who don't take trapper's education classes. "The biggest thing this day and age, dealing with the other users, is to keep in mind that whatever you do. Your actions should reflect that you are aware of the outdoors users that are out there—whether they are consumptive users or not."

Talks-a-Lot is a man who embodies the Montana trapping legacy. His love for the wilderness and the lifestyle that chose him is rare. He spent years on traplines and in remote hunting and logging camps, nestled in the most rugged wildlands the world has to offer. The wildlands and wild places he knows intimately are but a faraway place on a map to most. To him, they are the places that really matter. The source of his livelihood, the real world revealed. Montana's rich trapping heritage lives on, not in the storybooks of history, but through men like Talks-a-Lot with fur-laden mules traveling over a high mountain pass to sell his wares and resupply. It happened yesterday. It happened today, and it will continue to happen tomorrow.

"Trapper Walks-a-Lot"

> I see what you mean, but I do not think what you think.

> —Mason Cooley

In the early 1950s, American family gardens were nurtured more out of necessity than the more common elaborate hobby gardens of the twenty-first century. Backyards produced winter wares to be preserved in glass canning jars or freezers. It was at this time when Trapper Walks-a-Lot and his younger brother were given the responsibility to take care of the garden. His dad would till and fertilize the soil, but after that, it was up to Walks-a-Lot and his brother to make sure the vegetables grew until harvest time. Each year, along with the arrival of blooming flowers and fresh garden plants, came the inevitable arrival of hungry gophers. The rodents would pluck the efforts of the Walks-a-Lot boys every year, but not for long. Walks-a-Lot was paid 5¢ for each striped gopher, and 10¢ for pocket gophers, by his father. Traps began making him additional income at around age five, a recurring theme that would follow him throughout his life. The brothers were on the honor system for the number of gophers they caught, and they were instructed to bury them in the backyard once they were paid. Trapping to protect his family's produce was as much a part of daily life as going to church on Sunday.

Around that time, his uncles were long-line mink trappers who would run traplines that carried them 200-250 miles in their vehicles each day. They would work hard all summer, paving highways and all winter trapping wild fur. In those days, wild mink was a top-priced fur product, and these men made half their living via fur sales. At a point in young Walks-a-Lot's life, his uncle would board at his house and took Walks-a-Lot along to tend his traplines. "He showed me a lot of the blind setting, how to cover the miles, the creeks, the waterways, and how if we looked under a bridge along the way and someone had it set up. We would go upstream or downstream, making as little disturbance as possible and make a good set. He taught me a lot of that trade," Walks-a-Lot explained.

His uncle told Walks-a-Lot that when and if he started using lures and attractors on his own mink line to use Hawbaker's products out of Pennsylvania, a lure product that is still available to trappers today. "It took me a while before I learned that you not only have to have a good lure, you have to be in the right location," Walks-a-Lot added.

He rode his bicycle to manage his first traplines until he was old enough to drive. Then he started covering more ground. At that time, there were three local fur buyers in the area, and Walks-a-Lot remembers one distinctly: Ezra, who chain smoked cigarettes. "And he would light one off the other, and he was dying of lung cancer. I know he was, because you would walk into his fur shed—he had a mink farm—and he would cough and wheeze the words 'what do you got here throw it up here on the table—*cough, hack, cough, wheeze,*'" Walks-a-Lot mimicked.

Old Ezra would look them all over and make an offer before hacking and coughing again. "And you'd expect he was going to be dead of lung cancer the next year, but when the next year and the fall rolled around, my dad would drive us up there and sure enough—we'd go in there with our grocery sack with two to three mink and fifty to sixty muskrats, and there he was, *cough, cough, cough!* And it was quite a routine, I'll tell ya," he said with his distinctive scruffy voice and straightforward, matter-of-fact demeanor before roaring with laughter.

His uncle would take him along on weekends, and if he skinned his mink and stretched them—which he did on a basswood stretcher—and scraped the fat off with a spoon, Walks-a-Lot could have all the muskrats and raccoons caught on his uncle's trapline. "It wasn't a good quality fleshing. Now I take the saddle off and make them look clean, I've got a two by four that I made down for mink."

Number 1 ½ long-spring traps were set for muskrats in bank holes by Walks-a-Lot, but in that time period a grade 1 XL mink pelt was getting $42 on the fur market. In stark contrast were the muskrats, which received just 35¢, and even the best raccoon would receive $2.50, and that was a half a day's work getting, the raccoon skins prepared. "Our fur handling was extremely rough in those days." Walks-a-Lot remembers.

It was also at this time that Walks-a-Lot first learned from his uncles that there were people who didn't like trappers, regardless of whether they knew one or not. "My uncles would tell me, 'There's people out there who don't like us, they don't like trappers or trapping—keep that in mind . . .' But I just assumed everybody loved it. It didn't bother me. It was like in one ear and out the other."

It never really sank in that the animal rights movement had any effect on his trapping, hunting and fishing lifestyle. "It was a way of life for us," he recalls. "The whole family would jump in the boat on the weekends in the summer. We'd go out fishing, filling our baskets with our limits of fish. If the limit was twenty-five blue gills, we caught twenty-five blue gills. If our limit was fifty, we caught fifty. Ya know, we looked like a troller out there!"

When deer season came, his family had nine days to fill their allotted permits and put meat in the freezer. For the first two days of the season, each hunter could take a doe or a buck. Walks-a-Lot, his father, and his brother would usually all "fill up" on white-tailed does taken with 12 gauge shotguns and rifled slugs, which at best achieved twelve-inch groups at fifty yards, even when rested on sandbags at a rifle range. "That's the best you could do, it sounds like a joke, but that's how they shot!" he recalled.

Walks-a-Lot went on to proudly serve his country in the United States Marine Corps, in infantry platoon I-3-7, from 1966-1968. After thirteen months in South Vietnam, he returned home and got back to doing what he loves, trapping.

In the early 1970s, Walks-a-Lot met a man in South Dakota named Gerald, who worked nights at a radio station and spent his days trapping. Gerald would trap five hundred to seven hundred fox in the month of October before packing up his vehicle and heading to the Arizona desert to trap coyotes and bobcats all winter. Gerald bought furs and would also sell urine and lures, which he made himself. It was the accomplishments of Gerald which inspired Walks-a-Lot to really strive to make a profit trapping.

Walks-a-Lot worked at an auto-body shop, which allowed him to arrange plenty of time to trap. "That's what I did to support my trapping habits," he joked.

Even while his trapping skills improved and he began to take trapping more seriously, he still had a lot to learn about marketing his fur. Like many trappers, Walks-a-Lot sold to local fur buyers and dabbled in shipping furs to various sales around the country. But as he compared his fur prices received to the receipts of other trappers who had sent their furs to Canada for sale on the world market, he couldn't believe what he had been missing.

After moving to Montana from South Dakota, he immediately joined the Montana Trappers Association. One of the first Montana trappers he met was a man named Howard, the district 2 director at the time, who showed Walks-a-Lot his returns. "When he showed me some of his returns, I'll tell ya, he just blew the doors off me. I looked at that stuff in just disbelief—I couldn't believe it, I had been selling coyotes for sixty bucks, and he was averaging $120-140 apiece straight across the average." Walks-a-Lot shipped one hundred beavers to a fur auction in New York and received a $9-$10 average, while Howard received an average of $32-35 apiece for beavers from the same region of the country. Another shipment to a sale in Colorado paid him about $12.50 apiece, and that was the final straw. "I said that is it! If I'm going to be out there doing the work with the blood, sweat, and tears, I'm going to start making some profit, and the next year, everything I had went to the Dominion Soudack . . . and when my checks came back, I'd died and went to heaven!" He laughed. "So the lights went on, but it took a while," he continued.

"I feel somewhat guilty about not supporting the state sale here in Montana because I know they get darn good prices for quality stuff, and they keep it fair as far as the buyers—the amount of them—they come and you get legitimate good offers on your stuff there." Walks-a-Lot is loyal to NAFA and continues to market his fur on the world market through that auction house.

The late spring and early summer months are the off season for fur trappers, so when Walks-a-Lot saw an ad for nuisance trappers in Oregon, he sent in his resume. He initially thought the job was for problem coyotes but learned that timber companies struggled with black bears damaging their planted forests. They have tried to feed the bears with nutritious supplements and used nonlethal deterrents. However, like many operations in forestry and agriculture, they needed experienced trappers to remove problem animals. The bears would rip the bark off tender trees at a critical time of the year and the trees would die.

The head of the operation flew into Montana and spent time with Walks-a-Lot on his trapline and interviewed him at the same time. Walks-a-Lot was quickly hired, and he spent the months of May to July in Oregon for five years, helping the timber companies resolve nuisance bear issues with humane foot snares. All bears terminated during this time were used in their entirety. The meat was processed by a packing company and shipped to Portland to feed poor people living on the street. This is a fine example of using natural resources on a sustained yield basis to create jobs, feed the homeless, and all the while supporting overall wildlife health.

Walks-a-Lot's garage is primarily used for storing traps and putting up fur. Large chest freezers line the outside walls, and traps are piled in the middle of the floor, ready for use or modification. Skins are placed in the freezers and rolled up for fleshing and stretching at a later date. "I allow about a month and a half to two months. Basically, July and August are strictly to put up fur . . . but if I get both freezers full, then my back's against the wall, and I've got to start fleshing, stretching, and drying furs as it goes," he explained.

This system of catching and freezing fur to be put up at a later date also works well for his marketing strategy. "If you were only going to sell at one sale in Canada, you would do the February sale, every time," Walks-a-Lot advised, and he should know, he received and shipped fur for ten years for Canadian fur sales. In the early 1990s, the Northern European Economic Community tried to institute a ban on wild fur being shipped into Europe from countries that use foothold traps. "It's the animal rights mentality in Northern Europe thinking they can bully the rest of the world into not buying or using their fur product. And the thing they were trying to ban is probably the most humane, selective, best tool ever invented for trapping—the steel-jawed foothold trap . . . so many people don't realize that," he said emphatically.

Another thing people don't realize is that every individual pelt shipped out of the country has a bar code stapled to it, which traces that pelt back to an account owner. The fur industry is heavily regulated, in the U.S. and the rest of the world.

In 1994, Walks-a-Lot decided that he wanted to get more involved in educating people about the benefits of trapping and began teaching trapper's education. His reasons for getting involved were, in large part, to thwart the efforts of the animal rights movement slowly moving into the western U.S., as Walks-a-Lot explained, "All along I could start to see what I call 'Californication.' I don't mean to alienate people from California because most of them are probably good people. But when you get the bad ones that have been indoctrinated by Mickey Mouse and Donald Duck and anthropomorphisms that put animals on the same scale or level as a human being, they are really bad because they're not just satisfied to believe their agenda, they have to force it on other people. I could see that coming, and I could see the way we were getting blasted every time there was an incident with an unethical trapper, and I'm not sticking up for every unethical trapper you know, they are out there." He said.

Walks-a-Lot is convinced that the best way to preserve our consumptive wildlife lifestyle is by educating people, particularly young people. "Everybody just kind of laughs about Bambi, Mickey Mouse, and Donald Duck being human beings, but Walt Disney—in making his millions of dollars like most successful business people in the entertainment industry—I think he got to more of those people and their mentality, and it even goes deeper than thinking Mickey Mouse and Donald Duck are human beings and having feelings. A trapper feels a sense of accomplishment when he gets his fur check back. These people into this anthropomorphic cult feel good about themselves when they leave their entire estate to the HSUS. They really believe they're doing the right thing, and I think if we're going to combat these people, we've got to beat them at their own games," he said.

Walks-a-Lot later explained, "With this anti thing, don't ever, ever drop your guard, and don't ever think you've got it made. They're going to come at you with every angle they can." And it isn't just wild consumptive users. The animal rights agenda is far broader than hunters, trappers, and anglers, as Walks-a-Lot continued, "They are poisoning these young minds to where the trapper, hunter, or fishermen or any consumptive user is public enemy number one—they're just demonizing us. Why they picked us [trappers], I don't know. They won't stand a chance against the cattlemen yet, but they are knocking on the cattle industry's door . . ."

When Walks-a-Lot isn't educating people on the benefits of ethical trapping, he actively traps through the season. His success stands as evidence of his intimate understanding of animal behavior, but that doesn't mean that he gets them all. "One of these long walks down in a dark, cold little hole to check a bobcat trap . . . the year before I had just gotten top lot, $1,200 bucks for one really nice, big blue tom bobcat topped the market with it, and I was going down in the same vicinity to check a trap. It was a cubby, kind of a baited set. I looked, and I could tell by the way it was torn up, I had a cat. And all I had with me was my pistol, and the first thing I always do is look to see how well it is caught. And it looked to me like it was caught by one or two toes, and when I looked at the trap, I could not see anything under the jaws. I thought, *oh, I'm twenty feet away or so, it's a heck of a chance. If I fire this pistol and I miss, it's going to be gone.* I backed out of there real slow. It never moved a muscle, it just sat there and stared at me. I backed out real slow and got the .22 rifle, and I snuck real slow back down in there, ya know, 'cause I was thinking about $1,200-1,500 bucks sitting there, looking at me. And it's an old Stevens single shot, and I pulled back the thing to make it click. That cat went straight up in the air, out of the trap—I seen the tip of its black-tipped tail, one flash into the green, and it was gone! And I've never caught that cat yet!"

Luckily, for Walks-a-Lot, the furbearer numbers seem to be higher than ever in Montana. When it was suggested that maybe he was just getting better, he said, "I don't know. They call me 'Walks-a-Lot,' but I'm walking less and less every year. When my wife rides along, she makes that comment all the time, you're getting to be a lot more like the Drive-By Trapper!"

Wild animals are always a challenge for trappers to deal with, and domestic animals can be just as difficult. Walks-a-Lot often brings his dog along on his trapline and has had domestic horses attack his dog and destroy his vehicle while he was hiking along on his trapline.

Over the many years, Walks-a-Lot ran traplines from the Oregon Coast to Wisconsin, and countless areas in between. It's always been because he loves trapping that he continued on. Trapping is hard work and requires year-round dedication to make a profit, but the reason he loves trapping so much isn't because of the money he earns doing it. It's about learning, spending time outdoors, symbiotically participating in nature, and challenging himself to be the best he can be.

"Trapping's been so good to me over the years. I can't think of a profession that would have been more satisfying or more fitting for me than being a trapper," he said.

When asked why he loves trapping, he leaned back in his chair, spoke deliberately, and thoughtfully explained why after sixty years of trapping, he had no intention of hanging up his traps anytime soon. "Expectation, I love reading the sign. I love learning about the animals. I love making the sets. I love the learning aspect of getting to know your territory, your animal, and making the best set physically and mentally possible, and then coming back and checking it and seeing how you've done. It's sense of accomplishment. I'd rather have the animal teach me, he's the best teacher I ever had."

"Drive-By Trapper"

Judge not, lest ye be judged.

—Jesus Christ

A lifetime of sharing knowledge of wildlife has taken one Montana trapper from private ranches to public schools, and he continues to "pass it on" every chance he gets. After a walk through the "Drive-By Trapper's" home, I got the impression that this man loves the outdoors. Unique artifacts collected over the years adorn his home, including a whale vertebrae and a walrus skull—complete with long ivory tusks imprinted with genuine Native American artistry. More traditional hunting gems include deer, elk, and moose antlers, while a mountain goat taken by Drive-By in 1976 complement two antelope taken in 1965 by him and his wife on their honeymoon. Sitting at the kitchen table, surrounded by old photos and hunting paraphernalia, Drive-By shared stories of the army, welding, hunting, and trapping. His views on recent wildlife management and the politics of it all came out with strong ties to the local ranching community.

Around 1942, Drive-By was offered 10¢ for every rat he trapped around his family's barn. If he cleaned out the chicken coup, he was paid anther dime. He recalled the drudgery of cleaning out the chicken manure and the candy bars he could buy with the hard-earned money. One day, a local man told him that the muskrats swimming out in the lake eating aquatic vegetation could bring more money to a trapper than cleaning out the chicken coup. So it was in 1946 when Drive-By saved his money and purchased a number 1 Victor long-spring trap and a trapping license, and managed to trap three muskrats. He sold those first muskrats and used the money to order two more traps, which at the time, cost him 23¢ each.

As a young boy, Drive-By recalled hunting squirrels and rabbits near his home. A brand new J. C. Higgins 12 gauge, purchased for $25.88 from Sears and Roebuck in the fall of 1949, was his first shotgun. His earliest big-game hunting experiences were humble, Drive-By recalled. "Dad never took me out and got me shooting with a slug. When you're shooting squirrels on a limb, you just point the thing and bang, the squirrel just falls off. But with a slug, you've got to aim. Well, the first year we went deer hunting, I missed nine deer. I mean, I couldn't believe it! It sounds terrible, but it's the truth!"

In 1956, Drive-By was turned down by the Harley Davidson Motor Company for a job as a welder on the assembly line. As he walked out the door, he walked right back in again, following a group on a tour of the facility. The next morning, Drive-By stood in front of the foreman once again and explained that he knew he had the skills to perform the type of welding the job demanded. He was given five hours to prove himself. It only took three.

That same perseverance showed through again when after being drafted into the army in 1961, Drive-By decided he wanted to make corporal before his time was up. As 2,400 men marched off the U.S. Darby in 1963, there was just one double skeet wing corporal in the group—Drive-By Trapper.

Being a welder for local ranchers has its advantages, and soon, he found his way onto ranches that most people could only view from a distance. Coyotes are a major cause of lamb and calf mortality, and when a problem coyote starts killing domestic animals, it equates to a loss of revenue. Ranchers can't afford to lose livestock to predation.

Perhaps it is this agriculturally utilitarian-based mentality that led Drive-By to love coyote trapping so much. "My favorite animal to trap is a coyote. Whether I use snares or footholds, it doesn't make any difference either one. They are a neat animal to trap. And when you've got one in, either a foothold or a snare, you've done your thing proper," said Drive-By.

Drive-By makes his own gland scent from the coyotes he traps. He learned the recipe from an old government trapper, who told him not to tell too many people in his area or it will spook the coyotes. And the gland lure made from selected glands and meat from the coyote isn't only effective on coyotes, Drive-By explained, "Every bobcat I ever have ever caught in a foothold trap was caught with that coyote gland scent that I make up." Later on in the year, he adds glycerin to freeze proof his lure. And as the temperature drops, he also adds skunk essence for additional attraction.

One time, a man asked Drive-By if he had a place to put a mule that had died recently. Rather than allow the animal to simply be buried and go to waste, Drive-By utilized the animal in true trapper's practical fashion. "That was the best draw station I ever have had in my life. I don't know what it is with a mule or a horse, but that 'drawed' them coyotes in. I took thirty coyotes off of that carcass. The closest I put a trap or snare, I think was about one hundred yards. I even went farther on trails. And that was on a small ranch. It was only eight hundred acres, that was a good one," he said.

Drive-By builds his snares and locks using chainsaw links and heating them in ashes, which have an annealing effect on the metal. He then bends the links into a ninety-degree angle and has a tried-and-true method for making snare locks. The locks meet the state regulated break-away requirements and function perfectly. His favorite cable is a 5/64 inch, 7x7 cable.

Coyotes fascinate Drive-By with their behavior. "I've seen coyotes come down the trail in fresh snow and see that snare, and I can remember one. I can see it just like it was happening five minutes ago. He came down that trail, it was a cow trail, and he hit the skids. And I am certain he got his head right into that snare, but he backed up and he took right off, and ran right up the hill full bore. I don't know what the thing was, but he was truckin', and he almost got it! He slid, at least I would say, ten to twelve inches on all four, coming down that downhill grade," Drive-By remembers.

A small lock on snares seems to be less noticeable to wary coyotes. "You get some pretty dad—gum smart coyotes once in a while. One year I got there and there the snare hangs, and I was looking at that thing, and there wasn't any snow—it was early. I usually start at the end of October, and there was the snare hanging there, and it was chewed off. And I thought, *What the heck,* ya know, and I figured it out that this coyote come along and got into that snare. And he was very intelligent, he sat right down on the spot and chewed the snare in half—in two—and went on about his merry way." Drive-By explained that this coyote did the same thing again the following year, but was eventually caught by another trapper four miles away.

Drive-By has noticed that coyotes will travel in big circles. After seeing numerous coyote tracks and scat in an area, Drive-By would set out his traps. But sometimes he had to wait ten days before they came back through the area. But when they are moving through an area, Drive-By has caught as many as seven coyotes in one day in a small area. One day, Drive-By had several snares set in a location where coyotes were funneled into tight draws perpendicular to steep ravines. Coyotes were drawn into the area in late winter, following the deer herds. "They seem to run them deer downhill, and they get them running downhill. And right when they have to switch gears right in the bottom of the draw, that's when the coyotes get on 'em," he explained. Drive-By learned the habits of the deer and coyotes by observing the tracks in the snow while hunting and trapping. His familiarity with the area is remarkable—the result of more than forty years of wildlife study in close proximity to home.

Trappers like Drive-By, who spend years hunting and trapping on familiar lands, develop a real sense of the land and all the things happening on it. Few people—other than trappers—who have spent a majority of their lives studying the intricacies of the local ecology, have such a vested interest in the land and its inhabitants, whether wild, domestic, or human.

This knowledge, in combination with patience, culminated in several remarkable catches, as Drive-By recalled, "I had four up one draw. I hiked up that draw. It was about three-quarters of a mile up in there, and I got one way up at the end up there, and I was packing them down two at a time. And then I'd drop them, and then go back and get the other two.

Man, it was a kind of relay situation. I was tired as a buzzard when I got back to the four-wheeler!" he exclaimed.

Drive-By learned that coyotes, fox, and bobcats are creatures of habit, and when they cross under a fence once, they are likely to cross in that exact spot again and again. "I had one, one time, a bobcat came down the hill and crossed underneath the fence, and it was just a barbed wire fence. And I hung a snare at that barbed wire fence, and it was there about two weeks. And I had a fresh snow there one time, and I went up in there, and I had a snowmobile. And I seen my snare was gone, and I got a little closer and there was a bump in the snow, and there I had my bobcat. That cat came right through that area on that same trail that he passed through before . . . he could have crossed that fence at any place within a quarter of a mile, and was exactly through that spot where he had crossed before," he said.

When the snow piles up, Drive-By likes to spray-paint his snares white. He once had coyotes avoiding one of his snares for half a dozen checks. After painting the snare flat white, that snare location began producing coyotes.

Drive-By's snare preparation begins with boiling them in a solution of baking soda and water to take the sheen off, then he cuts the tops of alder brush and sage brush to make another solution and boils both traps and snares in it. This solution turns his traps and snares dark and eliminates scents. In the same solution, he adds pieces of denim for trap pan covers. The trap pan covers keep airspace under the pan to ensure the trap will fire when a coyote steps on it. Once the traps, snares, and denim pieces are boiled in the alder and sage, he takes great care not to get any human odors on them. Drive-By doesn't wax his traps. Instead, he carries coal slack with him to bed his traps in. A piece of aluminum foil laid under his traps keeps the frost from fouling them. A strip of denim goes over the pan, just before coal slack dust is poured over his trap. For a final touch, he adds waxed dirt over the trap to keep the weather out. Duff found under fir trees is a good substitute if he runs out of coal slack. This method gets his traps bedded solid and keeps them working even at extreme low temperatures.

At another time, his neighbor was losing sheep to coyotes every night for several weeks. He was certain that one coyote was responsible for killing thirty sheep, the rest of which were now housed in barns and not allowed to graze until the problem ceased. The coyotes had become wary of snares hung along the fence, and Drive-By had to problem-solve.

Instead of hanging the snare as he normally would, he decided to make the snare loop really big, but he tied monofilament fishing line across the opening. When that sheep-killing coyote came through there the next night, the sheep killing ended. Without the trapping skills of the Drive-By Trapper, who knows how many more sheep would have been killed?

The animal rights agenda is a hot topic with ranchers, hunters, and trappers—groups that Drive-By proudly represents. His opinion is as straightforward and direct as one might expect from a hardworking Montanan with close ties to the rural community. "I do not agree with any type of animal rights, I believe in taking care of animals. If you have a dog or a cat, I believe you should take care of that animal—make sure it's fed and watered, vaccinated, and that sort of stuff. As far as animal rights are concerned, an animal doesn't have any rights because an animal doesn't know the difference between right and wrong. Our dogs here—we've got three here, and one gets at the food bin here—they know their pecking order, but if one gets in the way too much, one of them is going to get gnawed on. They don't know the difference between right and wrong. If something gets in their way, they're going to chew on it. It's just that simple. But when you've got animals, you take care of them. That's the way I look at it. And when you've got animals out here in the field that are running wild, you take care of them also."

Taking care of animals is part of the agricultural communities' way of life. Domestic animals are raised for income and wild animals are nurtured for food and clothing. And for trappers—additional income.

Drive-By has spent a lot of time representing trappers at various venues, such as county fairs, schools, radio stations, and trapper's education classes. At a county fair in Bozeman, Montana, Drive-By had a booth with furs and trapping information on display and talked with people as they walked by. In a five-day period, he recalls five people who walked up to his booth who were against trapping. Drive-By invited them in and discussed the aspects of trapping that concerned them. "In that five-day period, we talked to five different people who had a negative attitude about trapping to begin with. Four of them went away with a positive attitude after I got done talking with them. And there was one person who didn't have a positive attitude at all. This person was against everything, including cutting trees and all the rest, and I believe she was possibly against motherhood also. We just weren't going to change her mind," said Drive-By.

Education is the best tool, in Drive-By's opinion, to change the minds of people and make a difference. One time, he was asked to be on a radio station in Missoula to talk about trapping. He expected to have to deal with a lot of negativity. "Ya know something? I was on there for an hour and didn't get one negative call," Drive-By remembered. When people called to ask questions, Drive-By provided straightforward information. "I told them what fur is used for, and that most of it goes out of the country, and it's one of the few things that we get nothing but finances back into this country. It's our natural resource. We're trapping as many coyotes and muskrats and beaver as we ever did. And then I gave them the information that there are more beaver in the state of Montana today than there was at the turn of the last century," Drive-By recalled.

Drive-By believes that trapping is either in your heart or it isn't. It's that simple. "Trapping ain't for everybody, nor is fishing or golfing or anything like that. I wouldn't go chase golf balls around for any money in the world. And I'm not out there trapping because I make a lot of money at it. It's something that's in my heart. And I love them animals, and I know what it is. I trap a few muskrats in the fall, and in the springtime, the rest are all dead. They die off, so I'm not hurting the population whatsoever," he explained.

These days, Drive-By traps a few muskrats to bring to the Youth Trapper Camp for demonstrations, and sets out snares for coyotes while at elk camp for two weeks each year. With the wolf population on the rise in Montana, the number of coyotes has been drastically reduced. Red fox are now more common on Drive-By's trapline than coyotes in areas where, for more than forty years, he rarely ever saw a fox track. The stories told by tracks in snow and patterns of other animals are easily discerned by observant trappers. With time, comes change. Changing seasons, weather, and animal populations ebb and flow like the lives of men. But it's the generosity of knowledge from outdoorsman like the Drive-By Trapper that will ensure the trapping heritage is carried on for generations to come.

The Drive-By Trapper epitomizes the spirit of trappers as he passes the torch still burning bright after sixty-six years on the trapline. "Pass on the knowledge that you have to people, to young people, old people, middle-aged people, anyone who will listen to you and can pick up on the knowledge and experience that you've had in all your life—and pass it on. That's the way I look at it."

"A Montana Trappers Day on the Line"

The morning sun timidly peered over the mountains, casting soft shadows on snowcapped peaks. A steamy river flowed through willows, the water cold and dark. A herd of elk chewed on wild grasses long ago buried under the white blanket of winter. Snowshoes pressed into the soft flakes, making an almost imperceptible whooshing sound with every step.

Around the next bend of the creek came the first fur of the day—a muskrat held in a body gripping trap that had been placed on a small run, trickling over a beaver dam, just wide enough for the small trap. Montana Trapper removed his pack before picking up the animal and admiring the thick fur. He always thought that muskrats had the most beautiful fur, in contradiction to their name. The 'rat was removed and placed in his pack. The trap was reset. A dozen more sets like this remained on this stretch of creek. Two more held muskrats, and the last, a mink. Mink were always a welcomed addition, and in midwinter, have the sleekest of fur.

Up the bank and through a stand of conifers, several traps were waiting. A dozen sets made for marten, bobcats, and fox held nothing as the faint snowshoe trail was again pressed with the woven imprints of rawhide and bended wood. The trail dodged snow-laden branches and led him around downed trees. The woods were quiet, and a white-tailed deer bolted at the sight of the figure moving through the forest. She blew a warning sound, sending three others running through the boughs of fir and pine. He thought about his freezer and the meat from the elk that filled it. Meat stores were full, and hunting season over. "You've no reason to worry, deer," he said to himself.

The last three checks had yielded nothing on this line except frozen traps and the experience of hiking though the forests in winter. But today was one of the good days. The kind of day he lived for. As he snowshoed along the edge of an old beaver flow, it changed from thick trees to willows and alders. Red fox tracks made since the snow yesterday followed the edge of nearly impenetrable forest and its more open reprieve. He knew there was a chance the next set would hold that fox. His steps quickened in anticipation, the snow and the heavy pack quickly reminded him to keep it slow and not overheat. Red fur glanced through the brush in the very place he had set a trap while first laying out this trapline three weeks ago. This was the second fox caught at this set since that time, reaffirming his reasons for placing it there. The trap had done its job, even in the wintery conditions, holding the fox by the foot, its bright-red fur in stark contrast to the world of white.

A sudden and accurate blast reported from his .22 caliber pistol just before he knelt down to remove the winter prime fox from the trap and laid it next to him. The set was remade in minutes, and he contemplated skinning the fox right then. He decided instead to press on, knowing darkness would surround him in a few hours.

Another mile of trail and four sets later, he had two marten added to his basket. The marten had also run along the edge and were lured to small boxes made of wood and guarded with the same type of trap used to capture and quickly kill the muskrats he now carried on his back. The boxes were wired to evergreen branches, five feet off the ground. Weeks of snow made them almost invisible to the human eye, but the essence of skunk and fresh beaver meat continued to lure the marten in. So many times marten had approached the boxes and not committed to the bait. Today was different, he had two. *A great day for marten trapping,* he thought.

Down a hill and another half-mile walk through willows and grass and snow lay five ponds separated by short and narrow creeks. Two of them had lodges made of mud and bright bark free sticks with long brushy feed piles extended out into deep water. The brush was frozen into the ice, and thin branches poked out even above the snow. *Winter beavers are difficult to catch,* he thought as he chopped another hole in the ice and peered into the dark water. Except for occasional forays, they only move from their sleeping quarters to feed piles and back again when the mercury drops, and so far, his beaver traps were empty.

He continued to snowshoe through the thick alders, occasionally tangling in the branches until he stood on the bank of the narrow creek, flowing between two ponds, created by his favorite animal in the world. It was winter, late December, and the snow was piling up. The moon was bright, and this was the last check of the day. Wearing a heavy wool shirt and long johns under his green wool pants, he peered into the slow trickle of water below a beaver dam.

The two sticks he had used to stabilize the trap placed in the anticipated beavers' path were gone. The ice had been broken and refrozen since his last visit, evidence that the trap had done its job. The trapper knew the heavy furred animal must be right there somewhere in the maze of cold water, snow, and ice. He swung his axe, hitting the hard ice. Chips flew in all directions. Again, the axe came down. This time, a splash of water accompanied the chards. A third and fourth swing began opening a hole, large enough for him to see what lay at the end of the wire fastened to a tree root close to the water's edge.

A tug on the trap chain revealed the brown fur of a beaver, the biggest one this season. He pulled the large animal up onto the bank and saw that the trap had worked perfectly, just as a mousetrap set to remove a rodent at home would. This large rodent had swum from a hole dug into the bank under the surface of the water and had made its way down the creek. It crossed the small dam constructed of mud and sticks cut and placed in summer, when the weather was warm and the water open. The beaver left tracks in the snow when leaving the water and just before sliding into the narrow channel below.

This trapper did what he always had, what he knew. He knew beavers, perhaps better than anyone. Miles from his camp, it was time to go. But not just yet, a few more traps to set under the ice on a cold winter's night beckoned. The moon was full, and the shadows of the trees danced as he walked.

Hours later, after skinning his day's catch, he sat by a campfire, a creek shushing his mind. A thousand times he's been here, he thought; right here, surrounded by earth. Trees tall, air cold, fire hot. He lives his life to absorb Mother Nature as much as he can before his own inevitable death. Human roots are eons deep. His senses were the result of a thousand generations who came before him. He uses nature, takes and gives as people always have. He had emerged from earth's ever-changing, ever-evolving lineage he knew.

He pondered the fact for a while that some humans disagree with his way of life. Animals are not to be a part of human existence, they say. They are not to be utilized, not entertainment and never food. Nature should be observed from a distance, man far removed.

We are people, are we not? Do these people wish that humans weren't human? They wish we were separate, that animals were not us, and we were not animals. They would change the history of man and nature in an instant if they could—and man would either not exist or would not be man at all.

Where would it change, this history, if it could? Would it change by a campfire like the one he sits by now, flames hot on his leg, smoke stinging human eyes? Would it be changed five thousand years ago when an African tribe danced in celebration around just such a campfire after a successful hunt?

Or would it change later in history, when a Sioux native carried a deer into his village just three hundred years ago on American soil? Perhaps it should have changed just after the Great Depression, when so many people were reliant on wild animals to feed their families.

Would it be changed instead in 1988, when an eleven-year-old boy trapped his first animal in a small American town, an event that changed his life forever?

Man and nature, life and death—not just parts of human evolution and earth's creation, instead, whole and never in the history of our natural earth separated. It is what we are. We are people. We are natural. We are wild. We live. We laugh. We hunt. We eat. We have emotion. We have animal senses. We are part earth. We always have been.

When and why would we ever try to become something we are not? To love nature is to take part in it, to use our emotion the way our natural instincts were meant to be used. At what intersection in our human lineage should man's separation from nature have taken place?

At what point should man and nature have separated? He wondered. He stared upward for a moment and noticed how bright the star-filled sky is, the moon casting shadows across the land. His furs hung from a pole and glimmered in the fire's glow. Boots dried by the fire as a coyote howled in the distance. Just then, he decided he doesn't know. And until he knows, he'll sit by this campfire and allow the creek to shush his mind. Tomorrow brings a new day, and it's impossible for him to imagine a better place to be than right there, right then, on his trapline.

Chapter 14

The Greatest Triumph

It's not what you look at that matters, it's what you see.

—Henry David Thoreau

Fear of losing our natural resources has not subsided since the first conservation groups were founded in the U.S. at the turn of the last century. Lands continue to be set aside for preservation, while hunting, trapping, and fishing seasons reduce populations where they are high and prevent taking too much where they are low. After one hundred years of conservation, our wildlife managers have learned a lot in the face of new challenges often more akin to sociology than biology.

There is perhaps no greater wildlife hot button anywhere than there is in western Montana. Wolves and wolverines are being trapped—wolves for proper management, and wolverines for trapping opportunity. Even with court cases and protests, the fact is that neither population will be irreparably damaged by trapping. In fact, trapping wolves may be the best way to prevent irreparable harm to Montana's ungulate populations. Beavers and muskrats are damaging public and private lands, including wildlife refuges while raccoons eat farmer's grain, and coyotes kill sheep. Trapping is often the most effective method to improve these situations, and the most practical. But it isn't easy to balance trapping with wildlife amid harsh political controversy.

No one knows that better than Montana Fish, Wildlife, and Parks' Regional Wildlife Manager Mike Thompson, who in 2006 became the man with responsibility to ensure healthy wildlife populations that fit the needs of western Montana's natural ecosystems and the expectations of the people living and visiting there.

In 2012, we sat in his office in Missoula, Montana—surrounded by photos of Montana's wildlife, FWP employees posing with trapped and collared large predators, and large maps of mountainous terrain. A digital picture frame flashed photos of field workers and wildlife above his desk. His relaxed demeanor and low voice spoke volumes about him in the absence of explanation. With more than thirty years' worth of experience with the ever-changing marriage of wildlife and man, Mike freely offered his insight as I asked questions about trapping in wildlife management.

I began by asking the man who openly advocates for trapping if he had ever spent any time trapping. Mike's father always hunted, and there were sportsmen in his family, yet no one in his family trapped Thompson began. "I was always interested in trapping, but I always thought that was the next step in expertise and knowledge, and I didn't know how to get there by myself. It was part of my dream, about who I would become, but that never quite happened."

When I asked Mike about his path to becoming a wildlife manager the floodgates opened as he recalled his early years in a competitive field. "When I was a kid hunting, trying to learn how to be more successful, I remember the day when it just came to me: Wouldn't it be cool to be the guy who knows where the grouse and the deer are right now when I can't find them? I supposed that there are people out there like that, and I wondered if I could learn to be that person. I assumed that maybe the wildlife department people know those things," Thompson recalled.

At that time, people went to theaters to view wildlife films and read magazines to learn what the world looked like. Mike usually had such magazines open on top of his English book in high school, and it was through these magazines that Mike first fell in love with Montana. He knew he wanted to work in the outdoors but wasn't quite sure how to go about getting a foot in the door. Four years after starting at Paul Smith's College, he had attained a bachelor's degree in wildlife biology from the University of Montana. He spent a lot of his time backpacking when he admittedly should have been studying, but he loved his first Montana experience.

He returned to New York, where he volunteered to ride around with a wildlife technician who was live-trapping beavers with Hancock cage traps for relocation. As time went on, he managed to get a temporary job with the NYSDEC, but those Montana outdoors magazines remained open and continued to lure him westward.

He made contacts with MSU in Bozeman, Montana, in hopes of continuing his education and, after proving he could make the grade, was accepted into the graduate program. As luck would have it, a mountain goat study sponsored by the Montana Fish, Wildlife, and Parks was available on the Rocky Mountain Front. This opportunity was a "dream come true" for Mike.

"I remember sitting up on a mountainside one time when my last summer was concluding, and I said, 'Well, I don't know if I'm going to become a wildlife biologist or not, but by God, whatever happens from here on out, they can't take this away from me!'"

He laughed before continuing with a nostalgic grin. "I still had a thesis to write, but I got through it and did well enough and worked my way into and up in Fish, Wildlife, and Parks."

Compensatory Mortality

His answer to my question about how he sees trapping fitting in with wildlife management was interesting. I expected an answer involving statistics and justifications. What I got was an answer focused on wildlife availability first and trapper opportunity second, and a list of variables both scientific and social.

"I think that you start from the concept of a harvestable surplus. By starting there, you start with the perspective that trapping is a legitimate use of the resource. It is not necessary to justify trapping by saying that the wildlife population needs trapping, although sometimes that is true, I believe. But what we're looking for, first and foremost, is a harvestable surplus that would allow a consumptive use. Muskrats, of course, are a good example. Paul Errington did the early research on compensatory mortality and reproduction in muskrat populations—the fact that a certain amount of natural mortality can be replaced with a harvest that keeps the population steady, tempering the natural highs and the lows. You can manage to make the lows not so low and the highs not quite so high and provide a consumptive recreational opportunity as a result," Thompson explained.

Wildlife Damage

Wildlife damage occurs around the globe every year and at times have had serious impact to human health and safety. Muskrats have dug through earthen dikes in marshes constructed for wildlife management and in other cases have flooded towns and villages with their digging habits. While muskrats are a prolific animal with a surplus available they aren't the only destructive rodent which trapping can alleviate.

"We were talking with a sportsman's club here a little while ago, and they were talking about how the beavers were wreaking havoc and asked if we would live-trap beavers. Well, we could do that if there are vacant suitable habitats. But we've got really strong beaver populations now, and they are widely distributed. I asked them to think about a harvest in this situation, where there really isn't room for beavers—and why not start thinking about recruiting kids into an outdoor activity like trapping, where they can learn something about wildlife? I don't think any one of them that were sitting in the room at that time trapped, you know? But they could be thinking about that. So we think about harvest as being something legitimate to do," Thompson said.

Abundance Management for Available Habitat

One of the biggest challenges facing wildlife managers is fragmentation of the landscape. We have the knowledge to grow high populations of animals but no place to put them. Mike went on to illustrate the challenges of having wildlife on a fragmented landscape with multiple land use perspectives. There are so many viewpoints about wildlife in Montana from so many places around the world each with its own merits and demerits.

"On the far end of the spectrum, we absolutely have to have trapping in order to manage wolf populations because it provides the most effective means for obtaining a meaningful harvest. If you're going to have fair chase harvest and management of wolves, it's going to be trapping that is effective. The wolf is perhaps the best example that we have of a species whose abundance needs to be managed for a balance in the larger system of predator and prey," Thompson said.

"When we talk about the wolf, we often hear about the idea of wildlife coming into balance on its own, some sort of self-regulating balance. And that can occur, I think, where the species occupy relatively little landscape with small home ranges and their system occurs in a small space.

"But the systems that supported large numbers of wolves are gone, and anything that might be called self-regulating were systems which included bison, elk, antelope, and deer across the heart of North America in unbelievable abundance. Those days are gone, and they're never coming back. The ground is farmed, it's settled. There are remnant habitats, and the remnants are significant, but they will never support the system that was there before, and we can't hope to get there again," Thompson explained, putting things in perspective.

"What we hope to manage now are the glimpses of that heritage, of the fragments of it that were once connected. And they can function, within limits, if we're careful. But they need help in the modern world. Wildlife management is what we do to mitigate for the tremendous loss of habitat—and in the case of wolf, prey—that occurred long ago. The wolves are here to stay, and so are you and me and human land uses. We're not going to go back in either direction. That leaves management."

Cooperative Compatibility

Deciding how many animals the available habitat can support for the long term is far easier than balancing the numbers people want to see with what the landscape can support. Further complexity begins to emerge when managers have to balance habitat, wildlife and humans all vying for occupancy of the same space.

"So to have wolves—for example—with management, is something that I think people can accept no matter where you're coming from. It's a huge conservation success to have wolves, just to have them and manage them. If you're greedy about it and you've just gotta have more, then we won't succeed at having them at all because they will over utilize their own prey in the small landscapes that we have left for them. If the prey existed by the hundreds of thousands or millions, that's a different ball game, but the land does not allow that now. Let's learn how to manage the fragments that were preserved and that we have left," Thompson suggested.

"Wilderness and preservation are only a small part of the picture. Expand that to cooperation, where human existence occupies the vast majority of the land, if you can find that compatibility—that's the challenge. Compatibility is the greatest triumph for wildlife and the greatest triumph for everybody, and trapping is absolutely essential in that big picture." Thompson said.

Trapper Contribution to Wildlife Management

Trapping provides a necessary knowledge base for biologists to work off of but biologists also appreciate the historic aspects of trapping as Thompson explained; "I just think it's so cool that the ancient craft of trapping—and it would have been the first thing that man learned to do when he got hungry—has endured in our culture. People want to say that trapping is cruel and inhumane and has run its course—that society has evolved beyond trapping and should stop. Well, it's relatively few people who have come out on the other end of all these generations, millennia of human evolution, of human societal evolution, and what's left are those few people who are the most connected to the land—who practice the ancient crafts—and it's ironic that those relatively few people are able to provide now through their craft a product that is a restored wolf population and a system within the fragments that are still available in the western United States. I think that is really cool."

The role trapper's play in wildlife management is critical now perhaps more than ever in especially in Montana. While the professionals who work closely with trappers understand and appreciate the knowledge trappers cultivate not everyone else does.

"Trappers have taken a lot of abuse for being trappers, but today, we all ought to go up and shake the hand of a trapper because can you imagine, if that had not persisted, if society had not made room for people like yourself to practice that craft, if we were starting from scratch and we had wolves, we'd all be scratching our heads. If I didn't have you [trappers] to bounce off ideas and learn from as a wildlife manager, and we were starting from absolute scratch to manage wolves, we're probably not very good cavemen right now in this period of history, and right now, we would probably be in trouble." Thompson said.

Thompson continued. "We talked about trapping and transplanting beaver, which is fine, there's a time and a place for that. Then when there are beaver problems, there are ways to mitigate beaver problems using the beaver baffler and these kinds of things. And again, there's a time and a place for those—all the kinds of preventative and mitigation measures that we take are most effective when you have lower, moderate densities of the animal that you're trying to baffle.

"With the beaver, the baffler does not work in place of beaver management. It is something that goes hand in hand so that people can live very nicely with beaver if we manage the total population.

"Bobcat populations track nicely with the abundance of their prey, and we're not managing the trajectory of bobcat populations with trapping. But what we're trying to do is just back off on trapping pressure when we see the population at a low level, so that we don't drive it lower and slow its recovery.

"Their reproductive rate and survival are lowered for a period of time when prey are low, and that's a point when mortality tends toward additive instead of compensatory. Then as you see the population increase, you can add to the harvest again," Thompson explained.

Living With Wildlife

"We make a lot of effort at consulting with people to adapt their lifestyles to include wildlife—changing their patterns of putting the garbage out and feeding the birds. But those folks also need our help with population management and harvest in order to maintain wildlife densities at a level where people can be successful at mitigating or preventing conflict for short periods of time in their own backyards. Otherwise, high overall wildlife densities can overwhelm the good efforts of well-meaning people just because there are too many animals, and you reduce support for preventative measures because they're not effective. Prevention and population management have to work hand in hand," Thompson said.

One pressing issue that I read a lot in antitrapping propaganda is that state biologists have no idea what the population is for species that aren't required to be individually tagged for data collection. So naturally I asked how biologists know the health of species which aren't required to be checked in. The answer was simple and puts an end to this public concern. "It's distribution. They're common species, they have a high reproductive potential. Generally, they live very well with people. So what you're looking for, generally as an indicator of whether a population is in trouble or not, is a sharp and noticeable change in distribution. And I mean range distribution, broad landscape distribution. You're going to have—and sometimes on purpose—some very localized declines in the short term. But if you've got common species that remain common in their distribution—as long as you have them in the places you expect to have them—casually observed and reported by trappers, landowners, biologists, and the general public, then those populations are in good shape." Thompson explained.

Trapping Saves Wildlife

The number one question that I hoped to have answered was what the ramification would be if trapping were not allowed on public lands in Montana. His answer was surprisingly pointed. "We are at risk of losing elk on some public lands in some places, and for a variety of reasons, the wolf makes it worse. It's not the wolf's fault. We're managing all wildlife, and if we could not trap wolves on public lands, wolf numbers—in combination with lions and bears—would rise to intolerable levels that would locally extirpate some species of prey and reduce prey numbers on public lands to a point where the wolf is subsisting more and more on private land. Wolves on private land eventually lead to conflict and will result in the wolf being removed. So in order—in particular with the wolf—for people to have wolves, trapping on public lands is absolutely essential to conserve prey on public lands. In some parts of Montana, the quickest way to losing wolves is to lose trapping." Thompson said firmly.

Trapping Preserves Human Insight

"In terms of marten, bobcat, fisher, the world would not end; and there would be bobcat, marten, and fisher. What we would lose on the human side are people with the clear insight into how those animals use the land in particular drainages. On a real, local scale, we would lose human knowledge about how those populations use the land—their ups and downs. Sometimes I think that people assume that wildlife science replaces oral history and local wildlife knowledge, but it cannot," Thompson continued.

"Wildlife science occurs at a broad scale. It provides conceptual sideboards within which we can explain and better understand the variations that we see locally. The local variations and the local appreciation and the local decision about whether the population is okay or not—whether it is acceptable or not—all come from the folks in the field, and those are the trappers—the trapper is the sharpest eye in the field—that is where the footsteps are occurring. We would lose that awareness, that important piece of wildlife management." Thompson explained.

Trappers Provide Fine Scale Detection

"Marten are tied real strongly to land use and particular habitat—mature forest stands. I've noticed this too, that marten trappers in particular are a conservative bunch. They've got marten in a particular place where they trap, and they want marten to always be there. They set their own standards about female harvest in that spot at a level that occurs on a fine scale, finer than management dictated by regulation. And so they are trapper by trapper, forest stand by forest stand, setting their own standards to try to maintain marten in those places. And they will back off if they don't see good numbers of marten, so they'll be the first ones to report if they are seeing habitat changes affecting marten populations." Thompson said.

"Big habitat changes or small habitat changes that could affect marten could be missed, and an opportunity could be lost if we don't have trappers in the field paying attention and if we didn't have that constituency voice speaking for furbearers," Thompson explained.

Keeping it all Together

The perspective of a wildlife manager is one of uniqueness, where every user group has a stake in the health and well-being of wildlife and wild lands. At a time of shrinking habitat and growing public expectations, the balance between human perception and nature's reality is tough to find. In Montana, the answer lies somewhere between wildlife sciences and firsthand wildlife intimacy.

Deer and elk numbers are detected first by the hunter, fishery health by the angler, and furbearer health by the trapper. The omission of any of these user groups would be a detrimental loss to biologists, and a major loss of firsthand human experience.

Mike Thompson's early childhood dream of becoming a master woodsman may never have come to fruition, but perhaps finding ways to have wildlife and people coexist is a much greater contribution to Montana's wildlife than knowing where the grouse go when no one can find them.

The most important message from this Montana Fish, Wildlife, and Park's wildlife manager may be that biology and wildlife science are as reliant on trappers and hunters as trappers and hunters are on wildlife science and biology. They can each exist without the other, but when they complement each other—when trappers seek out wildlife managers and wildlife managers listen—that is when wilderness and preservation expand to that cooperation where human existence occupies the vast majority of the land yet achieves compatibility. "The greatest triumph for wildlife and the greatest triumph for everybody."

Chapter 15

Common Ground

Education is the most powerful weapon which you can use to change the world.

—Nelson Mandela

Wildlife population control must take place in one way or another. The eventual "boom and bust" phenomenon occurs in isolated areas around the country, but not without severe negative results for humans and their domesticated animals, and certainly not without potential wildlife population crashes due to starvation and disease. Like it or not, there is no alternative to death for any animal. When populations exceed their natural carrying capacity, they die. When they exceed their perceived carrying capacity, they die. This life cycle developed by nature is simply how it is.

Regardless how large and fancy our skyscrapers become; we are still limited to a small and relatively short time on earth. Humanity generally agrees that human life is inherently valuable. An extremely small portion of people also believe that animals are equally and inherently valuable. The differences in mind-set are so contentious that some people attempt to destroy other people's lives over the use of animals by other humans.

The natural order established by nature certainly lends itself well to trapping, provided that humans are considered part of nature and not outsiders. Most trappers I believe view themselves as another animal on the landscape, at least from the perspective of predator and prey interaction whereas non-trappers seem to view things differently. As if man is somehow separated from nature and therefore cannot participate in the life and death cycle that every other species on earth can. It is an interesting concept that man and animal are equal yet man must not interact with animals in a natural way. Until a few hundred years ago, most of human existence relied on sharing the same landscape and natural predator prey relationship as all other animal species do now.

So far, a compromise has been made—that if we choose to use animals and wild places, we are obligated to conserve and perpetuate the existence of as many species as possible and take on the responsibility to be good stewards of the land. Trappers love wildlife and wild places. Some antitrapping advocates love wildlife and wild places. Neither can stand to see it wasted. Both sides agree. It is the idea of how our natural resources should be conserved that pulls the ever-present human emotion from passionate nature lovers and casts it into the throes of political controversy.

Is there room for compromise between the conservationists and preservationists? The terms conservationist and preservationist may have negative connotations, depending whose side you're on. When local and world economies are factored into the equation, it is difficult to argue that the conservationist's mentality works. People can use wildlife and wild lands sparingly, and if they overuse, they must back off until flora and fauna populations recuperate. Wildlife management dependent on hunter, trapper, and angler dollars has been so successful in the United States for the last century—the continuation of that relationship seems logical. Wildlife numbers have increased for many species to the point that some once-rare species have now reached nuisance status. Habitat restoration projects have improved waterfowl numbers to recent all-time high numbers. The success of the North American Model of Wildlife Conservation is irrefutable. We've got it pretty good. The problem is that, some people cannot accept that humans kill animals. They want balanced nature without hunting and trapping. This would require a severe reduction in wildlife populations and the total exclusion of humans from nature interference, with the exception of human wildlife fringe areas. That might be the saddest and worst possible situation ever, where man is severed from his natural place in nature. Man's position in the realm of the animal world is a matter of debate, one in which I would argue that man should continue his natural nature-developed relationship. Because we can't truly love something we don't understand, and you can't understand something that you don't know intimately.

In order for nontrappers to peacefully coexist with trappers, both sides must learn and accept the facts, not the pseudo "my-way-or-the-highway" facts used in propaganda campaigns to promote a cause at the expense of the truth. I am talking about the real truth, facts—the third side of the story. In reading letters to the editor; attending workshops; viewing websites, books, and magazine articles purporting to be the disseminators of truth, it is difficult to know what is real and what is made up. That goes for trappers and nontrappers alike.

With that said, I have created a list of statements that are commonly used, and I have done my best to explain the reasons for each statement's lack of integrity, regardless of which side is wrong. The first thing that anyone can do to find compromise is to understand the opposing view. This, I believe, can only be accomplished by sifting through the mire of half-truths and disinformation from your own side and the other side. I stand firm in my belief that education is the answer to every issue facing America today, and that it takes a willingness to teach *and* learn to resolve conflict. Compromise is a matter of give and take, and neither side needs to take the crap-scraps left over from the fact table. The following statements and explanations are true, accurate, and complete, based on the best information available. This is not a guess. It is not propaganda. It is the truth in simple terms.

Trapping is no longer necessary in our society.

Trapper Facts:

When your sink is plugged from hair and soap scum, you call a plumber. When your creek is plugged by beavers, you call a trapper. It takes the right tools and experience to remedy any situation. And trapping is often the best solution for human-wildlife conflict. Case in point: If you have a mouse infestation in your house, you could sit and wait to shoot the mice as they go by, you could place toxic substances in the mouse's path, or you could trap them. Traps are the easiest, safest, and most effective means to reduce the numbers of mice. You could choose to use a cage trap or a body grip trap. But live relocation is difficult, and the mice may die, regardless of your best efforts. Foothold traps, body gripping traps, and cage traps are acceptable by wildlife agencies around the world as humane and necessary tools for wildlife control. Fur trappers help to quickly control localized populations of wild animals and have helped restore and preserve numerous species, including furbearers, game and nongame species, waterfowl, and wetlands habitat and domestic animals. You can't justify your mousetrap and condemn a beaver trap. Trappers provide an invaluable service—this is irrefutable. Although the demand for fur garments in the U.S. has subsided considerably, many countries rely on fur as part of their culture and practical necessity, as well as fashion. Trapping is absolutely needed currently and in the future.

Nontrapper Facts:

Trapping is not always the best management tool for every occasion or for every species. Some species essentially "self-regulate" their own populations and produce very little in the way of "surplus" (defined as the number of animals above the carrying capacity at the beginning of the next breeding season) and maintain a balance within their natural carrying capacity and human-perceived carrying capacity. In these situations, the trapper may neither help nor hinder the overall population and could in fact decrease the population too much, resulting in overharvest. Other long-term methods may be more suitable to help other species—like ducks—as a whole, such as increasing habitat size and stopping the loss of wetland habitat. In cases where trapping is not necessary for certain species for wildlife management, trapping is done on a sustained yield basis for trapper opportunity, and not due to a need for management.

Wildlife agencies' trapping techniques bear little resemblance to the methods used by the fur trade.

Trapper Facts:

The traps, techniques, and tools used by wildlife agencies are exactly the same as the traps, techniques, and tools used by trappers in the fur trade. There is *no* difference. Recently successful wolf, lynx, and otter reintroduction programs in the U.S. used foothold traps set up identically to the traps commonly used by trappers. In fact, many animals are trapped by volunteer fur trappers and relocated by wildlife professionals in a joint effort. Wildlife agencies may use foothold, body gripping, and cage traps and/or snares to effectively and humanely remove problem animals. By following trap designs, configurations, and modifications set forth by the Better Management Program standards, traps are humane;

don't break bones, cause lacerations, or unnecessary damage; and are far more selective and effective. Game agencies check traps on a regular and frequent basis, as do responsible trappers.

Nontrapper Facts:

Not all traps used by fur trappers are suitable for use. Traps purchased off the shelf are often not ready to be used in the most humane and effective manner and require modification, but are used by trappers anyway. Trap jaws should be laminated (made thicker) and/or have rubber pads added to prevent lacerations to an animal's foot and eliminate the possibility of breaking bones. Chains should be fastened to the center of the trap frame to prevent injury. In-line shock springs should be fastened to trap chains to prevent unnecessary muscle damage. Certain traps are poorly designed and should be avoided. Some uneducated trappers use traps that don't meet the recommendations set forth by the Better Management Practices (BMPs) to prevent injury to trapped animals. The fact is, not all trappers have the same work ethic when it comes to trap modification and use. Perhaps it would be better to limit the trappers in the field to those who demonstrate that their tools meet these industry standards and possess the skills to trap in a way that doesn't damage trappers' reputations.

Furbearers are being trapped to extinction.

Trapper Facts:

Furbearer management is extremely successful in the United States. Furbearing animal harvests are strictly regulated, and the data from trappers ensures the long-term sustainability—and even increases—of wild furbearing animals. Trapping techniques, many of which are state regulated, prevent the capture of various species of nontarget catches. By setting pan tensions to certain specifications, using appropriate trap size, and techniques, while avoiding trapping in areas where threatened or endangered species are present will ensure that species of concern are allowed to flourish. Trapping can be *very* selective.

Nontrapper Facts:

Furbearing animals which are low in numbers may be caught and killed in traps set for other animals. Trappers who catch nontarget animals must report their catch, but the only real way to ensure it happens is if the trapper who catches and unintentionally kills one has integrity and turns it in as the law requires. This is important to ensure that all species are properly monitored. By having corridors available that are trap free, these species can travel without additional mortality (to the already innumerable ways an animal can die, including automobile accidents, predation, starvation, disease, old age, etc.).

Animals chew their feet off to get out of a trap.

Trapper Facts:

No animal has the capacity to reason that if it chews off a limb, it will get out of a trap. Poorly designed traps with jaws that are "too high" and poorly used traps stop circulation to the trapped animal's feet, and they become numb. When this happens, animals may chew on their feet below the trap jaws. This is not at all desirable or ethical. In cases where muskrats or beavers "wring out," which mean they twisted their foot off in a trap, this happened not because the animals chewed on their feet. Rather, the trap design and size was not suitable. It has happened to trappers prior to advancements in traps and techniques, which virtually eliminated this rare but no less unacceptable fact. Better traps with "stop loss" devices and quick-kill trapping methods have eliminated this from occurring on responsible trapper's lines. Trappers today should not be held accountable for things which used to occur in trapping fifty years ago.

Nontrapper Facts:

Not all trappers are responsible or take the time to set their traps in a way that will prevent injury from happening. Those trappers should not be trapping. Whenever people are hunting or trapping, wild animal accidents can happen, and animals can be injured just as they can on the highway with vehicles. Every effort must be made to be as humane as possible. Only ethical trappers should be allowed to trap with properly modified equipment.

Traps will chop an animal's foot off.

Trapper Facts:

No, they won't "chop" any animal's foot off. First of all, what good would a trap do any trapper if it had the ability to "chop feet off"? Any animal getting in the trap would just run away without a foot—the goal of the trapper is to catch and hold the animal, not cut their feet off. Second, trappers commonly get stuck in their traps while setting them and come away with all their digits.

Nontrapper Facts:

Improperly modified traps can cause lacerations to animal's feet, and if traps are not checked frequently enough, a trap that is not modified appropriately could result in preventable injury. Trappers must check their traps regularly and ensure that only appropriately modified traps are used.

There has not been a threat to public safety due to wildlife in one hundred years.

Trapper Facts:

The cases of animals threatening public safety are so widespread and irrefutable that I am not sure where to begin. Beavers flood roadways that can cause destruction to bridges, pavement, and buildings and create ponds in areas dangerous to humans. In addition to physical threats to public safety, beavers can and commonly do threaten public water systems when they inhabit these areas and bring human communicable disease with them. They have also flooded sewage systems that polluted human water sources, such as wells. Muskrats are also a source of disease and can threaten public safety when not controlled. Animals such as moles and gophers destroy lawns, cemeteries, and golf courses. Raccoons can enter houses and cause fires when they eat insulated wires. Rats, raccoons, fox, coyotes, and skunks carry diseases that threaten the safety of people, pets, and other wildlife. Gophers and badgers have dug through levees and flooded towns, causing extensive damage. Trapping is one of the most effective means of reducing these threats.

Nontrapper Facts:

Sorry, nontrappers, there are no facts on your side here. Many wild animals absolutely threaten public safety and have as recently as this morning.

Trap design hasn't changed at all in the last century.

Trapper Facts:

While the basic design of a foothold trap has essentially remained the same, numerous trap and chain rigging design changes have been developed, tested, and added to the BMPs for nineteen species of animals, and the list is growing. By using a combination of swivels; shock springs; laminated, offset and/or, padded trap jaws; center-mounted baseplates; friction beads; and many combinations of other modifications makes traps more humane and selective. Trappers have come a long way from the Jeremiah Johnston days. Foothold traps are commonly used to catch, relocate and release animals unharmed. Additionally, foothold traps are the only efficient, practical, humane, and environmentally benign live capture restraining devices currently available for many species. Dog-proof traps, trap boxes, and other modifications have eliminated the risk of dogs getting into body grippers while still ensuring quick and humane species-specific harvest of furbearers.

Nontrapper Facts:

Trappers may do everything they can to prevent injury and make traps selective, but those opposed to it just don't like it. Crushing animals to death with a body gripping trap may be a quicker death than shooting with a bullet or an arrow, but these traps can catch and kill unintended animals if set improperly or in areas where unintended animals live. There is no chance of releasing animals alive if they are caught in this type of trap. Snares do not kill animals quickly every time, and animals can chew through the cable. Deer, elk, moose, caribou, mountain lions, and bears have been caught in snares and killed. Foothold traps seem cruel. An animal caught in a foothold trap is stuck there until a trapper comes to kill it. It is difficult to change a person's mind that is dead-set against foot traps, body gripping traps, or snares. The fact remains that some trappers are irresponsible and use poor equipment.

Trappers are greedy and only care about money.

Trapper Facts:

The trappers I have talked to do enjoy getting money for their furs, glands, meat, and urine. But trapping is a mix of adventure, animal tracking, constant learning, physical challenge, and a craft with a rich and deep heritage. It is who they are, what they love. Trappers also hunt, fish, hike, camp, float rivers, work regular jobs, and have friends, families, and pets. Trappers are a practical group of people who love wildlife and wild places. A typical trapper's house may have several tanned skins from animals they have hunted or trapped adorning their walls—deer and elk heads, fish, photos of wildlife, paintings, old decoys, decorative traps, and antiques. Trappers seem to love rustic decor, old log cabins, and snowshoes. It's a lifestyle. They are drawn to it, and for most, it's not about money. Some trappers trap only when the fur prices are up, but it is often because they cannot justify the costs involved in setting traps unless they can be assured that they can recover their costs through fur sales.

Nontrapper Facts:

Trappers kill animals and sell their skins to the world market. When fur prices go up, the number of trappers out trapping goes up. This is an indication that for those trappers, it is more about the money than the experience of the trapping lifestyle.

Trappers don't follow fair chase ethics.

Trapper Facts:

In hunting, there are rules of fair chase that are followed. Laws must be adhered to, and animals that are killed must be taken under fair chase conditions. Fair chase conditions require that certain rules are established, such as no animal shall be taken while contained inside a fence, in deep water, in a trap, in deep snow, or on ice. No animal may be taken under motorized power, using electronic calls, or equipment. This fair chase ethic is designed and accepted by hunting organizations to define rules for ethical hunting of game. Nontrappers say that trappers don't follow fair chase rules, but they are applying rules for hunting game to the rules of trapping and fishing. While hunting, hunters may get a shot at an animal and must decide whether or not that shot is ethical.

A trapper who catches an animal gets a shot at three feet with the animal standing still. There is no chance of wounding the animal with a fleeting shot. Instead, a quick and ethical kill is made every time. The goal of the hunter is to challenge his skills to stalk and shoot, play the wind, and learn his quarry. Trappers use their skills to place traps exactly where an animal will step, learn their quarries' path and habits, and test their wits against wild animals just like hunters do. Trappers have certain rules of fair chase that they must follow, depending on their state and federal regulations. In some states, you may not trap within fifteen feet of a muskrat den entrance or a beaver lodge entrance. While in others, you may place a trap directly in front of it.

Some species in the country may be harvested by hunters and trappers in an unlimited number by individual trappers. Those species which are plentiful in an area have been determined by biologists to be able to absorb a heavy harvest, while others are not. While hunters may take unlimited numbers of some species, anglers may also take unlimited number of certain prolific fish that can absorb heavy harvest. Furbearers are managed in the same way.

It is obvious that there needs to be different harvest rates and techniques for different species and in different regions of the country. For large game, it is by bullet; for fish, it is by hook; and for furbearers, it is by traps. The numbers removed from the population vary for each one, based on biology.

A person cannot just go out and set a trap and expect to catch something. There are few highly skilled trappers in country who are consistently successful at trapping certain species. Those trappers who have excelled in their understanding of predators may not do well in trapping beavers or mink. Trapping is a very difficult activity to become proficient at. Any member of any group pursuing any activity can be unethical, but only if they are held to the ethical standards of the activity they are involved in.

Applying the rules of hunter's fair chase to trapping and fishing is no more accurate than applying the rules of baseball to football. While each sport has their rules for fair play, they are not interchangeable.

This statement is used by antitrappers to divide sportsmen.

Nontrapper Facts:

Trappers are the only group of people who can harvest numerous animals with unlimited traps. Hunters use one gun or bow and must get close enough to his or her quarry to shoot it. Anglers are limited to a maximum number of fishing poles, a maximum number of hooks, and have bait restrictions in certain areas as well. Anglers must get within striking distance of fish to cast to them or net them. A trapper can set as many traps as he or she wants in many states and is limited only by ethical considerations as to how often he checks traps and how long animals may potentially be held in a trap. Not all trappers, hunters, or anglers, are ethical. Poaching occurs within all these groups, and animals are wasted. When compared to the fair chase rules of hunting, it doesn't seem like fair chase to a nontrapper when one person can set as many traps as he wants, baited with meat or lure that can attract multiple species. This is especially concerning when fishing with trot lines and nets is also not a fair chase endeavor in many states.

**For every one target animal caught,
two nontarget animals are caught.**

Trapper Facts:

This is not true. This number was derived from records maintained by government trappers in the 1960s who set snares and traps close to large bait stations. The rate of non-target catches can be high in certain situations such as huge bait stations but the records of trappers through the end of the last century also resulted in recommended setbacks from bait stations. And in many states, it is now law. Not only do setting traps and snares far away from bait stations along predator trails prevent nontarget catches, it also serves to improve the trapper's success rates because other target animals in the area are less likely to associate the bait station with danger, thereby increasing the trapper's success. In addition, the longer traps are working and free from nontarget catches, the longer the potential for catching the intended prey is. Many old studies, or studies that don't apply to other areas of the country, are used by the protest industry to gain support for their cause, and this one is a classic.

One Montana trapper and his partner reported that out of one hundred fifty coyotes caught in foothold traps, only two incidental kit fox were caught. Kit fox are much lighter than coyotes, and by setting the pan tension to about 3 to 4 pounds of pressure, fox may step on the trap but do not weigh enough to set it off. (Kit fox do have a season in which they can be trapped, so they are only "nontarget" when their season is closed.) While simply adjusting the pan tension can avoid the vast majority of nontargets, many other methods such as bait selection, location, and trap specificity can eliminate nontarget catches. Examples of these are using sweet bait to avoid cats while trapping raccoons or setting traps four feet above the ground to target one species and avoid others and the use of dog-proof traps. There are many more examples like these that can make a trapline extremely selective and humane.

When a trapper sets a trap for coyotes but catches a badger, the badger may have been a nontarget animal. However, the badger is a welcomed furbearer on a trapline—as are skunks, red fox, bobcats, mink, otters, raccoons, and others. If a furbearer is caught in a trap intended for a different furbearer but that furbearer is in season, that animal should not be considered a nontarget. If a deer hunter is sitting in wait for a white-tailed deer but an elk walks by, the elk is not a nontarget, just as a bass angler who hooks a walleye would not consider the walleye a nontarget fish. Multispecies harvest potential adds an element of surprise to hunting, angling, and trapping.

Nontrapper Facts:

While it is true that groups opposed to trapping do commonly misrepresent scientific data to manipulate "facts," nontarget animals may be caught in traps, and it is impossible to eliminate this completely. Federally funded research shows that approximately 6% of captures with foothold traps are nontarget animals.[15] This includes the summation of combined nontarget catch averages by poorly educated trappers and well-educated trappers. Although many nontarget catches can be released unharmed, not all can, and this must be accounted for with wildlife management data and subsequent calculations to ensure long-term sustained yield harvest.

Trapping nets about $94,000 per year in Montana, while wildlife watching brings $376 million a year.

Trapper Facts:

This value has been used to describe the economic contrast between trapping and wildlife watching in Montana by animal rights groups. The data to support either value has never surfaced. However, at one fur sale in one small town in Montana in 2012, fur trappers were paid $225,000 for their fur. There are multiple other outlets for fur trappers, such as international auction houses, private buyers, craft shows, tanneries, etc. This doesn't count the economic stimulus generated by trappers and predator hunters from fuel, food, and accommodations during their travels. There are also numerous trapping supply stores and sporting goods stores, which also see financial benefit from trappers. And let's not forget that the fur trade is a $14-billion industry worldwide in retail sales alone. Trapping has a huge economic impact on local and global scales.

Nontrapper Facts:

Wildlife watching brings a lot of money to the state of Montana and to other states. Some people have stated that they will discontinue tourism in Montana if the state allows trapping of certain species, such as wolves. When photos of trappers with their trapped animals are exploited by members of the protest industry, it is certainly negative publicity.

Traps just hold an animal's foot. They don't cause lacerations or break bones.

Trapper Facts:

If the proper trap size is selected and used according to BMPs, the trap will hold the animal without lacerations, broken bones, or any other damage—provided that the trapper checks his traps routinely. Even if trappers take every precaution, it is not 100% preventable—neither is any hunting, fishing, nor agricultural activity 100% free of accidental injury. Responsible trappers do everything they can to avoid injury to the animals they trap, just as hunters, anglers, ranchers, horse and dog trainers do.

Nontrapper Facts:

While most animals caught in foot traps can be released unharmed, domestic animals are brought to veterinarians every year with lacerations, broken bones, and broken teeth. Trappers cannot deny that this can occur on their traplines. Even if trappers take every precaution, it is not 100% preventable. The trappers are the ones who place the traps on the landscape, and they are responsible for the well-being of the animals they trap. This statement may be true for some traps, but not all traps. This is reality. Trappers must do everything they can to prevent unnecessary injury to the animals they pursue, just as hunters, anglers, and stock growers do.

Traps are checked every day to ensure that animals are treated humanely

Trapper Facts:

Many states require that foot traps or traps set on land must be checked within certain time frames but vary from twenty-four 84 hours or there is no mandatory trap-check requirement. Checking traps every day, especially in remote areas, is not feasible for many trappers, especially in large mountainous areas such as those in Montana, Idaho, and Alaska for example. The cost of running a trapline is high, and to be effective, trappers must have flexibility to check less frequently. In some cases, such as in marten trapping—where small body grip traps are used—the traps are very selective, and the marten is dead within seconds. In cases like this, especially in midwinter when temperatures remain near zero, the animal will be killed instantly and frozen within minutes, and there is no need to check more frequently than once every week. In cases where traps are placed and the animal is held alive, the likelihood that an animal will be caught in the trap, minutes after a trapper checks it, is extremely low. Few trappers would ever go longer than seventy-two hours between land-set trap checks because the longer an animal is in a trap, the longer that trap is out of commission. It benefits trappers and the animals they trap to check traps routinely. The average time animals are held in traps is about eight hours in the U.S., according to an NTA publication [15]. Regardless of trap-check requirements, there are laws against wanton waste, and virtually all trappers do not want any animal to die needlessly.

Nontrapper Facts:

Not all trappers check their traps every twenty-four to seventy-two hours, and multiple states do not have a mandatory check requirement. Animals caught in traps may be subject to predation and death due to the elements. Not all trappers are responsible and maintain their traplines in an ethical manner. Because of the irresponsible behaviors of unethical trappers, no trapper can argue that all traps are checked routinely by all trappers.

Dogs and children can get caught in traps

Trapper Facts:

As more and more people frequent trails and forest service roads where once only trappers and hounds men roamed after big game season closed, the rate of pet-trap interactions have undoubtedly increased. While there is a leash law in Montana requiring pet owners to keep their dogs on a leash or under the owner's control, many pet owners don't follow that rule, and the result of this irresponsible action can range from unwanted interaction with wild or domesticated animals and people to an encounter with a legally set trap or snare.

The Montana Trappers Association has been working hard to find common ground with recreational nonconsumptive users and take the threat to their way of life seriously.

Several recreation areas have been made trap free by the Montana Trappers, in cooperation with the U.S. Forest Service (USFS)and the Montana Fish, Wildlife, and Parks (MFWP), for pet owners including the Blue Mountain, the Rattlesnake and Pattee Canyon areas north of Missoula, and the Bass Creek Recreational area to the south. The Montana Trappers are working in conjunction with genuinely concerned citizens, the USFS, and MFWP to improve public relations through education and land use agreements. But the designated trap-free areas don't always provide a positive experience for pet owners.

Recreationists at these areas have to deal with too many people and unruly dogs. The reasons for using these areas are to get pets out and let them exercise without worrying about traps. But anytime too many dogs congregate in one area, conflict is certain to occur. Dogs fighting with other dogs lead to people fighting with other people.

204   TOBY WALRATH

The same individuals who can't control their dogs at trailheads while at other areas in the state show up at these designated areas and let their pets run free without control. The irresponsible dog owner, it seems, is irresponsible wherever he goes.

As for children being at risk, it is highly unlikely that a child small enough to become caught in a trap would be crawling through the woods unsupervised in midwinter.

Nontrapper Facts:

Pet owners are afraid that their pets will get into traps because of local antitrapping rhetoric, which leads people to believe that their children, pets, and livestock are also at risk. Hopefully, Montana will follow the lead of other states and require a trapper's education class be taken prior to purchasing a license. But the classes must be taught by experienced trappers to be effective.

When an unleashed dog finds its way to a legally set trap or snare on public or private land, the controversy between trappers and pet owners is fueled. When trappers place traps that can attract dogs where dogs are present, dogs can and do get into traps. It will take a concerted effort between pet owners and trappers to eliminate this from occurring. The responsibility is on both sides.

Resolution

There are many more statements like these that are stated and repeated, argued from both sides, and then regurgitated time and again. The preceding examples were intended to shed some light on current trapping conflicts with the omission of emotional propaganda. Not all trappers are ethical or really care about trapping or its rich heritage. If trapping were gone tomorrow, they wouldn't care. They would just find some other way to make a dollar.

For the trappers who truly love what they do because they are infatuated with nature and wild animals, the loss of trapping would be devastating. Years of learning passed from generation to generation would be lost, as would their cultural identity. The American society seems to be on a path of nature disconnectedness, a path which has resulted in the denaturalization of our nation's children, and is drawing lines of separation between humans and wildness. A fact that has resulted in a generation that has little or no vested interest in understanding wild life and wild places however, they seem to have developed a sense of urgency to save and protect it due to the loud voices of preservation advocates.

The elimination of people who rely on a deep understanding and fascination with wildlife would destroy a critical link between "saving nature" and "using nature." If we don't use nature in some way, nature will be devalued, and the risk of destruction would increase (as has occurred in many countries around the world). Give nature value, and it is safe.

So how can we protect nature and use it without putting it on a pedestal or loving it to death? The situation is a matter of delicate balance. On one hand are the people who have more knowledge about wildlife than any other single group, and on the other hand are people who want nothing more than to preserve nature and let it continue on without human interference.

From a trapper's perspective, we must champion good ethics, sound conservation, and cultural preservation. Perhaps stringent education courses and mandated equipment modification should be incorporated into law. Surely the cost of equipment maintenance will be far outweighed by the long-term continuation of trapping. Mandatory trap-check requirements have been instituted across North America, but not for all states. While sets made in water are distinctly different than sets made on land, so too are body gripping sets on land different than foot traps set on land. The ethical responsibilities are therefore also different.

A marten caught in a body gripping trap at eight thousand feet in the mountains is dead almost instantaneously, whereas a coyote caught in a foot trap is held alive until the trapper returns. There should certainly be different requirements—personally, ethically, and perhaps legally—for the dead marten versus the live coyote. A beaver set made to kill the beaver quickly under ice shouldn't require as frequent a check as an animal that is snared.

It seems unreasonable to be required to check marten traps every forty-eight hours when marten are killed instantly. There is no way it is alive, and most likely, it is frozen and preserved. Likewise, it seems unethical to leave a coyote in a trap for five days out in the elements. Aquatic furbearers are quickly and humanely killed and preserved by ice-covered ponds for extended periods. A blanket rule for trap-check regulations is not reasonable or necessary to fulfill ethical considerations.

I struggle to find resolution to these concerns because of the "slow chipping" effect by members of the lucrative protest industry. Ever so slowly, sportsmen's rights are being whittled away, just as promised by powerful anti-animal use groups. By allowing a trap-check requirement and equipment requirement to become law, it opens the door to even more restrictions.

Trappers in Montana support many recommendations for things, such as a forty-eight-hour trap check and pan tension devices, but refuse to accept them as mandatory regulations. Not because they support unethical behavior, but because these laws aren't necessary for ethical trapping and don't take all trapping methods into consideration.

In some states, trapping regulations were made so restrictive that they essentially destroyed the ability of trappers to trap effectively and has resulted in the elimination of hundreds of trappers and halted the passing of valuable wildlife knowledge to the next generation. In other states, foothold trap or body grip trapping bans have destroyed the heritage and effective wildlife management tools available for would-be trappers to embrace.

The results have been severe increases in predator and rodent populations, increased threat to public safety and health, and the further chipping away of the American outdoorsman culture, a culture whose continuation is necessary if we are to perpetuate our nation's long-standing history of producing and maintaining large numbers of wildlife and preservation of wild places. The reasons for these severe restrictions and the choking out of sportsmen's heritage are due to the plethora of disinformation presented to government officials and an unsuspecting public—which, together—change laws.

Countless stories perpetuated by the media are questionable, but when asked why more coverage isn't made for the positive roles trappers play in protecting public safety and improving wildlife habitat, one reporter in Montana said, "That won't sell papers."

Montana law states that body gripping traps greater than seven inches may not be set on land, unless it is recessed seven inches inside an enclosure with an opening no greater than fifty-two square inches. This regulation prevents dogs from entering the trap while remaining highly effective for target species. Traps may not be set within fifty feet of a public trail or a roadway either.

Leash laws are established to protect pets from many hazards, including wildlife, other dogs, and other recreational users. So in areas where leash laws require dog owners to keep their pets leashed, there should—theoretically—be no conflicts. Unfortunately, that is not always the case. Old forest service roads make for great cross-country skiing and snowshoeing opportunities. Miles of maintained trails draw hordes of winter recreationists to the forests. When these users choose to let their dogs run free against posted laws, problems can and unfortunately do happen.

The trapping culture has remained relatively safe in light of controversy surrounding the use of traps because fur trapping is promoted and regulated by fish and wildlife agencies as an important management tool and wildlife data collection resource. Wildlife managers use the harvest numbers to calculate the rise and fall of local populations. In turn, the quotas are adjusted when necessary to keep the management objectives in check. The fact that biologists and wildlife managers use trapping information to keep track of the health of furbearers and other game means that trappers can keep doing what they love to do while ensuring the long-term sustainability of wildlife.

The Montana Trappers Association has held trapper's education classes for more than twenty five years to inform trappers about how and where to use traps—perhaps more importantly, where not to set traps. Many nontrappers attend these classes to learn about trapping in a nonthreatening environment. The MTA welcomes anyone who wishes to learn, and encourages people to attend and/or call with questions.

Educated trappers know when and where to set traps and snares and where not too, and educated trappers do not fuel the opposing groups' fire. The unfortunate fact is that inexperienced trappers may not realize the impact that their mistakes are creating, and without a mandatory trapper's education course requirement in Montana, it takes a bad experience to teach them the lesson. Trapping violations are handled with fines, but the cost to trapping privileges can't be paid for with cash.

Great strides have been made by the MTA to make a hands-on, instructor-led training course a requirement, just as hunting education and bow hunting education classes are required prior to the purchase of a hunting license. The MTA trapper's education is supported by the MTFWP. Many other states have excellent trapper education classes provided by their respective state game agencies in partnership with state trapping organizations as well, and many states require that a trapper's education course be completed prior to the purchase of a trapping license.

Trappers must use the most up-to-date trapping equipment and methods available if they are to carry on their lifestyle. It is better for the animals they pursue and better for trapper's image. Use of best practices will yield acceptance of trapping. Trappers who are not willing to improve poor methods and equipment should not be trapping.

The need for resolution is clear. Both sides must accept when their own side is wrong and must work to improve. So too must we accept that we all want our wildlife to flourish and wild places to be forever beautiful. Trappers are not mean, nature-hating, money-grubbing slobs. Neither are environmentalists radical, control-driven, granola-eating anthropomorphists. Trappers and nontrapping nature lovers both love nature and cherish their experiences in the wild. Although there are certainly individuals who fit the stereotypes on either side, there is commonality.

And while neither side may ever agree nor reach a state of cohesiveness, the fact is we need a little of both in order to perpetuate value-added understanding and protection of wild places. Trappers see the details of the forest quite well, and environmentalists see the whole forest. If only we could accept opposing views and combine our energy to protect our cultural heritage—which includes the stewardship and perpetuation of our natural resources and cultural connectedness—instead of constantly defending our own one-sided approach to conserving the beautiful things we have inherited.

Hopefully, cognizant, rational human beings can find common ground and work together to protect the wildness that we have all inherited without resorting to the use of hate-filled rhetoric.

Chapter 16

Cultured by Nature

No culture can live, if it attempts to be exclusive.

—Mahatma Gandhi

Humans who choose to live their lives within the boundaries of nature's laws are more natural than those who don't. It can't be any other way. The more time we spend participating in nature, the more we become part of it, no longer strangers looking in but rather natural members looking out. For eons, human life has drawn sustenance from the flora and fauna provided by the earth. Although man has slowly separated from the very core of his existence, the yearning to commune with nature has not subsided; instead, it has grown immeasurably. People seek the unsophisticated spontaneity of nature amid complicated unnatural lives to fulfill the wildfire that feeds our hearts.

Every fall, right about when the nights start getting cooler and the first dusting of snow appears on the mountaintops, the rich heritage of Montana's mountain men is preserved by the skillful hands of natural historians. They go to work, not for fame or fortune, but to carry on the legacy of people and places wild. The best are rarely seen, their accomplishments unknown. It's neither fish nor feathers nor trophy game that brings these secretive and often quiet, natural consumers out into the most intimate reaches of nature's bounty. Their silent pursuit is unique, just as it is for hunters, anglers, and hikers. In search of solitude, love for creatures' wild and adventure, these outdoorsmen and women carry on the tradition that defines who they are. The reasons why are as deep and varied as the individuals themselves, but for each of them, it's a way of life. They have a close-knit relationship with nature that is often misunderstood and isolated even among other outdoorsman.

Fur trappers spend their days reading the stories hidden on the forest floor, articulated through the tracks left by wild inhabitants. Sights and sounds stimulate sensibilities. For these men and women, the chill from mountain air and the excitement of feeling wild places with human senses is a part of daily life. The effect of living wild in wild places brings trappers closer to natural fulfillment. The natural building blocks of the trapping culture are people with close ties to the land. They utilize animals not in an act of violence or egotistical dominance, but as natural participants in the circle of life. Animals caught may be utilized for food, glands, and fur. Man can consume or be consumed. Trappers know this firsthand, not through abstract conceptualization; they know it because they are part of it.

Slowly, the diversity of our planet's people is becoming lost forever as the mono-culture melting pot tears down cultural walls and melds them together. The American trapping culture is made up of people who possess an intimate understanding of wild animals and their habitat, an understanding that is out of reach from most urban Americans. Their skills are unique and necessary, their passion for what they do unrivalled, their culture worth preserving.

Montana, once a trapper's paradise and destination for tough men looking for adventure, is currently one of the great strongholds of the trapping culture. The Montana trapper's way of life has roots deep in a proud heritage of consumptive use, woodsman skills, lore, and passion for wild places and wildlife. The wilderness is no more foreign to a Montana trapper than city streets are to a Wall Street trader. The rare knowledge gained by studying wild animals every day for weeks on end imbues the trappers' minds with wonted skill to the point that they can predict when an animal is going to move through an area, and not just where, but exactly where.

The men and women who participate in trapping in Montana and around the globe are knowledgeable students of wildlife, their understanding of furbearing animals and natural processes are from firsthand experience. These people are intertwined with nature, how could they not be?

Successful trapping doesn't happen by accident. Successful trappers must know their quarry intimately. What's more, their level of understanding of natural history must be exceptional and will rival, if not leave wildlife biologists in the proverbial dust. Certainly, a well-trained biologist who knows his subject matter can create models, perform field studies, and write papers filled with data and conclusive findings. Trappers, on the other hand, study the habits of animals, assess the weather and its impact on furbearers, learn the details of tracks and trails, and prove their understanding of this information not in scientific journals but in their ability to place a trap in the right place at the right time.

The trapping culture must be preserved because it is a keystone subculture of American outdoorsmen. Trappers, hunters, and anglers are the foundation of America's wildlife legacy. When we preserve and nurture our great trapping heritage, by default, we preserve and nurture hunting, fishing, agriculture, and rural America. Trapping preservation is rural preservation, and the implications of not preserving the skills and history of people with strong ties to the land are far reaching. The effect of our nation's de-naturalized children has yet to be seen, but the cure is often found in wilderness immersion programs, statistically the most effective therapeutic experiences available. Participating in nature is a necessary component of preserving the human spirit.

But that is not the only reason to preserve trapping or even celebrate it. There are many more. The historical and cultural significance alone would be enough reason to preserve America's rich fur-trapping heritage. Perhaps the trapping skills used to remove nuisance wildlife when they threaten public health would be enough. Or the fact that wildlife officials often need trappers to capture animals for research, relocation, or wildlife restoration would be enough reason. But there are many more reasons to preserve and even enhance trapping and trappers.

Trappers possess in their hearts a love for the outdoors, a yearning to learn more about wildlife, tracks and tracking, and the habits of wild creatures. They are different than the average recreationist or hunter. Give a trapper a couple days on a rancher's property, and he'll know the wildlife there better than anyone. A few short weeks afield are not enough for these rugged souls and their pursuits carry them into the remote reaches of the wilderness. In the middle of winter, packs are loaded with steel traps, lures made with secret ingredients, dirt sifters, wood boxes, axes and trowels, and steel stakes and wire. The work is hard. The days are long.

The goal is to catch wild furbearing animals to sell, tan, or trade. Furbearing animals are defined differently state by state due to differences in requirements for wildlife management principles and social factors. These furbearers are for the most part plentiful, and at times, even today, are quite valuable on the world market. But money is not necessarily the reason these hardy souls deal with frozen fingers, sore backs, and muddy clothes.

Many trappers end the season with little financial gain to show for the extreme effort of the season. Unknowing onlookers can't understand what could possess someone to stand in the middle of a beaver pond in January with an axe in his hand to chop through the ice day after day, checking traps for beaver, or riding a snow machine for miles through remote forest service roads when it's 20 below zero checking traps set for marten, only to come home in the evening to thaw the daily catch and stay up half the night to skin, flesh, and stretch the wild fur before retiring for a few short hours, only to return to another section of trapline the following day to start the whole thing over. And all of that for a few hundred to a few thousand dollars' worth of overall profit. While some fur trappers do make a significant portion of their annual income from trapping, what is it really about the trapline that draws these woodsmen year after demanding year?

The trapping culture in Montana is a tight circle of men and women who arguably possess more knowledge and understanding of wildlife than all other outdoor enthusiasts combined. The insight of these few individuals is staggering, and it doesn't take long to respect a successful trapper's knowledge about his natural surroundings, regardless of one's views of trapping itself. Who could know more about wild places and the creatures that inhabit the land than the people who spend virtually every day studying tracks and learning the habits of animals and their interaction with the topography of the land?

A trapper's world is made up of huge mountains, open prairies, tight draws, dry creek beds, trails, and a single two-inch diameter trap pan. When a bobcat commits to stepping in a two-inch circle out of hundreds of miles of free range, the trapper has succeeded—succeeded in figuring out where that cat had been and where he was going. The trapper predicted where his quarry would be days or weeks into the future, not just where, but exactly where, and it was no accident. The trapper proves it by repeating the act again and again throughout one of the toughest seasons there is—trapping season.

The trapping culture has never consisted of a large number of people. Over time, there have been fur booms and busts where trapper numbers rise and fall like the cycle of rabbit populations. Those who trap when fur prices are high are, for a time, trappers. They set traps and put up their catch and sell it to a waiting market and reap the reward of hard work and know-how. But despite their enthusiasm when the prices are high for their efforts, they are not the heartbeat of the trapping culture, not even a faint pulse. For when the fur prices drop, their traps remain hung in the shed. Trapping season comes and goes, but their traps never move. For these trappers, trapping season is over until the prices rise again.

It's the trappers who trap no matter what the fur prices are or are predicted to be, who make up the heartbeat of the trapping culture. These men and women don't trap because they want financial gain, although a few extra dollars in their pocketbook won't be turned down, mind you. Just as an elk hunter may sell the hide and antlers of their trophy that is not the reason they hunted. A hunter could choose to buy domestic meat at a grocery store instead. But that is not what hunting is about. It's about taking responsibility for the food the hunter eats, immersing one's self in nature, being part of it and not separate. The same is true with trappers.

Trappers trap for the enjoyment of being outdoors at a time of the year when many people are snuggled up in blankets at home on the couch. They trap to fulfill the trapper's call. Trapping is in their hearts, and there isn't anything a real trapper can do to shake it loose but go trapping. With prices high or prices low, the traps come down off the shed wall when the fur is prime. Heavy coats and warm hats are pulled on, and the ground falls away behind them as trappers are drawn ever closer to whatever lies ahead on the trap line.

The historical and cultural significance of trappers, especially in Montana, cannot be overstated. It was primarily the search for pelts that spurred European explorers deeper into the western United States. The settlement of the West was based on the relationships developed between trappers and Native Americans. The history of the modern-day American West is a compilation of events which trappers and trapping cannot be separated from. On the contrary, it was *because* of trapping and the stories of mountain men that those events ever took place.

Four hundred years ago, fur trappers and hunters ventured into the wilds on foot or horseback in search of wild fur. This tradition which shaped the United States and Canada continues today. Trappers are truly wild and proud caretakers of wildlife who carry on the richest wildlife legacy in the world. The intimate relationship between man and nature spawned by early explorers is continued through a few hardy souls lucky enough to know the thrill and excitement of a trapline.

Few can know—really know wild creatures and places. What it is to intimately know the environment in all its harmonious convulsive functioning is reserved for people who choose to spend much of their time immersed in intense and passionate study of wild details seen only after extended observation. Trappers are one of the few remaining subcultures in tune with their natural surroundings. They are not casual observers who rarely visit to randomly catch a glimpse of nature's beauty. Instead, they are astute participants educated about the ways of nature and its inhabitants. They are more comfortable figuring out the mystery of tracks and scat on the forest floor than dressing up in business attire and belting out financial jargon.

Montana trappers are people with stories as wide and varied as the mountains surrounding them. Their stories are vivid and their passion for wildlife contagious. They share freely their knowledge and celebrate the rich heritage received and passed on.

The story of the fur trapper didn't end in the 1800s. Not even close. Montana trappers proudly continue their wild heritage today, along with men and women in virtually every state of the U.S. and every province of Canada, across Europe, and around the world. The wildly adventurous lifestyle of modern-day trappers is the culmination of nearly four hundred years of producing the most sustainable natural product on earth. It is exciting to run a traditional trapline high in the mountain country, to battle weather and rugged terrain, to snowshoe for miles with a heavy load, and to bring the season's catch to sale as an extension of America's trapping heritage. Perhaps the only thing more exciting than the melded natural and human history of the American fur trapper is the continuing wild and proud story of trappers yet to unfold.

Works Cited for *Wild Pride*
by Toby Walrath
2012

1. BEVINGTON, A. Frank Ralph Conibear (1896-). ARCTIC, North America, 36, Jan. 1983. http://arctic.synergiesprairies.ca/arctic/index.php/arctic/article/view/2301/2278. (Accessed: Oct 01, 2012)
2. Montana Fish, Wildlife, and Parks Furbearer Regulations, 2012. http://fwp.mt.gov/hunting/planahunt/huntingGuides/furbearer/default.html?regulationsTabHeader (Accessed Oct 01,2012)
3. Moore, Bud, The Lochsa Story. Missoula, MT: Mountain Press Publishing Company, 1996.
4. James W. Boyd, Christopher S. Guy, Travis B. Horton and Stephen A. Leathe (2010): Effects of Catch-and-Release Angling on Salmonids at Elevated Water Temperatures, North American Journal of Fisheries Management, 30:4, 898-907.
5. Casselman, S. J. Catch-and-release angling: a review with guidelines for proper fish handling practices. Fish and Wildlife Branch. Ontario Ministry of Natural Resources. Peterborough, Ontario. (2005): 26 p.
6. Association of Fish and Wildlife Agencies Best Management Practices for Trapping in the United States (BMPs), 2006 http://www.fishwildlife.org/files/Introduction_BMPs.pdf> (Accessed Oct 01, 2012.
7. McMillion Scott. Mark of the Grizzly, Kingwood, TX, Falcon, (1998).
8. Dahl Thomas E., Technical Aspects of Wetlands History of Wetlands in the Conterminous United States Geological Survey Water Supply Paper 2425; *1990. http://water.usgs.gov/nwsum/WSP2425/history.html (Accessed October 01, 2012)*

9. McCulloch, Linda 2010 Ballot Issues Montana Secretary of State http://sos.mt.gov/elections/archives/2010s/2010/initiatives/I-160.asp (Accessed: 10 Jan 2012).

10. Young, Julie K. Predator Damage Management National Wildlife Research Center, United States Department of Agriculture FY2010: 2010 http://www.aphis.usda.gov/wildlife_damage/nwrc/research/ predator_management/content/WS_Research_protect_livestock-7. pdf (Accessed October 15, 2012)

11. National Wildlife Control Operators Association. http://www.nwcoa. com/ (Accessed: October 15, 2012).

12. MacCallum, Wayne F., 2012 http://www.mass.gov/dfwele/dfw/ wildlife/facts/mammals/beaver/pdf/beaver_citizens_guide.pdf (Accessed December 15, 2012)

13. Lariviere S. "Ranch Mink: Friend or Foe?" *Trapper and Predator Caller Magazine Vol. 36 No. 10* (December 2011): *page 32.*

14. J Trapping News Business Survives Arson Attempt. *Trapper and Predator Caller Magazine* Vol. 36 (November 2011):No. 9 page 7.

15. National Trappers Association (2012) "Traps Today Myths and Facts" [Brochure].

16. 2012 Brainy Quote http://www.brainyquote.com/ Accessed: October 01, 2012.)

17. Reid Edwin. Hello Adirondacker!, Wanakena, NY. Reid Publications, (1998).

18. Montana Trappers Association. *http://montanatrappers.org/* (Accessed:November 2012).

19. Posewitz Jim. Beyond Fair Chase, Helena, MT, FalconGuides, (2002)

20. Amazon Rain Forest. *http://www.amazon-rainforest.org/ indigenous-tribes.html*(Accessed:November 2012)

Edwards Brothers Malloy
Thorofare, NJ USA
June 14, 2013